The
Competitive
Mind

The Competitive Mind

Strategy for Winning in Business

Andrew Crouch

John Wiley & Sons, Ltd

Email (for orders and customer service enquiries): cs-books@wiley.co.uk

Visit our Home Page on www.wiley.com

Other Wiley Editorial Offices

John Wiley & Sons Inc., 111 River Street, Hoboken, NJ 07030, USA

Jossey-Bass, 989 Market Street, San Francisco, CA 94103-1741, USA

Wiley-VCH Verlag GmbH, Boschstr. 12, D-69469 Weinheim, Germany

John Wiley & Sons Australia Ltd, 42 McDougall Street, Milton, Queensland 4064, Australia

John Wiley & Sons (Asia) Pte Ltd, 2 Clementi Loop #02-01, Jin Xing Distripark, Singapore 129809

John Wiley & Sons Canada Ltd, 6045 Freemont Blvd. Mississauga, Ontario, L5R 4J3 Canada

Wiley also publishes its books in a variety of electronic formats. Some content that appears in print may not be available in electronic books.

Library of Congress Cataloging-in-Publication Data

Crouch, Andrew.
  The competitive mind : strategy for winning in business / Andrew Crouch.
    p. cm.
  Includes bibliographical references and index.
  ISBN 978-1-4051-8562-2 (cloth : alk. paper)   1. Strategic planning.   2. Competition.   I. Title.
  HD30.28.C764 2008
  658.4'012–dc22

                                                                              2008022825

British Library Cataloguing in Publication Data

A catalogue record for this book is available from the British Library

ISBN 978-1-4051-8562-2

Typeset in 11/15 pt Goudy by SNP Best-set Typesetter Ltd., Hong Kong
Printed and bound in Great Britain by TJ International Ltd, Padstow, Cornwall, UK

Contents

Acknowledgements

Philip Yetton's encouragement to think seriously about a manager's role set a direction for this book, although strategy had hardly entered our conversations those many years ago. Depth of understanding is your scholarly legacy, Phil. I hope some of that is conveyed here.

The idea of strategic thinking presented in this book came to life through conversations with my students. This generous and talented crowd of people joined me with enthusiasm and energy in my endeavour to make sense of strategy. You, my friends, will recognise echoes of many of our discussions in what follows.

A book writing enterprise can strain domesticity. Thank you, Barbara, David, Clare and Elizabeth, for supporting me and steadying the ship throughout my obsessive immersions.

And to Claude and Madeline, for sitting faithfully at my feet during all those hours of my insanity, seen from their canine perspective, rest in peace.

AC

1

Introduction

This book is about competition between businesses. Thinking about competition between businesses is what I call Strategy, the interaction between competitive minds. Skilful strategic thinking is mindfulness that provides a basis for succeeding in commercial competition. In this book I offer advice in the form of Principles, or guidelines, for outwitting commercial rivals and also, importantly, a mindset for discouraging rivals from doing the outwitting.

The principles offered here apply equally well to large companies and small. Among the large, for instance, there is no doubt that the future of Nokia depends, on the understanding Nokia's executives have of Sony Ericsson's, Motorola's and LG's future intentions.[1] The earlier and better these are known to Jorma Ollila, Nokia's chairman and chief executive, and others charged with thinking about the firm's competitive manoeuvring, the more fully these ideas can become plans factored into Nokia's outlook for future business advantage. Executives in Sony Ericsson and the other competitors are likely to have a similar outlook.

Among smaller companies, the proprietor of that familiar small business located near where you live will also, no doubt, be mindful of the activities of commercial rivals.

While the ideas which follow concentrate on ways in which senior managers might create and sustain a successful competitive orientation towards commercial rivals, this kind of thinking is, of course, not all that executives think about. Other considerations are vital: customers and clients, markets, supply chains, finance and staffing, together with numerous other matters. All are essential. However, strategic thinking is cardinal. To overlook the plans and progress of a business competitor invites risk; commercial opportunities might be ignored and threats could go unseen.

In this introductory chapter, I concentrate on two main topics: the heritage of strategy, and essential concepts for explaining what strategy means. I firmly believe that useful thinking about strategic thinking should take account of the fact that strategy has been studied and discussed by scholars and practitioners since the beginning of written history. It would be a mistake to overlook this heritage while attempting to distil an essence of value for strategic thinking. It is also important at the outset to clarify the conceptual domain of strategy.

Heritage

In recent times strategy has received much scholarly attention in a quest to explain and prescribe means for securing commercial advantage. However, human competition has a long history and distilled advice on strategy is available from deep in antiquity. In my view, a thorough understanding of the topic of strategy will benefit from an appreciation of our heritage.

I begin with a commentary on the place of strategy in relevant contemporary business literature. Then I offer a series of introductory sketches of the contributions of a small number of historical figures, chosen for their enduring reputations. This section provides the foundation for the content of the Principles of Strategy which follow in subsequent chapters.

Contemporary perspectives

The idea of strategy, as applied to business, has received substantial scholarly interest since the 1950s. Originally subject to academic study in the United States at that time, and primarily centred in the Harvard Business School, the evolving themes have spread throughout the business world. This American influence can be readily seen in the published work of Porter,[2] and Hamel and Prahalad.[3] Contemporary views have been integrated into textbooks such as that of Johnson, Scholes and Whittington.[4] They have also received thorough comparative analysis by Mintzberg[5] and a critique of their philosophical basis by scholars such as Calori.[6]

The main thrust of early scholarly activity during the 20th century began with a notion of improving business direction. Inspiration for this came from the enormous and successful military efforts which were conducted during World War II; this was surely a powerful influence for thinking about how to achieve large scale commercial objectives.

Three particular scholarly themes which have arisen are of special interest: the idea of management of strategy, the possibility of principles and a logical structure for strategy.

Strategic management

Early development of thinking about strategy after World War II took place alongside practitioners, the executives in large companies who were charged with shaping corporate direction. As scholarly interest in strategy grew, it is interesting to note that little time passed before the study of 'purposefulness', the essential reason for corporate direction, was displaced by 'management of purposefulness'. This was, perhaps, an inevitable result of intersecting scholarly inclinations among evolving academic disciplines. Thus the field gained the title Strategic Management.

Contemporary literature on strategic management is diverse. This is not surprising since it draws insight from a range of intellectual disciplines which range from Porter's background in industrial economics to Freeman's[7] intellectual base in sociology. Henry Mintzberg is one of the more creative thinkers in the field of management and strategy. He and his colleagues point out that conventional views of strategic management comprise at least 10 different perspectives.[8] There is therefore potential for great confusion if one falls into one of the twin traps of either seeking a grand all-encompassing model which integrates the different perspectives, or of trying to decide which one of the perspectives is correct.

Principles

Although the aim of scholarship in strategic management has been to inform good business practice, the distillation of principles is rare. Unusual among contemporary prescriptions guiding business strategy is that offered by Gilbert, Hartman, Mauriel and Freedman.[9] These authors discuss the problem of principles in strategy and offer a set of three principles for evaluation of so-called strategy frameworks.

These principles are outlined below since they were a valuable source of guidance for the writer's development of the six Principles of Strategy which form the essence of this book:

Principle about Persons. This idea points to a requirement that guidelines for strategy and strategic thinking should accommodate the fact that people, their motivations, decisions and stakes are an essential strategic consideration. Strategy and its context are not abstract and isolated. Advice guiding strategy will comply with the Principle about Persons if it acknowledges people in their context and complexity.

Principle of Business Basics. This principle is a reminder that the game, as it were, is one of commercial competition. The essential features of commerce: markets, products and services, customers and suppliers should be given full recognition in evolving strategic direction and action.

Principle of Timely Action. Strategy implies action, but analysis is not necessarily action oriented. A useful and effective guide to development of strategy will acknowledge the need to decide when to act and when not to act. The intent of strategy is to influence the course of events in a longer term as well as immediately. Such time span considerations should form an integral part of strategic thinking.

Persons, Business Basics and Timely Action are clearly helpful reference points for appreciating what one needs to take into account when thinking strategically. Note that these principles weigh up the value of different theoretical perspectives in terms of conceptual relevance; they do not evaluate prescriptions which follow from these frameworks.

Principles like these are, of course, available in the form of guidelines for thinking in other fields of human competition. In the field of military business, for example, organisations around the world employ similar guidelines for strategic thinking.[10]

Logic for strategy

A purposeful logic for strategy was proposed by Mitroff.[11] He offers the idea that strategy, or as he refers to it, policy, can be formulated in terms of the formal logic of argument. As such, a policy position or line of strategic direction is a *claim*, supported by *warrants* based on *evidence*, and surviving against *rebuttal*. This idea also carries weight as a contributor to strategic thinking because it requires precise specification of the elements and considerations in formulating a strategic position, incorporating explicit rejection of alternatives. This logical basis does not solve the problem of formulating strategy; it simply assists by providing a framework for thinking.

More recently, a further framework for the logic of strategy is proposed in terms of harmony and confrontation in commercial competition.[12] This idea is based on the observation that much of corporate behaviour involves peaceful co-existence among market-oriented firms. While a firm's vital interests are not placed under threat from the behaviour of rivals, a harmonious pattern of market-based interaction persists. If, however, interests are threatened, the pattern of competitive interaction shifts radically to a mode which is confrontational. This idea is developed further in Chapter 2.

The literature on business strategy is enormous. Its growth has been motivated by curiosity among senior executives about how to guide their businesses to succeed. But despite the quantum of scholarly effort and writing, I believe most executives are disappointed by the result. Principles are rare and the logical structure of advice is abstract. The literature on strategic management refers to many rather abstract aspects of the management of businesses, but it offers very little advice about dealing with the most difficult aspect of securing business success: dealing with direct competition from rival firms.

Classic perspectives

Although the connection between business and strategy is relatively recent, our heritage in strategic thinking has a very long history. It is over 2500 years since Sun Tzu[13] wrote his military treatise. At about the same time Kautilya[14] was providing comprehensive advice to King Chandragupta on the Indian subcontinent. This included a guide for prevailing in competition with enemies. Alexander the Great[15] undertook his great enterprise in empire building between 334 and 323 BC, leaving a history rich in evidence of strategic thinking. A little more recently those with responsibility for the protection of state sovereignty have been advised on strategy by Machiavelli[16] and von Clausewitz.[17]

This group of scholars of strategy is neither exclusive nor comprehensive in their insights; no doubt others also have had considerable influence in their times.[18] It is clear, however, that Sun Tzu, Kautilya, Alexander, Machiavelli and von Clausewitz are historical figures with enduring reputations and this is the basis for their selection to contribute to Principles of Strategy.[19] A background sketch for each author is offered below.

Sun Tzu

Some raise doubts about the identity of the author of work attributed to Sun Tzu, but few dispute the power and wisdom of the insight handed on from around 500 BC. Sun Tzu's thinking evolved from his observation and participation in struggles among warring states. He dwelt on the sources of success in such rivalry. This thinking has been distilled into a rather abstract, even poetic form, which expresses principles which are both profoundly powerful and plainly practical.

Sun Tzu recognised war as a recurrent conscious act and not a passing and painful aberration in human affairs. This rationality is the basis of the detached analysis which forms the essence of his theory. Most importantly, Sun Tzu is aware that armed struggle is always costly and should not be undertaken recklessly. Because of the inevitable cost and mutual disadvantage arising from application of direct force, he sees it as a last resort. Far better, he argues, to attack the plans and ideas of a rival and even better still to undermine an opponent's morale. Attack a rival's intentions rather than his army or cities. The objective is elimination of the will to resist, not annihilation of the enemy.

Accomplishment of military success depends first on societal unity, order and harmony under a ruling sovereign. Sun Tzu then prescribes with clear insight and in simple representation, the contingencies for victory: the mental, moral, physical and circumstantial factors. His emphasis is placed on the general's creativity in formulating deceptions in the imagination of his rivals: surprise, uncertainty, arrival of the unexpected and continuous change is the means for undermining a rival's sense of stability and security of command. Sun Tzu advocates that his students move with balance, speed, decisiveness and flexibility to create fear among their opponents. Victory, he argues, should be a foregone conclusion resulting from careful and imaginative preparation and the exercise of calculated risks.

Kautilya

Kautilya's book, *The Arthashastra*, was written for King Chandragupta as a manual for statecraft on the Indian subcontinent in about 350 BC. It contains detailed advice on almost every matter of concern to a king, ranging from management of the economy and treasury, to securing and housing elephants. While much of the detail refers to the particular time and location for which it was designed, Kautilya discusses timeless issues, most importantly: how a king should conduct his relationships with neighbouring kingdoms.

He takes a pragmatic view, based on his clinical observation of human nature and how people are inclined to behave. For instance, Kautilya observes that a neighbour is a potential rival and diplomacy should be based on this supposition. He recommends caution, therefore, in dealings with other kings. As part of his care in safeguarding the interests of his kingdom, Kautilya recommends that a king foster relationships with the heads of other states, near and far. Cultivation of advantage through diplomacy builds a power base which can be employed to benefit when times require it.

The essence of Kautilya's recommendations in managing foreign affairs is based on enhancing and preserving the kingdom's interests; simply put, he advocates securing power in relationships with others.

Machiavelli

Nicolò Machiavelli's writing, especially *The Prince*, convinced many, in his own time and since, that he was an evil counsellor of statesmen, inspired by the Devil. When he wrote,[20] reactions to his proposals drew passionate objections, particularly from those with a religious voice.[21] But much of this criticism overlooks Machiavelli's motivation and the circumstances in which he wrote.

As his interpreters point out,[22] Machiavelli was not a detached political philosopher. He was a man who was deeply concerned about the disaster facing the Italian states and particularly Florence. He wrote at a time when the states lay at the whim of invaders from Spain and France. For Machiavelli this situation was a deep threat to personal pride and esteem, an intolerable, shameful humiliation of the city states. *The Prince* is a passionate, even obsessed plea to restore autonomy, harmony and power to the states. It is a statement of hope.

Machiavelli was an astute observer of political affairs, though with little direct participation himself. He was an outsider and perhaps his psychological insight benefited from this detachment. His thinking was focused primarily on corporate success and the means by which a leader might accomplish it. *The Prince* is a formula designed to appeal to his political patrons who, should they be convinced by his argument, might act decisively to begin to turn the tide of national defeat. His treatise is a theory of power and the need for power: how a prince might acquire a principality, how it is maintained and how it might be lost.

Concerned that one of the contemporary failings of the Italian states lay with leadership, Machiavelli called for stiffened resolve and discipline, but that a state could not be rebuilt without the goodwill and respect of the people, the *Prince*'s subjects. In view of the stakes, shame and the prospect for renewed self esteem, Machiavelli advocated ruthlessness and toughness to repel the invaders. He also pointed out that in the long run there is possibly a greater benefit from action that might at the time be considered cruel, rather than the considerable cost of uncertainty and loss of morale resulting from indecisiveness and weakness.

His advice is consistent with the bald observation that successful governments are always prepared to act ruthlessly to achieve their ends. In the final analysis, as Bull[23] observes, whether action is evil can only be decided in the light of what it is meant to achieve and whether it is successful in achieving it.

Von Clausewitz

Carl von Clausewitz was a Prussian soldier who witnessed, first hand, the effects of Napoleon Bonaparte's crushing purposefulness of military expansion throughout Europe early in the 19th century. His unfinished book, *On War*,[24] was written as his attempt to come to terms both theoretically and practically with the nature of war.

It is commonly argued that there are three broad theories of war;[25] those of the so called *pessimists*, *optimists* and *realists*. The pessimist marks progress towards a single final event in which mankind will eventually meet its destruction. Optimists propose a set of conditions, as yet incompletely defined which will draw humanity into a subsequent state of harmony, free from further conflict forever after. Realists accept the inevitability of struggle among humans to maintain and enhance interests, and consequently their rivalry for power and influence. Von Clausewitz was a *realist*.

He categorically rejects war for war's sake, seeing military activity as an extension of politics: war is an exercise of force for the attainment of a political object, regardless of whether this object is ethically right. If war is a rational instrument of national policy, then it is based on a balance of benefits and costs of military action, it is purposeful and goal oriented, and it is intended to advance the nation's interests by seeking and seizing opportunities, most likely to the disadvantage of others. Military action is instrumental in a struggle for national interest, that is, for power.

A direct observer of Napoleon's transformation of war from tactical melodramatics with an emphasis on manoeuvre to decisive action through actual application of irresistible force, von Clausewitz formulated his philosophy with great clarity and simplicity. He advocated bringing requisite force together in the shortest possible time and with maximum momentum to a decisive point of action. An army therefore, as an instrument of politics, is an instrument applied with a single intention; to win, in final, absolute and unambiguous terms.

Blunt, brutal and single minded about victory, von Clausewitz is also sensitive to the subtle aspects of command. 'Everything is very simple in war, but the simplest thing is difficult.'[26] Among his central interests is the challenge to leadership; the requirements of a great commander who is responsible for guiding the spirit of an army. Effective leadership demands decisiveness, while resisting the inevitable emotional effects of the tumult of battle with detached rationality. All the while, the aim needs to be maintained: to undermine and destroy the enemy's will to resist.

Alexander III of Macedon

Alexander's influence on contemporary strategic thinking comes through example rather than theory. Unlike Sun Tzu, Kautilya, Machiavelli or von Clausewitz, Alexander did not leave behind him documents explaining his aims or practices. What remains of his accomplishments is their history; discovered, described and debated comprehensively by scholars for over 2000 years.

A controversial figure even in his own time, Alexander has attracted both strong criticism and flattering praise since his remarkable campaign for growth of Macedonian influence which began in 334 BC. Some have challenged the reputation of the man as a violent and destructive conqueror, prone to drink to excess, and driven by such ambition that by the end of his career he harboured divine aspirations. Others hold Alexander in heroic esteem, citing his leadership, generosity to the defeated Persian royal family and the loyalty shown by his followers as indicators of his lasting high approval. Even today Alexander's campaigns are viewed with a combination of admiring regard, especially by those who appreciate his military accomplishments, and political cynicism by those whose values challenge Alexander's motivations and methods.

Although some aspects of the Macedonian King's reign attract competing interpretations, there are others about which there is little disagreement. Acquisition of the Persian Empire, and territories beyond, was an outstanding feat. At its peak, the Macedonian empire extended from modern day Italy and Libya in the West, to India in the East; from Germany in the North, to the Arabian Sea and Ethiopia in the South. To control this area in its diversity is a monumental feat in any terms. Moreover, the influence of Alexander was one of lasting achievement. It generated both political and economic opportunities. The unity of the empire might have been lost and become fragmented after his death, but evidence of Greek culture is still evident in widespread areas under Alexander's previous control.

Alexander's political skills are often underestimated or overlooked. The League of Corinth which was forced on the Greek states by his father, Philip II, was an unstable inheritance. It was ready to split into hostile factions at any moment, its unity already undermined by the belief that the Macedonians were uncultured barbarians. Yet this fragile alliance was maintained by Alexander over the eleven years of his Asian campaign. It also yielded him supplies and military support. A further dimension of Alexander's political intelligence was his attempt to bring together the people of Greece, Egypt and Asia in a 'policy of fusion'. His apparent design was to create a harmonious partnership which would bring economic, social and political benefits to all.

The highest admiration is usually reserved for Alexander's military accomplishments. His methods at all levels from empire building to campaigns and battles typically receive great respect. Napoleon and Julius Caesar are most notable among those who studied Alexander's campaigns and who are known to have modelled their thinking on Alexander's designs. Detailed study of Alexander's battles, sieges and counter guerrilla campaigns are generally recommended as models in military circles, even today.

Perhaps most outstanding is Alexander's generalship. He clearly had a capacity above most people to inspire heroic behaviour in others. Through his own confidence, determination, persistence and courage he was able to motivate his followers to succeed in the most unlikely situations and overcome the almost impossible. Ruthless at times, guided by unlimited ambition, demanding of his army, he never asked more than he himself was prepared to give. Yet balanced with compassion and sensitivity to the psychological aspects of leadership, his influence was little short of inspirational.

Alexander's campaign in empire building is an enduring model.

The reader will detect a contrast between the brief overview of contemporary literature and the so-called classics. The essence of the difference is the emphasis by the latter on competition.

Delineation of strategy

The central proposition I offer is that strategy is about succeeding in competition; no more and no less. It is the creation of a design that takes account of capabilities and contingencies, it anticipates the behaviour of competitors, and so improves the prospect of relative success in accomplishing corporate direction. The outcome of strategic thinking is a compelling argument for securing corporate purpose.

Placing this supposition in a commercial context, consider Nokia once again; it is a large Finnish manufacturer and marketer of mobile telephones. We do not know what Jorma Ollila thinks about when he thinks about strategy, nor do his commercial rivals know what he thinks.[27] However, we can speculate about his thinking process and its content; how he thinks and what he thinks about. Most importantly, we can reasonably assume that his purpose is to see his company succeed in the face of determined competitors.

Strategy is the appropriate word used here to describe an executive's orientation towards business competition. The word has its roots in the Greek *strategos* which refers to the work of the general.[28] Generals command armies to protect and enhance sovereign interests; their aim is to prevail in competition, should it arise.

The reader will note that this is a particular choice for meaning of the word strategy at a time when, in common business language, '*strategy*' is associated with almost everything anyone considers important. This choice therefore excludes many topics which are relevant for study elsewhere.[29]

Primary concepts

I propose that strategic thinking involves four interrelated primary concepts:

Purpose

The publicly apparent purpose of Nokia is to maintain its very substantial share of the mobile telephone market. No doubt Mr. Ollila is much more specific in his thinking with his senior strategy staff about particular aims for the company and its stakeholders: objectives in commercial outcomes, aims in time and ambitions in position relative to Nokia's main rivals.

The essential goal which is inherent in strategy is to strive to maintain one's discretion in independent action, unconstrained by rivals. Such commercial liberty stands in contrast with a much more unfortunate situation where one's commercial actions are constrained, or worse, dictated by others.

The achievement of the goal of freedom of commercial movement is complemented by a simultaneous and self-evident aim which is to achieve a circumstance of safety and security, rather than be placed in a position of vulnerability.

It would be a very unfortunate business indeed for any company to have its commercial actions shaped entirely according to the desires of rivals. One might argue that this is most unlikely for Nokia, given the size and stature of the company in its industry. But constraint is not inconceivable. A vital element of strategic thinking is, therefore, to devise courses of action which avoid this unpalatable future.

Reasoning

Strategy is a thinking process which employs both concepts and content for systematically devising plans of action aimed at securing and maintaining competitive advantage. Ideally there is a rational process by which information about the competition is arranged and interpreted in a logical manner to form a reasoned argument for proceeding in one direction rather than any other.

Strategy is thoughtful and deliberate, founded on premises and proceeding to valid conclusions. We would expect an argument for a course of action for Nokia, mounted by its strategists, to aim to pass tests that ensured its premises were true and that the direction selected was not spurious.

Concepts which comprise strategic thinking are abstract ideas which help to make sense of the elements of competition, what it means and how it is engaged by participants. For instance, one of the ideas which will be explored more fully later is the concept of *flexibility*. This is an idea which, for Nokia strategists, would refer to beliefs about the degree to which the company can shift from one apparent direction to another, for example, from manufacturing its own products to a greater emphasis on buying from unbranded handset manufacturers.

Content refers to the specifics of competition: the kind of confrontation which is under way. In the case of the mobile telecommunications industry the content of strategy would include reference to the speed with which strategists at Motorola are anticipating its business position in 3G technology. Content would also include the strength of ambition among LG's strategists to increase its market share.

Advantage

The priority in strategic thinking is the view to rivals. To disregard one's competitors could place the business in jeopardy through inattention to the designs a rival might have on one's enterprise. The aim therefore is to achieve relative advantage over rivals.

Strategy takes account of how this aim is to be achieved. This is in part a matter of relative capability of competitors and of the conditions under which competition proceeds. The work of a strategist is to conceive of paths to create a state of relative commercial advantage. That is, for example, to see to it that Nokia is positioned to prevail in competition with its rivals.

While the essential emphasis in strategy is on rivals, to disregard one's clients could render a business unviable through inattention to the market's needs. Here, then, I draw a distinction between marketing and strategy: whereas *marketing concentrates a firm's attention on its clients, with an eye to its competitors, strategy concentrates attention on competitors, with an eye to clients.*

Nokia's marketing outlook refers to the company's orientation towards its clients and customers; network operators and mobile phone users. Strategy refers to Nokia's particular orientation towards its rivals, concentrating particularly on the plans and activities of Motorola, Sony Ericsson and others.

Our interest in strategic thinking will therefore concentrate on competition from here on, but clearly, not to the exclusion of the market.

Future

Strategy is oriented towards advantage at a time which is yet to arrive. As such it is an abstract concept dealing with a future reality which is as yet only imagined and anticipated.

Strategy does not deal with the past or present. Nokia's current situation is the outcome of past strategic thinking; its current strategic thinking is the design for competitive manoeuvres to achieve future outcomes. Not for tomorrow, but for the longer term.

Strategy is abstract: it is an idea about imaginary actions in an imagined future with imaginary implications. It is prospective. That is, strategy refers to thinking in the present about future actions; thinking now about what to do at some future time.

Thinking about the strategy of Nokia is therefore thinking about what actions this firm might take in a future where competitors act according to predictions and possibilities. As a consequence, strategy is not real and it cannot therefore be judged true or correct. Evaluation of strategy is meta-level thinking about the future value of those future actions. And, strictly speaking, strategy can only be evaluated after the consequences of plans unfold.

Levels of direction

Strategy, Policy, Tactics and Operations are often confused with one another. There is a degree of arbitrariness in distinguishing between them because they all refer to aspects of corporate direction. I choose to separate these concepts, for convenience, in terms of the criteria which follow.

Policy is the term I will use to refer to the highest or most general level of corporate direction; for instance, directions from the Board of a public company. Policy forms an envelope of direction within which strategic objectives are formed. These, in turn, define the conceptual space within which Tactics are decided, and Operations are determined. Strategy therefore takes its general direction from purposes set by Policy, and it in turn, sets the direction for Tactics.

To illustrate, let us hypothesise that Nokia's Policy is to achieve a certain return on investment in a particular future year, say 10 years hence. This goal frames Strategy. To achieve this Policy objective, Nokia will need to contend with several ambitious current and future rivals. Strategic direction formed within this Policy might be to dominate 3G technology before its competitors are able to gain a foothold in this emerging market. Tactically, actions would need to be taken to secure advantage in relevant technology and to draw so closely to mobile operators that competitors would find it difficult to negotiate a position of advantage. Tactical objectives would be turned into Operations, that is, into the particular practical steps needed to ensure that technology and relationships with mobile operators are secured.

Ideally, Policy, through Strategy to Tactics and Operations, should be aligned with one another so that Policy directions are eventually accomplished at the lowest level by Operations. Non-alignment at any level requires resetting direction either above or below.

Hierarchical relationships among Policy, Strategy, Tactics and Operations can be distinguished by three criteria:[30]

1. *Time Horizon*: Strategy is concerned with the longer, rather than shorter term outlook. Its considerations lie between Tactics which are short term, and Policy which has a time perspective as long as is possible for the enterprise.

2. *Size of Asset Commitment*: Strategy is concerned with a larger, rather than smaller asset commitment; larger than is needed for Tactics and smaller than the entire asset base of the firm which is the concern for Policy.

3. *Decision Reversibility*: Strategic decisions are substantial and therefore rather difficult to reverse. They are more difficult to reverse than those of Tactics, but not of the great trouble to reverse which is typical of Policy.

Table 1.1 *Interdependence among Strategy Concepts.*

Concepts of Strategy	Purpose	Reason	Advantage	Future
Purpose	Aspirations of corporate stakeholders inform corporate aims			
Reason	Direction logically created as a path from aims to compelling claims for specific action	Rational, logical argument for direction using valid information and explanation		
Advantage	Direction secures interests of stakeholders relative to rival aspirations and capability	Systematic appraisal of interests of competitors revealing threats and opportunities	Benefit to corporate interests relative to intention and capability of specified rivals	
Future	Direction secures enduring protection of stakeholder interests	Systematic assessment of alternative likely linked events through scenarios	Interests secured relative to actions of current and future rivals in anticipated situations	Anticipated outcomes of action, situations and likely events in longer term

Finally in distinguishing among levels of direction, scale matters; while the concept of Strategy, enveloped within Policy and guiding Tactics, is a useful abstract device for showing what is required for unity of direction, distinctions cannot be universal. What is Strategic thinking in a small firm might be Tactics in a larger one.

These four primary concepts help to explain what strategic thinking entails, as I intend to show. They are not independent of each other; in strategic thinking they form an interdependent cluster, a holistic idea, rather than one comprising a set of discrete elements. Each concept relates to each other, as Table 1.1 shows in sketch form. The combination of concepts forms a basis for the discussion of Principles which follows in subsequent chapters.

Principles

Now I invite the reader to take a short leap of faith; I am about to assert a set of Principles before fully explaining them. It is my view that a deep and diverse heritage in strategic thinking, such as has been introduced above, offers to enrich our understanding of the essence of strategy. The product of my own analytical and integrative effort in drawing insights from these various sources is a set of six Principles of Strategy. These are the main topics of the chapters which follow. But before proceeding I first introduce the Principles themselves. Since there is much ground to cover exploring each one, and because of the interdependence and overlap among them, I urge the reader to suspend critical judgement about these ideas until they have all been fully explored.

The Principles of Strategy are asserted as guidelines for both the development of strategic thinking and for evaluating strategy. They are prescriptive propositions, which, taken together, incorporate both the four essential concepts of strategy distilled above, and the recurrent themes about strategy identified in contemporary and classic sources.

The Principles are as follows:

1. *Principle of Competition*: Strategy is a purposeful activity; it is aimed at achieving beneficial corporate goals in competition with rivals aiming to gain the same objectives. Corporate purpose therefore, is to outwit out-manoeuvre and outperform the competition.[31] Competitive intelligence is required to inform strategy about the intentions and capabilities of rivals. Strategic thinking must also take regard of the competitive context to appreciate the effects of potential opportunities and pitfalls.

More formally stated, *Strategy ensures that the enterprise maintains its orientation towards those rivals who could interfere with corporate aims.*

2. *Principle of Assessment*: Assessment involves two components: design, which is the formulation of a logical argument for action; and evaluation, the estimation of relative value of alternative courses of action.[32]

In essence, *Strategy ensures that the enterprise creates a compelling and logical argument for choice of direction to achieve aims.*

3. *Principle of Integrity*: A central idea in strategic thinking is devising initiative; designing decisive pre-emptive thrusts while adapting to circumstances to dislocate a rival's activities. Strategic thinking is unified through building and maintaining competitive momentum, flexibly adapting to changing circumstances, and by maintaining competitive readiness.

Thus, *Strategy ensures that the enterprise maintains unity of thinking which concentrates on progressive enhancement of competitive advantage.*

4. *Principle of Security*: Progress towards goals is secured through main-tenance of freedom of action and balance. Time in all its aspects, is central to strategy. So also is the ability to influence a rival's perception of the competitive circumstances he or she faces. Out of impressions they form, a rival is overpowered. Efforts to shape rivals' perceptions and their conse-quent choice among courses of actions should be designed to restrict com-petitive freedom of movement. Such influence is designed to increase a rival's perception of perceived dependence.

Thus, *Strategy ensures that the enterprise secures its position from a condition of psychological strength and stability.*

5. *Principle of Feasibility*: Assets and abilities necessary to enable accom-plishment of aims need to be acquired and maintained. Strategic capability is enhanced by securing systemic uniqueness in assets and through developing the ability to outwit rivals. Alliances strengthen strategy to the degree that they reinforce strategic assets and abilities. Allies will support strategy to the degree that they are satellites which extend competitive influence.

In brief, *Strategy ensures that the enterprise acquires and maintains sufficient capability to accomplish aims.*

6. *Principle of Morality*: Strategy will be judged on whether its aims and associated actions are good and right. Strategic thinking therefore needs to be ethically defensible.

Finally therefore, *Strategy ensures that the enterprise acts consistently with ethically principled judgement in achievement of aims.*

The Principles introduced above are constructed on a foundation formed from the primary concepts discussed earlier. The essence of this foundation is explained and illustrated in Table 1.2.

The statements of Principle and Table 1.2 are intended to guide progress through the chapters which follow, each dwelling on one of these Principles in turn. The final chapter employs a case study which shows how the Prin-ciples relate to one another to form a combined interdependent whole.

Table 1.2 *Relationships between Strategy Concepts and Principles.*

Strategy: Concepts and Principles	Purpose:	Reason:	Advantage:	Future:
	Aspirations of corporate stakeholders inform corporate aims	Rational, logical argument for direction using valid information and explanation	Benefit to corporate interests relative to intention and capability of specified rivals	Anticipated outcomes of action, situations and likely events in longer term
Competition: Orientation to those with rival claims	Purpose in competition is to secure enterprise and its aims against others with rival claims	Commerce is a potential intersection of interests among competing rivals	Benefits accrue to a competitor able to reduce own weaknesses and exploit rival vulnerabilities	Commercial competition contains the potential for rivalry over interests in the indefinite future
Assessment: Compelling logical case for direction	Construction of convincing, logical and rational argument supporting purposeful course of action	Explanation of basis for choice of intended direction ensures non-rational elements are avoided and motivation is raised	Evaluation of benefits and limitations of alternative courses of action underpin advantage	Appraisal of competitive circumstances as they exist, and as they could be, is the basis for design of action for anticipated benefit
Integrity: Concentration on advantage	Initiative, flexibility and balance are purposeful activities designed to secure competitive momentum	Explicit reasoning reveals the basis for creation of direction intended to upset rival equilibrium	Maintenance of initiative secures control of competitive momentum	Competitive momentum keeps a competitor disadvantaged for the time it can be maintained

Table 1.2 *Continued*

Strategy: Concepts and Principles	Purpose: Aspirations of corporate stakeholders inform corporate aims	Reason: Rational, logical argument for direction using valid information and explanation	Advantage: Benefit to corporate interests relative to intention and capability of specified rivals	Future: Anticipated outcomes of action, situations and likely events in longer term
Security: Psychological control of impressions	Purposeful management of rival's impressions of time, reality and dependence to cause disorientation	Creation of impressions relies on formulation of logic of interpretation from rival's viewpoint	A competitor deprived of an accurate sense of reality is vulnerable to loss of advantage	Creation of false impression is designed to temporarily disable a rival to secure a better position of future advantage
Feasibility: Maintenance of capability	Purposeful assembly and maintenance of assets, abilities and allies to secure advantage	Capability underpins rationale for securing interests through transformation of circumstances	Maintenance of advantage depends on ensuring relative capability is superior	Capability declines over time, undermining competitive effort and advantage; must therefore be sustained
Morality: Action consistent with principled standards of behaviour	Purposeful identification of values and standards of behaviour to secure reputation	Adoption of assertive or defensive posture logically maintains finite game within infinite game	A competitor's reputation as an acceptable player in an infinite game depends on articulation of values and standards of behaviour	Reputation is a future appraisal of a competitor's acceptability as a member of a competitive commercial community

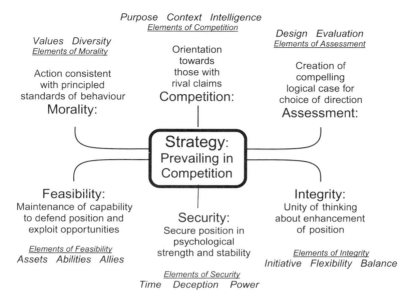

Figure 1.1 Concept map for Strategy.

There the reader will find a comprehensive basis for understanding and evaluating strategic thinking.

The diagram above is a concept map[33] (Figure 1.1) guiding the visualisation of the following chapters.

Reflection

Can there be competition without strategy?
Can one have a strategy to climb a mountain?

2

Competition

Principle of Competition: Strategy ensures that the enterprise maintains its orientation towards those rivals who could interfere with corporate aims.

An orientation towards competition builds on the concept of a strategic threshold, a moment for contemplation of future competitive direction. It involves three components: purpose; the essential aim of interaction with a commercial rival; understanding of competitive context, that is, the circumstances in which competition occurs; and competitive intelligence, the estimation of the intentions and capabilities of a rival, and masking of one's own intentions and capabilities from a competitor.

Companies which sell chocolate delights to treat, indulge and please their customers might be expected, themselves, to be generous and friendly participants in a kindly and charitable industry. Not so; at least, not so all the time. The two largest firms in the confectionery industry in the United States, Mars Inc and Hershey, share a century-long history which began with mutual support fostered by their founders. Mars is a private company and Hershey is publicly listed. Today, and for the past 30 years, these two companies have been engaged in a sometimes brutal struggle for supremacy.[1]

Both companies have cultures which were shaped by their founders. Hershey was the dream of a utopian idealist; Mars emerged from an indomitable will to succeed. Elements of these different ideas survive today in each of the firms. However, what both have in common is a simple strategic objective: to prevail over the other in commercial competition.

Although rivalry is their common orientation, this is not to say that executives and staff in both companies care less than a great deal about their products and their customers. In different ways and at different times, both companies have invested very substantially in initiatives designed to invent new products, improve production efficiency and enhance product quality. But the competitive eye, each for the other, has not wavered.

Battles between the two companies have erupted periodically as each has attempted to secure its interests.[2] In 1964 Forrest Mars, son of the founder, took control of Mars and immediately decided to end his firm's dependence on Hershey for chocolate. Until that time its commercial competitor had been the supplier of one of its most important ingredients. Mars was determined to secure control of all of his business. This affected Hershey badly because Mars was a major customer. Shortly afterward, two of Mars' key senior staff defected to Hershey and proceeded to instil an aggressive market discipline which was common in Mars, but which had never been seen before in Hershey.

Over the years commercial attacks against each other continued. One such struggle took place over a very large contract to the United States military for supply of confectionery to soldiers at the time of the first Gulf War. Accusations of unfairness and underhanded practices were exchanged. Shortly afterwards, Mars relaunched one of its products in packaging with a similar style and colour to one of Hershey's best selling items. Another vigorous struggle ensued. Bitter accusations were expressed by both sides; 'fair and legal' was the claim from one side, and 'desperate and illegal opportunism' from the other.

The object of the competition throughout has been market share, especially the proportion of sales controlled by each in the United States. Mars and Hershey both take the view that the major share is rightly theirs; 'rightly' is a sense of the natural order of things, it almost has an ethical dimension. When one regains dominance, even by a very small margin, it is met by celebration in the winning camp, and disbelief in the other. In 1973, for instance, Mars surpassed Hershey's market share after a very successful marketing campaign. Staff at Hershey found this state of affairs difficult to acknowledge.

Purposefulness is a primary element of strategic thinking in each firm. So also is attention to environmental circumstances. Both firms rely on a relatively small set of vital ingredients for their products, principally, cocoa and sugar. Prices of these raw materials are very volatile, fluctuating significantly on world markets. An important element of competitive orientation has been the effort of each firm in trying to outperform the other in managing uncertainty in these commodity prices. Mars developed very sophisticated models for predicting their raw materials prices. Hershey tried integrating backwards into raw material production.

Attempts to better anticipate shifts in relevant commodity prices were designed, of course, to improve competitive position. In 1973, when Mars overtook Hershey's market share, the success of one over the other occurred in conjunction with a sudden and generally unexpected rise in world prices for cocoa and sugar. Mars was much better prepared for this event than Hershey. This was a valuable opportunity for Mars to capitalise while Hershey was vulnerable. Its initiative was swift and brutal.

The confectionery industry is well known for its secrets. Formulae for combination of ingredients, subtle methods of blending and forming, technology; each has the potential for success or failure. The chemistry enabling chocolate to 'melt in the mouth but not in the hand' is an example of one such vital product secret.

Just as the industry is notorious for its secrets, so also are its efforts to protect them. Competitors are extremely suspicious of an attempt by any outsider to learn about methods of production, not to mention results of market research and product launch plans. Mars is perhaps the most secretive of all; the extent of cloaking of all its activities is well known, to the point of near corporate invisibility. It goes without saying that intelligence gathering is a well practiced art in the industry.

Competition in the confectionery industry illustrates the point that executive thinking about business dwells on two principal ideas: markets and rivals. When does concentration on rivals occur and what is the trigger for confrontation?

As I explain in this chapter, harmonious and orderly relationships between businesses are disturbed through disruptive action when executives in one firm or another perceive that their sense of commercial order has been threatened by another business. Then competitors position their commercial rivals in full view. This emerging situation comprises a threshold for strategic thinking, that is, thinking directed towards taking a position to prevail in competition. As we shall see, the consequent competitive orientation can be usefully explained in terms of purpose, context and competitive intelligence.

Strategic threshold

In this section, I present a detailed theoretical argument which leads to the specification of the term *strategic threshold*. Beforehand, a state of commercial harmony describes an ongoing steady state in relationships between businesses. Then, as the reader will see, a psychological moment might arrive when an executive realises that relationships with other businesses in his or her industry now need to be considered differently. It is a point where confrontation, and therefore strategy, comes to mind.

The steps in the following discussion are: first, to outline the features of harmonious commercial behaviour. Next, I describe confrontational competitive behaviour between businesses. Last, the strategic threshold is the trigger which leads to a shift from harmony to confrontation.

Dynamics of harmony

A view which attracts widespread support among scholars of strategic management is one of competition among firms in a market, going about the business of satisfying the needs of customers. Rivalry, according to this perspective, comprises efforts by competitors to outperform potential alternative suppliers to customers in terms of a range of products and services with such attributes as price, quality, service and product performance.

The perspective would provide an acceptable and typical description of the aluminium industry,[3] for instance. The two largest businesses in this industry, Alcan and Alcoa, perform in markets alongside each other, acquiring alumina, converting it to aluminium and selling it to their clients. The main issues that face them both are the cost of supply of alumina, the cost of conversion to aluminium and the level of demand from manufacturers who buy their product.

Within this view relationships among competitors are harmonious as each firm accepts certain rules of competition which provide for peaceful coexistence. Certain aspects of such commercial behaviour recur, including reference to objectives and markets, a coping response to environmental variability and a striving for a stable equilibrium among intercorporate relationships which are accepted as mutually dependent.

Objectives and markets

Both Alcoa and Alcan are public companies and as such perform to meet the expectations of stakeholders, while aligning objectives with market conditions. As circumstances alter so also do performance targets.

The idea of alignment of corporate strategic purpose with environmental conditions is a common theme in strategic thinking as it has evolved over the past decade or more. Porter[4] frames the goal of competitive strategy in terms of positioning in relation to industry forces and effort to gain a return on investment which is superior to other options. Return on investment, in Ansoff's[5] view, is typically the basis of corporate objectives, determined in part through aims at business growth and stability.

Ansoff's customer and market focus is somewhat narrower than the perspective taken by Andrews[6] who identifies corporate strategy in terms of relationships among a much broader range of stakeholders. Andrews argues for a long term perspective, as well as a view to the short term:

> Management of a corporation with a future better than its past requires clarification of company objectives, confidence that comes from commitment to a future oriented program of action, and determination that careful formulation of plans rationally supports it.[7]

Much of this sense of direction is developed in an attempt to maintain alignment between internal goals and the aspirations of external stakeholders. The concept of alignment is also a common theme in the outlook of Miles and Snow[8] who propose that firms seek structural, strategic and process alignments with their customers in product markets. Through emphasis on customers and product markets attention is centred on maintenance of supportive business relationships.

Environmental variability

From time to time prices of alumina supply change with the various fortunes of bauxite miners. Alumina transformation is strongly affected by energy costs. Demand is influenced by national goals for productivity, such as those evolved in China. Economic conditions worldwide also have an impact on demand for aluminium as manufacturers respond to changes in product requirements. Change in technology will also bring a further consideration for the aluminium firms.

Inevitable acceptance of variability and uncertainty in a firm's commercial environment has been accommodated in theory in a variety of ways. Miles and Snow,[9] for example, view a firm as developing ways with which to cope with such change, suggesting a responsive stance, notwithstanding the strategic behaviour of their Prospector category of business strategy. This outlook is similar to that of Ansoff[10] who certainly acknowledges the significance of turbulence in formulating strategic objectives, but who barely recognises competitive rivals within his market orientation. Andrews,[11] in contrast, identifies choice of strategic group as a critical decision taken by a firm in preserving its strategic advantage. It is this group of rivals which defines the firm's market and the parameters of competition in its industry. In the case of aluminium, Alcoa and Alcan would comprise the prominent members of this group. Porter[12] and Henderson[13] also recognise environmental variability as a source of sustainable competitive advantage which permits a firm to succeed after recognising and reinforcing the elements of its relatively different history, objectives and behaviour.

Stability, continuity and equilibrium

As well as linking to their markets, Alcan and Alcoa also relate to one another and a wider array of industry-related participants. It is clearly in the interests of all participants that their relationships be stable and as predictable as possible.

Henderson[14] argues that 'Business is a system in equilibrium', a view which is also taken up by Porter[15] who refers to the idea of balance among industry forces and a firm's competitive position being in equilibrium among its commercial rivals. More recently, Kay[16] develops an argument based on the idea that competitive advantage is itself dependent on maintaining stability and continuity in value enhancing exchange relationships with suppliers and customers.

Although equilibrium has been advanced as a characterisation of relationships among firms, and this relationship is stable, it is also clearly acknowledged that the equilibrium is dynamic: firms seek continuity with continuing effort to sustain relative advantage. The process of accomplishment of stability is an adaptive cycle which, in terms of the model proposed by Miles and Snow,[17] involves a cyclic relationship among selection of market domain, creation of technological process to deliver products and an administrative function to control and co-ordinate.

Mutual dependence

When adopting the particular perspective of firms competing in strategic groups, several writers have pointed to the importance of appreciating mutual dependence among the strategic interests of competitors. Porter,[18] for example, underlines the idea that successful strategy depends on competitors choosing non-destructive moves. In his later book[19] he characterises firms as 'good competitors' or 'bad', that is, good or bad for the strategic group and for industry stability. He identifies factors which operate to the benefit of all competitors, including an understanding among firms of the prevailing rules of competition in the industry, a realistic estimate of potential market growth, moderate stakes in the industry, an acceptance of current levels of profitability and comparable ROI targets. It is in the interests of all competitors, he argues, to remain 'good' competitors. These views are consistent with Henderson's[20] earlier views about what comprises the goal of good strategy: a set of stable relationships favourable to one's own firm which are supported with the tacit consent of competitors.

The point here is that it is to the benefit of both Alcoa and Alcan to behave predictably in relation to each other. If either one was to deviate from an *acceptable* range of behaviour, then the expected outcome would possibly harm one or the other, probably both; at least such would be the rationale among executives in both firms.

Drawing together the elements of strategic thinking presented above, the overlapping interest among firms in an industry centres primarily on customers and product markets. One aspect of the strategic problem facing a firm is maintaining its distinctive relationships with its markets. Another is the problem of maintaining its place in mutual dependence with other firms in the industry.

Conditions of commercial harmony which comprise a collective solution by competing companies to maintenance of equilibrium can be represented

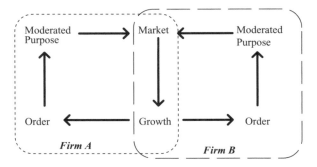

Figure 2.1 Dynamics of harmony.

by a cycle of relationships among four clusters of variables drawn from the discussion above. These are hypothesised as groups of related ideas which are recognisable as distinct elements of a strategist's cognitive map.

Figure 2.1 represents relationships among these variables: Markets, Growth, Order and Moderated Purpose. For simplicity, it refers to strategic relationships among two firms (such as Alcan and Alcoa). Four variables are associated with Firm A (for instance Alcoa), and the same four are associated with Firm B (Alcan). Order and Moderated Purpose are internal variables for each company. Growth and Markets are also associated with each firm, but they overlap due to the interaction of choices made by each company separately. The diagram illustrates the mutually interdependent problem solving within the intersecting market interaction and growth aspirations of Porter's 'good' competitors in a stable industry. Order and Moderated Purpose are separate for each competitor, comprising each firm's view of itself, the industry and its competitors.

Further explanation of each of the four variables follows:

Markets: Industry participants such as Alcan and Alcoa establish prices, produce to a certain level of quality and offer products and services in particular quantities. This cluster of variables includes the outcome of strategic choices affecting internal and external issues such as production, distribution, organisation and finance associated with a firm's product or service. Choices affecting this cluster of variables are governed by corporate objectives (*Moderated Purpose* below).

Growth: Alcoa and Alcan set explicit or implicit goals for such indicators of growth as profitability and return on investment. This cluster of variables includes the set of indicators which a strategist chooses to represent corporate performance. The general label of *'growth'* is an indication of a performance position which is perceived as progressive and beneficial to the firm. Growth is an outcome of the interaction among *Market* variables as influenced by the actions of firms, such as Alcan and Alcoa, competing for customer loyalty.

Order: In broad terms a firm strives to maintain its self-perceived stature or place in an industry through such indicators as acceptable levels of market share and participation in particular product markets. Executives in Alcoa and Alcan would hold particular views about the status of their companies within the aluminium industry. This cluster of variables incorporates historical and political influences, the values of the senior executive group and strategic aspirations. In essence the cluster is the referent for vital interests of the company and defines stability from the company's strategic perspective. It will therefore be dependent on indicators of *Growth*.

Moderated Purpose: Corporate purpose is not unconstrained. Competitors strive for stability in their industry to allow a level of predicability and to seek protection of their own market position, often through seeking a niche. This cluster of variables is a translation of perceived *Order* into a set of objectives which will ensure protection of the current equilibrium in the firm's industry.

The pattern of relationships among the four clusters of variables representing the hypothesised thought process of executives in a firm can be explained as follows. A firm (say Alcan) formulates its objectives in the context of industry expectations, moderating its own purpose to maintain order for the benefit of industry stability. The collective purposes of firms (Alcan and Alcoa) interact through market activities where adjustments occur in price, quality, service and location through attempts among competitors to sustain relative advantage in a way which is acceptable to rivals. The outcome of the interaction among market processes is a set of relationships among growth paths for competitors (Alcan and Alcoa), where once again, firms strive for mutually acceptable growth. The next step in the cycle is an examination by each firm (say Alcan) of its place in the order of affairs of the industry. In this phase a firm would determine whether it

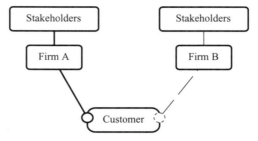

Figure 2.2 Harmony among businesses.

was prepared to accept its market share, for example, or instead initiate a shift in its objectives for incremental improvement in the next round of continuing mutual adjustment of purpose.

Based on the model presented in Figure 2.1, a harmonious and stable strategic relationship among firms in an industry derives from activity associated with stakeholders on one hand and customers on the other. Kay,[21] for example, refers to the concept of architecture of relational contracts networking the firm with suppliers and customers. Figure 2.2 represents the patterns of activity by two firms with their separate stakeholders and the actual and potential interaction with customers. A customer with a need or preference for a product or service typically has the option to choose between two or more suppliers in an industry; the chosen supplier develops an active relationship and the other remains a potential alternative.

Dynamics of confrontation

There is no doubt that activity represented in its simplest form in Figure 2.2 captures the essence of much commercial behaviour. But other aspects of commercial behaviour, perhaps not exhibited so commonly, but nevertheless real, are not reflected in Figure 2.2.

Behaviour which is overlooked in a model of harmonious equilibrium includes action illustrated in Figure 2.3 which is clearly confrontational. This diagram identifies three varieties of confrontational behaviour which supplement commercial actions shown in Figure 2.2. The combination of actions shown in Figure 2.3 is advanced as a qualitatively different variety of commercial behaviour which is not taken into account in Figure 2.1.

What kinds of action are conceivable in the competitive initiatives mounted by Firm B in Figure 2.3?

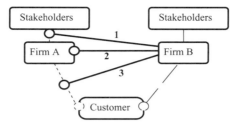

Figure 2.3 Confrontation between businesses.

Illustrations follow referring to the numbered points of confrontational activity shown in Figure 2.3:

1. *Firm B acts against Firm A's relationship with its stakeholders:* Firm B, for example, acquires control of a supplier to Firm A. The supplier is no longer free to support Firm A as a preferred provider through a conflict of interest with its new owner.

2. *Firm B acts directly against Firm A:* To illustrate this action, Firm B attracts key staff away from Firm A or begins purchasing shares in Firm A giving the impression of a move towards acquisition.

3. *Firm B acts against Firm A's relationship with its customers:* Firm B, for instance, offers incentives to current customers of Firm A to draw them into new relationships with Firm B. For example, advance publicity of a new product which would incorporate all of the functions of the current offering of Firm A with additional attractive features would comprise an action by Firm B against Firm A's customers. To illustrate further, Firm B encourages the spread of rumours about operational difficulties currently facing Firm A which call into question the likely long term viability of Firm A as a supplier to the customer.

How does the literature account for these forms of confrontational corporate behaviour?

Despite its traditional preoccupation with competitiveness, scholarship in the field of strategic management has, until recently, largely overlooked interaction between rival companies.[22] Porac, Thomas, Wilson, Paton and Kanfer[23] note that competition has largely been viewed from an environmental perspective with competitiveness inferred from resource transactions in the tradition of population ecology.[24] Likewise, Chen and his associates[25] observe that aggregate studies of industry competitiveness have overlooked issues which shape actual exchanges of action and response among competing firms.

Rivalry has perhaps been put aside through an apparent reluctance among scholars of business strategy, apart from Chen and his colleagues, to openly admit to the existence of the phenomenon of confrontation in commerce. Perhaps scholarly distaste arises from analogues of corporate behaviour which evoke visions of violence and destruction. Comparison between business and military strategy sometimes draws fleeting reference,[26] but more typically reactions are extreme. The idea that commerce is anything like warfare is often dismissed because it is claimed that business is about continuing co-existence among competitors and mutually beneficial relationships with customers and suppliers,[27] not elimination of rivals.[28] Furthermore it is claimed, the principles and theory of military strategy are too simplistic to be applied to the more complex activity of business.[29] Some even claim that use of the metaphor is simply unethical.[30]

Yet the language of aggressive rivalry is frequently used among observers and commentators on business competition, suggesting that interaction among industry competitors includes, at least on occasion, behaviour which is not harmonious and less than mutually beneficial for industry rivals. *The Economist*, for example, refers in recent times to feuds between business software development firms Oracle and SAP.[31] In the same issue the longstanding struggle between Boeing and Airbus continues.[32] In Japan intense rivalry is reported in the broadcast industry.[33] These are not isolated references to intense intercorporate struggle.

Business leaders themselves admit to being influenced by military thinking.[34] Writers of popular books and articles on the military metaphor, including Ramsey and James,[35] and Clemons and Santamaria,[36] draw attention to common references among executives to military terms when referring to business competition. The reality of commercial confrontation has encouraged those who recognise the parallels with military warfare to enthusiastically embrace well established military principles as a guide for business strategy. Adoption of the military metaphor is considered by Cohen[37] and Kotler and Singh,[38] for instance, to offer perspectives on ways of formulating solutions to pressing problems of aggressive business competition.

The more typical interpretation of aggressiveness in commerce has a relatively limited market focus. Ansoff,[39] for instance, refers to the aggressiveness of a firm's marketing capability in terms of its costs, its number of independent customers and its application of new technology. Similarly, Miles and Snow[40] refer to aggressiveness in terms of creating new markets and vigour in serving customers. While a market focus and competitive harmony appear to be the prevailing view in perspectives on strategic management, there is acknowledgement among some that the preferred stable equilibrium among competitors can sometimes be disturbed. This involves direct action against confrontational rivals who threaten commercial interests.

At times such as this the rules which govern behaviour change. Reference to the metaphor of war is not uncommon. In the introduction to his book, *The Philosophy of War*, Clark[41] refers to war as a transition from normal (peaceful) order of society, under one set of rules, to life under a different (war) set of rules. Importantly, war does not refer to the absence of rules altogether. No doubt the same is true in commerce. War is goal-related since it does not refer to indiscriminate violence; it is constrained and restricted. Under the regime of rules of war, the strategic problem for a competitor is how to create and maintain advantage. A number of commonly accepted themes are available to support this point of view. They refer to advantage deriving from competitor intelligence, activities to disadvantage rivals, psychological aspects of confrontation, secrecy and deception and the concept of limited competition and voluntary restraint.

I introduce, for speculation, the relationship between two firms: RIM (Research in Motion) a Canadian firm, and Microsoft.[42] Of particular interest is the posture of both companies over hand-held e-mail devices. The essence of the situation is that RIM has introduced BlackBerry, the first such device, and Microsoft is most likely motivated to respond to its benefit and RIM's disadvantage.

What factors and forces are likely to be in operation in this increasingly tense relationship?

Competitor intelligence

Both RIM and Microsoft will undoubtedly be trying to find out as much as possible about the intentions and capabilities of each other in relation to e-mail devices.

In a commercial context, Henderson[43] stresses the importance of preparation for rival confrontation. He advises firms to go to great lengths to collect information to form a detailed estimate of the capabilities and intentions of rival companies. Only through gaining knowledge of relative strengths of competitors can one prepare for defensive action. Most important is an appraisal of a rival's likely reactions to strategic initiatives one might take. Porter[44] goes so far as to encourage firms to develop a Competitor Intelligence System which formally monitors rivals as an ongoing corporate function. Gordon[45] translates this imperative into practical advice.

Sun Tzu,[46] in an ancient military setting, also calls for thorough understanding of the dispositions and distribution of power of the opposition. O'Dowd and Waldron[47] refer to this as knowledge of *hsu* (emptiness in the sense of weak line in a strong formation) and *shih* (solidness – strongly defended position with high morale, leadership and action according to moral code). The strategic advantage offered through this knowledge is concentration of *ch'i* (life force) while the enemy disperses his *ch'i*, allowing occupation of a favourable position creating the prospect of a victory from disadvantages created by the enemy's own tactics.

For von Clausewitz,[48] intelligence is necessary to form the basis of plans and operations. Information of every sort about the enemy and the country is vital; but such information is typically unreliable and transient. The reality of false, contradictory and uncertain reports is worst when incorrect reports reinforce each other. Only judgement can form the most reliable interpretation of incoming intelligence.

Disadvantaging rivals

Microsoft has a history of severely disabling its commercial rivals; the fall of Netscape is a well-known example. RIM is aware of this and must prepare.

Once a confrontational struggle develops Porter[49] advises taking action which will disadvantage a rival, preferably by taking initiatives to which the rival will be frozen from responding. This is consistent with the theme of attempting to take pre-emptive actions which will prevent a battle from ensuing. A range of options are identified by Porter. These include such tactics as denying the rival a base.

Henderson[50] is forthright in stating that commercial strategy must include the means for upsetting competitive equilibrium and re-establishing it on a more favourable basis. Foremost among his tactical advice is to concentrate a firm's effort and resources against a rival in such a way as to avoid a spirited counterattack, through first eliminating the ability and the willingness of the rival to respond. The value of this initiative depends most importantly on knowledge of how and when a competitor is likely to respond. All action, according to Henderson, is designed to persuade a rival to desist.

As O'Dowd and Waldron[51] observe, the strategic advice of Sun Tzu is founded on the value of preserving harmony by inducing chaos in the camp of a rival. Sun Tzu acknowledges that war is a serious concern because it risks the economic, social and political harmony or stability of a state. War should therefore be fought to minimise the risks to one's own state and create chaos to shatter the enemy. Warfare is a last resort.

In the view of von Clausewitz[52] the military object of war is determined by political objectives; importantly, war is not an independently defined military affair. But once military objectives have been formulated they will inevitably be framed in terms of overcoming or disarming the enemy. To overcome the enemy it is necessary to match effort against the rival's power of resistance, that is, the total means at his disposal and the strength of his will. Military activity is never directed against material force alone; it is also aimed simultaneously at the moral forces which give it life. Von Clausewitz views the material and moral as inseparable.

Psychological aspects of confrontation

RIM executives express confidence in the likely success of their BlackBerry product over possible rival devices; Microsoft is edging predictably towards release of its own comparable product. Microsoft executives are not speaking about BlackBerry. Such is the public posturing stemming from the mind game in play.

Successful strategic response to confrontation depends as much on a rival's psychological and emotional state as it does on the availability of material, financial and human resources. Porter[53] recommends meeting a confrontational rival with a form of competition for which they are ill prepared and least enthusiastic. This, he argues, will have the most damaging effect on morale. This initiative must display a demonstrated determination to respond: it must be unambiguously interpreted as a commitment by a firm to preserve and protect its interests.

Of course emotional bias will be a relative matter. Henderson[54] refers to the tactic of demonstrating a very strong and emotionally committed demand of a confrontational rival, most importantly, without drawing an emotional reaction from them. He argues that the rival will be most disadvantaged if placed in a position to rationally choose to desist from destructive action when faced with an emotionally committed rival.

Among the varieties of knowledge which must be assessed, the strength of a rival's will, a purely psychological dimension, must be taken fully into account. In the view of von Clausewitz, this is a critical calculation in assessing power of resistance and the effort required to overcome it. It should not be underestimated. But strength of will is not easy to determine; being unable to be counted, it can only be seen or felt. Spiritual and moral effects arise through qualities of an army, a general or government, the temper of the population and effects of previous victory or defeat. It can only be gauged approximately by the strength of motive animating it. Assessments of spirit and temper of one's own forces and those of the opposition are based largely on experience.

When assessing strategic capability, it is a mistake to underrate professional pride, which is the training, discipline, esprit de corps, confidence through practice and immersion of personality in the appointed task. It is all the more necessary when an army's forces are dispersed and therefore less directly influenced by concentration and direction by the general. Military spirit is one of the most important elements in war. It derives from previous victories and frequent exertions of an army to the utmost limits of its strength.

In von Clausewitz's view war is a matter of assessing probabilities: chance makes it a gamble and this means that guesswork and luck play a great part. Uncertainty places great emphasis on human attributes of courage, boldness and even foolhardiness. But in the final analysis, uncertainty is balanced by courage and self-confidence.

Secrecy and deception

BlackBerry has been sold for some time now; the device has no doubt been studied in intimate detail by Microsoft engineers and marketers. But RIM's plans are not so public. Microsoft has demonstrated a tendency to publicise new software in its forthcoming products to try to pre-empt rivals. Each company tries to influence the perceptions of the other, at the same time, revealing as little as possible.

While it is important to learn as much as possible about a rival, Henderson[55] recommends that information made available to strategic rivals must be kept to a minimum. Only selective information should be disclosed. In fact techniques of diversion and dissuasion depend on creating impressions and appearances of intent that mislead the confrontational rival. Churchill referred to this attribute of great commanders as *legerdemain*.[56]

In the view of Sun Tzu, 'All warfare is based on deception. Therefore, when capable, feign incapacity; when active inactivity. When near, make it appear you are far away; when far away, that you are near.'[57] He refers to the creation of circumstances which are attractive to an opponent in order to draw them into a trap: '. . . those skilled in making the enemy move do so by creating a situation to which he must conform; they entice him with something he is certain to take, and with lures of ostensible profit they await him in strength'.[58]

Von Clausewitz observes that the desire to 'take the enemy by surprise' is a universal military desire; it is basic to all operations '. . . for without it superiority at the decisive point is hardly conceivable. . . . whenever it is achieved on a grand scale, it confuses the enemy and lowers his morale'.[59] The achievement of surprise is integral to Liddell Hart's[60] conclusions about the strategic military advantage in dislocating a rival's forces through indirect approach rather than direct attack.

Henderson[61] is clear about the need for a firm to have the ability to disturb competitive equilibrium to further its interests. But he is also convinced that aggressive commercial behaviour is not unlimited. 'Brinkmanship strategies', as he calls them, are based on voluntary self-restraint whereby action is taken by all confrontational parties to co-operate: the ultimate objective is a return to harmonious stability with coexistence, not annihilation.

This is consistent with Liddell Hart's interpretation of the objective of war:

> . . . nations do not wage war for war's sake, but in pursuance of policy. The military objective is only the means to a political end. . . . The object in war is a better state of peace – even if only from your own point of view. Hence it is essential to conduct war with constant regard to the peace you desire.[62]

This inevitably implies self-restraint, an outlook found also in Sun Tzu's advice:

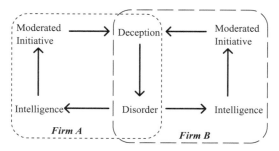

Figure 2.4 Dynamics of confrontation.

Generally in war the best policy is to take a state intact; to ruin it is inferior
to this. . . . For to win one hundred victories in one hundred battles is not
the acme of skill. To subdue the enemy without fighting is the acme of
skill.[63]

Drawing together the ideas presented above, four clusters of variables are
proposed to explain a dynamic and self-sustaining pattern of relationships
among confronting rivals.

The four elements of confrontational competition are: Intelligence,
Moderated Initiative, Deception and Disorder. They are linked with each
other as shown in Figure 2.4. In the simplest case of confrontational
competition between two rivals, each maintains a cycle of intelligence
leading to a moderated initiative, enacted as far as possible through deception
and resulting in disorder for the rival. Intelligence gathering and initiative
lie within the separate domains of the rivals. Deception and disorder occur
in the interaction between the rivals:

Intelligence: The first element in the sequence of processes comprising
confrontation is the assembly of knowledge of all aspects of a rival's
competitive disposition and the circumstances in which the competitive
struggle will take place. Competitive intelligence will be primarily focused
on assessment of the level of *Disorder* experienced by a rival as a result of
previous *Deceptive* action.

Moderated Initiative: Based on *Intelligence* and carefully calculated estimates
of the relative strengths and factors limiting the actions of rivals, and the
likelihood of responses to alternative courses of action, initiatives are taken
with the objective of disturbing and disorienting the rival. This action is

constrained by the level of effort required to accomplish specific long-term objectives.

Deception: Actions are taken with the goal of deliberately misleading a rival about one's intentions. Such action is dependent on maintenance of an *Initiative* which leaves an opponent unbalanced. This cluster of variables incorporates the element of surprise; without surprise, superiority at the decisive point is hardly conceivable. The essence of deception is secrecy and speed.

Disorder: The objective of confrontational action is to bring disarray and 'chaos to the camp' of one's rival, directly resulting from *Deception*. Such disturbance encompasses material and psychological dimensions: disorder to both resources and morale.

Threshold of confrontation

The hypothetical models of harmonious and confrontational competition proposed above are presented as separate dynamic and self-reinforcing relationships among relevant clusters of variables. Both competitive themes are offered as representations of aspects of commercial reality. In the following discussion I make a proposal which accounts for relationships between these coexistent mental maps. Specifically, an argument is developed to explain a shift from harmony to confrontation, and to account for a return to harmony.

In a stable industry comprising Porter's 'good' competitors, relationships between rivals are characterised by the dynamic processes of mutual adjustment which occur in what might be labelled a Plane of Harmony (Figure 2.5). The character of competition can alter fundamentally when one competitor re-evaluates its sense of order and determines that its perceived vital interests need to be protected, defended and action can be taken with reasonable cost to improve them.

In practice, confrontational behaviour emerges under particular sets of conditions which include the following:

- arrival of a new rival;
- slowing demand for a product or service;

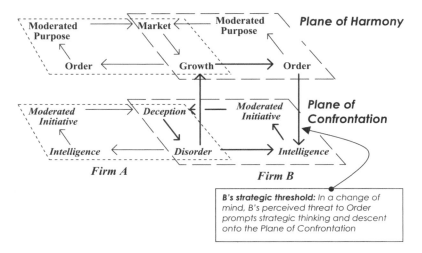

Figure 2.5 Firm B's step into strategy by confrontational initiative.

- industry overcapacity;
- threat to supply;
- corporate distress; and
- during orchestrated rivalry such as occurs during tendering for contracts and sales.

At times such as these, a firm's interests are most sensitive and exposed and threat will most readily be perceived. These will provide the conditions for confrontation as firms attempt to protect or advance their interests. Porter's[64] recommendations for discouraging 'Bad Competitors' would apply.

To return to the example of the aluminium industry, I speculate that the character of relationships among the businesses in the industry, most likely among the minor firms, would shift if there were to emerge a dramatic slowing of demand for the finished product, aluminium. Under these conditions the experience of threat among executives in the minors would be palpable. This would be the threshold of a shift in thinking.

This is a strategic threshold. It is the point where executives in a firm face two broad options: one is to think strategically, responding assertively to the perceived threat to interests. The other is simple acceptance of the new state of affairs, revising the firm's sense of order and establishing new expectations through moderation of purpose.

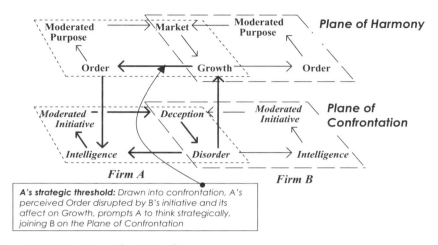

Figure 2.6 Firm A's confrontational response.

If the first course is chosen the aggrieved firm (Firm B in Figure 2.5) initiates a shift in the form of competition into the Plane of Confrontation. Here the cycle of intelligence gathering, initiative, deception and disorder becomes the primary focus of rivalry from Firm B's perspective. The objective of this policy initiative is to act against rivals in such a way as to restore harmony with the firm's interests placed on a more favourable footing. Firm B's action in creating disorder is aimed at redefining the nature of Growth in the Plane of Harmony so that it becomes relatively advantageous to Firm B. Order will be enhanced from Firm B's perspective. At this point the first cycle of confrontational action by Firm B is complete.

Firm A, previously a harmonious industry co-participant, must now respond to the confrontational initiative of Firm B. One option is to decide not to retaliate, accepting the new order created by Firm B and revising corporate objectives accordingly. The other is to join Firm B in the Plane of Confrontation. Figure 2.6 shows how Firm A's response would mirror that of Firm B in a cycle of intelligence gathering, action initiatives, deceptive action and the creation of disorder for Firm B. The mutually reinforcing action involving both firms in the Plane of Confrontation would continue until one firm or the other moderated its objectives in line with those of its rival. In military terms this would be equivalent to a victory to one firm and capitulation by the other.

Henderson[65] points out that it will be most unlikely that the rivals will struggle together 'to the death' when only one competitor will remain.

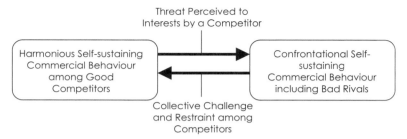

Figure 2.7 Cycles of harmony and confrontation.

There is a process then, by which rivals will challenge, posture and struggle, before voluntarily imposing self-restraint and the relationships among competitors return to harmony. Figure 2.7 represents a continuous cycle of harmony and confrontation.

The overall pattern of possible interactions among firms as they shift between the Planes of Harmony and Confrontation is illustrated in Figure 2.7. It summarises the phenomenon of mutual dependence among firms in harmonious commercial competition, a pattern which is only interrupted by perceived threat to interests by at least one firm through the actions of another. This perception acts as a trigger which shifts the character of competition into a new field with new rules. In Taoist philosophy Lao Tzu warns that this step should not be taken lightly:

> There is no disaster greater than taking on an enemy too easily. So doing nearly cost me my treasure. Thus of two sides raising arms against each other, it is the one that is sorrow-stricken that wins.[66]

While one should be cautious about responding with confrontation, Machiavelli warns also that reluctance can be disastrous. He[67] argues that it is necessary to anticipate troubles likely to arise in the future; if so these can be easily remedied, but if one waits then the problems will become incurable. 'There is no avoiding war', he says, 'it can only be postponed to the advantage of others.' The consequences of being ill prepared for war are clear in his warning to the *Prince*: 'The first way to lose your state is to neglect the art of war; the first way to win a state is to be skilled in the art of war.'[68] When states are lost, he argues, it is not misfortune which is to blame, rather it is indolence. Having never imagined, when times were quiet, that they could change, the first reaction to adversity is flight, not resistance. 'The only sound, sure and enduring methods of defence are those based on your own actions and prowess.'[69]

Confrontational competition persists, then, until there is mutual agreement that the objectives of firms will be moderated with a return to harmony. As a result of the confrontational interlude some firms might return to harmony with greater advantage than they had previously while others will be worse off. However the cessation of confrontation signals mutual acceptance that no further claims for advantage will be made, at least for the time being.

The explanation I offer above provides a reason for a shift in mindset from harmony to confrontation. The point of that shift is called a *strategic threshold*. There is cause to believe that strategic thinking, which is what occurs as competitors engage with one another in the Plane of Confrontation, does not persist indefinitely. It continues only until both, at least tacitly, agree that they have had enough and are unwilling to continue the confrontation.

The Plane of Confrontation is the domain of strategy and strategic thinking. It is what competitors think and do while engaged in this Plane that is of primary interest to us here. The next steps involve further discussion of competition and competitiveness, beginning with why and where: purpose and context.

Table 2.1 is a diagrammatic representation of the intent of the Principle of Competition once a strategic threshold has been reached. It gives an impression of the holistic sense in which Purpose, Context and Competitive Intelligence relate to one another. The diagonal cells represent the essence of each idea, and the off-diagonal cells refer to the relationships between these elements for a competitor with an *assertive* or *defensive* posture.

Aspects of the strategic thinking of both Mars and Hershey, particularly their views of competition, can be interpreted through this Table. Both were accustomed to taking *assertive* and *defensive* postures. Almost through turn taking, one would push to define the shape of their competitive relationship; the other would defend. Then the initiatives would be reversed. Their aims were common: the purpose was to dominate the confectionery industry. An assertive thrust by one would combine creation of discretion to build advantage, by redefining some aspect of the context in which rivalry occurred, with clear insight into the other's intentions and capability. A defensive response would comprise an attempt to deny the other's freedom of

Table 2.1 *Interactions among Purpose, Context and Competitive Intelligence.*

Competition: Orientation towards rivals to secure interests	Purpose	Context	Competitive Intelligence
Purpose	Essential aim in competitive engagement is to prevail over rival	*Deny a rival the freedom to shape circumstances to their advantage*	*Understanding of rival's intentions and capability enables identification of competitive threat*
Context	Choose and shape the competitive situation to ensure that likelihood of prevailing over rival is enhanced	Appreciation of circumstances in which confrontation is to occur	*Appreciation of competitive circumstances enables projection of likely threat in rival strategy*
Competitive Intelligence	Understanding of rival's intentions and capability enables identification of competitive opportunity	Appreciation of competitive circumstances enables projection of likely vulnerability in rival strategy	Securing an accurate understanding of rivals' intentions and capabilities

Assertive strategic posture
Defensive strategic posture

commercial movement by identifying the context in which the thrust was designed to take place, all with some knowledge of the other's strategic thinking.

Having sketched the combination of elements which comprise a framework for competition, and thus strategic thinking, I now invite the reader to join me in conceptually dismantling this cluster to examine each separately and more closely.

Competition

I begin with a definition. Competition is defined here in its elemental form as a particular type of relationship existing between two or more human entities seeking relative advantage in a common situation. Sport comes easily to mind.[70] Each participant has the aim of employing his or her capabilities to enhance value, while being both vigilant to the activities of others, and also being willing and able to protect interests if necessary.

How has competition in commerce been viewed by prominent scholars in contemporary business literature? How, for instance, would these various scholars interpret rivalry between Carrefour, Wal-Mart and Tesco, the world's top three supermarket retailers?[71]

Kenneth Andrews[72]

Kenneth Andrews and his colleagues at the Harvard Business School were the founders of contemporary thinking about strategy in business. The concept of corporate strategy which Andrews presents is his explanation for the way in which business executives consider and conduct strategy. His ideas are based on research conducted after World War II with senior executives in Fortune 500 companies, those leading the largest and most successful firms in the United States.

The formulation of corporate direction, according to Andrews, is based on an assessment of company circumstances, primarily an evaluation of industry trends. Strategy is, then, the creation of a proper fit between the aspirations of the senior executives and commercial opportunities.

In the view of Andrews, therefore, the strategy of Tesco, for instance, would emerge from reflection on growth trends in retailing and the aspirations of the company's executives for Tesco's expansion. It is a matter of fit.

It is interesting to note that this early view of strategy makes no reference to competition. One possible explanation is that at the time Andrews was formulating his ideas the post war economy was booming and commercial opportunities were so attractive that most could do well, and few firms needed to be concerned about commercial competitors.

Bruce Henderson

The Boston Consulting Group was founded in 1963 by Bruce Henderson. BCG has gone on to provide advice to some of the largest and most successful companies in the world. One of the keystones of BCG's consulting activities is advice based on a high level of intellectual argument.

In his article which deals with the origin of strategy,[73] Henderson uses metaphor to set out his view about strategic thinking. Two propositions are presented. One is that if two entities compete on equal terms for resources, the weaker will eventually be displaced. The second is that imagination, logic and commitment of resources by competitors enable shifts to occur in competitive equilibrium. This occurs through creation of mutually exclusive, differentiated advantages. It therefore fosters competitive coexistence.

For Henderson, therefore, the competitive relationship between Carrefour and Wal-Mart, the two biggest in retailing, involves the possibility that one or the other would eventually be extinguished through competition for the same market. However, since both firms can rely on human capacity for logic and creativity, both will endeavour to differentiate themselves from each other to pursue separate markets and thus achieve peaceful coexistence.

On closer inspection, the two propositions Henderson proposes carry another interpretation. First, avoiding competition on equal terms for resources reduces the likelihood of the weaker eventually being displaced. And the second proposition implies that imagination, logic and commitment of resources by competitors enable a shift in competitive equilibrium by avoiding competition.

Henderson argues that business strategists, since they are human beings, are able to avoid natural selection which results in a dominant species. To do this, human competitors behave in such a way as to differentiate themselves, and to compete, not with each other, but with the environment. The main thrust of this argument appears to be a call for advantage through differentiation, avoiding competition and therefore ignoring strategy.

Michael Porter

Porter's five forces model[74] is one of the most widely recognised in strategic management. It is often proposed as an analytical framework designed to support strategic argument for the direction of a firm. However, the model is not one centred on competition. Rather, it is centred on influences on the economy of an industry. Rivalry does figure in the model, but largely as a factor influencing the likelihood of a new investor achieving unusually high industry returns.

Michael Porter argues that strategy is essentially a matter of developing and maintaining distinctive activity systems.[75] He proposes that an improved strategic position will be based on a unique set of activities, which are different activities or performance of some activities in different ways to those of competitors. For Carrefour, for instance, strategy would be based on the unique activities and methods which enabled the firm to maintain its supply chain. These are skills, competencies and resources which cannot be decoupled from the system of interlinked activities. Porter encourages the deepening of distinctiveness of activity systems, without compromise.

It is useful to recognise that Porter is an industrial economist. His work which led to the development of the five forces model was designed to address the question: should investment be made in this industry based on expectations of abnormal returns? Note that this is an industry level question; it is not centred on the individual firm. It is a model which is designed as a framework for investment, not strategy. Yet, remarkably, the model has been enthusiastically adopted as a guide for strategic thinking at the business level, without reference the different nature of theoretical arguments required at different analytical levels.

Resource-based view

This theme in strategic thinking follows the work of Wernerfelt, Grant and Barney.[76] According to this view, firms are regarded as unique clusters of resources and capabilities. Within an industry, therefore, such differences between enterprises form the basis for creation of strategic advantage as firms appraise the opportunities for exploiting unique resources and capabilities. Strategic thinking accordingly, involves identifying resource gaps and investing where required to replenish or augment the resource base.

For Wal-Mart, the resource-based view calls for concentration on identifying the firm's resource gaps and investing to fill them. Again, this is an inward looking view which disregards external factors in competition, including consideration of rivals.

Hamel and Prahalad

Aligned with the resource-based view, Hamel and Prahalad promote the view that strategy should concentrate on the development and maintenance of a firm's core competencies.[77] This should be achieved through leveraging skills and resources through concentration on a small number of unique adaptable skills.

The corollary to this proposition, although not advanced directly by Hamel and Prahalad, is that those competencies, which are not core competencies, can appropriately be outsourced to others.

The issue of core competencies is therefore a separate quest for each of Tesco, Carrefour and Wal-Mart. As a view of strategy this perspective limits itself entirely to matters internal to a company; competitors are not considered, therefore strategy is overlooked.

Competitive groups

Contemporary scholarship reaches its closest point to recognising competition among firms in discussions of competitive groups.[78] Within this analytical perspective, the strategy analyst is encouraged to identify direct competitors, and to group them according to key characteristics. Wal-Mart, Tesco and Carrefour would therefore recognise themselves as members of a competitive group: global retailers. Analysis of this kind, conducted in each company, yields results showing that different competitors have different geographic coverage in their market, they exhibit different levels of diversity among their products, they serve different numbers of market segments, use different distribution channels, they apply different levels of marketing effort, exhibit different levels of vertical integration, and so on.

Although this approach refers to competitive groups, it does not really refer to competition among the groups: it is a matter of analytical description and categorisation; there is no reference to rivalry.

Through their concentration on matters of internal corporate activity, Hamel and Prahalad, Grant and Porter, make no explicit reference to competition. These views are therefore *myopic* perspectives in their relation to strategy. To take a sporting analogy, these views are equivalent to a football team competing for a premiership win by going to great lengths to develop the skills and abilities of players, ignoring the capabilities of the opposition.

Industry analysis and competitive groups provide no basis for competition, and therefore no basis for strategy. Strategic thinking based on these forms of analysis alone are at best competitive ambitions based on *hope*. Taking up the sporting analogy once again, the parallel is one of a football team aiming to defeat its rival by the choice of colour of players' jerseys.

The view I adopt, is that strategy is concerned with the relationship among competitive rivals, a relationship that leads to resolution, not myopia or hope. This perspective is reflected in only one recent viewpoint, to the writer's knowledge.

Stalk and Lachenauer[79] take an uncommonly aggressive view of commercial competition. They assert that companies should focus relentlessly on competitive advantage, avoiding direct attacks on rivals, but taking positive steps to devastate profit sanctuaries, plagiarise, deceive, apply overwhelming force, and take whatever action is needed to greatly raise competitors' costs. This would clearly provide a different insight into the strategic thinking of Wal-Mart, in its relationship with Tesco, for instance, than the views of the contemporary scholars outlined above.

To view strategy as based squarely on competition is relatively uncommon. I therefore choose to return to basics before proceeding further. Simply put: what is competition?

Competition and games

Are games a form of competition? Taking a broad philosophical view of human interaction, Carse[80] distinguishes between *Finite and Infinite Games*.

Finite games are those which have the following characteristics:

- willingness to play;
- bounded field of interaction;
- fixed and pre-agreed rules of behaviour;
- mutually exclusive interests;
- agreed criteria for achievement;
- definite start and conclusion;
- a title for the winner.

Carse distinguishes a finite game, which is familiar to most as the basis of competition in sport, from infinite games which are designed to maintain continuity of engagement between participants. A finite game can be played within an infinite game, but an infinite game cannot exist within a finite game. An infinite game is required to sustain competition.

To return to retailing, a finite game played between Tesco and Wal-Mart, through its Asda chain, would comprise the struggle in Britain for dominance. An infinite game would be the one based on at least a tacit agreement that the game of retailing will go on and Tesco and Wal-Mart will remain participants.

At a similarly elemental level, Fahey[81] offers the idea that competition in the business strategy game involves five key elements:[82]

- competitors or rivals;
- arenas in which they confront each other;
- stakes they win or lose;
- chips that are needed to participate in the game;
- methods by which score is kept.

In retailing, therefore, Fahey would view competition as comprising: competitors including Carrefour and Wal-Mart; geographical locations where they compete, such as China and Europe; stakes to be won or lost, such as establishment of a loyal customer base in China; physical, financial, knowledge and human resource capabilities to establish in the Chinese retail market; and a scoreboard for retailers, such as market share and profitability.

Competition also involves interaction; participants make decisions from among alternative courses of action, much as Dixit and Nalebuff[83] explain from a game theoretic perspective.[84]

Competitive thinking involves learning the capabilities and intentions of a rival, investment in the enhancement of one's own capabilities, hiding intentions from a rival, inducing a competitor to act against their own interests and, of course, a selection of a course of action to promote one's own interests. As Fahey says in a commercial context:

> To win against opponents, companies need strategies for three related tasks: outwitting, outmanoeuvring and outperforming competitors.[85]

As I explain above, finite games which characterise competition in commerce typically have limited duration. Vigorous, and especially confrontational, competition between firms does not last forever. It is normally interspersed with periods of relatively harmonious interaction as each company goes about its business of producing and marketing its goods and services to customers.

Confrontation is a self-sustaining state of rivalry between competitors. This kind of competition, so it is proposed, will only revert to harmony under the condition that *both* competitors perceive their critical interests are no longer under serious threat.

History shows that wars between countries come to an end when both decide that enough is enough.[86] The outcome will no doubt be one in which both competitors are prepared to tolerate a new equilibrium, a new state of relationship between them. One will be better off, and the other worse. But a new tolerable equilibrium is achieved, at least for the time being.

This view of competitive rivalry accounts for the possibility that companies are in the continuous process of forming and reforming their competitive relationships. Strategy is the thinking process which leads from one competitive resolution to the next.

It goes without saying that the finite game comprising business competition is played by human players, so the question of how the game is played is a question of human behaviour. The literature on interpersonal conflict[87] offers a useful distinction among four orientations towards competition; I refer to Wal-Mart and Tesco for illustration:

- *Aggression*: a conflict orientation designed deliberately to cause harm to a rival, without respect for the rival's rights. An aggressive orientation by Wal-Mart would aim to destroy Tesco.
- *Assertion*: an orientation in confrontation to pursue one's own interests, yet taking regard of a rival's aims and claims; the objective for the assertive competitor is to prevail without harm. Assertiveness among the retailers would exist in the aim by Tesco to prevail in the British supermarket field by discouraging Wal-Mart's growth.
- *Defensiveness*: willingness to act to protect one's interests when faced by a rival; the objective for the defensive competitor is to secure and safeguard valued interests while preventing a rival threatening them. Carrefour would exhibit a defensive orientation in its Chinese market by endeavouring to make the entry of Wal-Mart as difficult, costly and time consuming as possible.
- *Submission*: willingness to yield, without resistance, to a harmful aggressor; a form of collaboration with an aggressor. Submissiveness in retailing

would be revealed if a supermarket chain passively accepted that it would be overwhelmed and eliminated from the market by an aggressive competitor without a struggle.

Neither aggression nor submission can sustain an infinite game because one participant or the other is harmed, maybe both, and only one competitor exists in the long term. Therefore, no further finite games are possible.

In this present discussion on competition between businesses, I take the view that aggression is morally unacceptable because it is *wrong* to aim to do harm, that is, to adopt a purpose which is to deliberately destroy the business livelihood of a competitor and so undermine the continuity of the game of business. Harm is an unacceptable policy objective. And while submission might be unavoidable in some circumstances, my view is that as a deliberate choice of purpose it is, at least, *not right* because it represents unwillingness to protect stakeholders' rights to autonomy.[88]

Consequently, I refer to strategy hereafter only in terms of assertive and defensive thinking.

We are now in a position to turn from what competition is, to the matter of purpose: What is the aim of competition?

Purpose

Adobe Systems launched a desktop publishing revolution in the 1980s and early 1990s, and introduced with it the ubiquitous PDF file. The company is poised for a new initiative.[89] What is Adobe's *strategic* purpose?

From the perspective of Andrews,[90] a benign maintenance of fit is a company's generic aim. From this viewpoint one would expect that the aim of Adobe would be to continue fashioning fit between its capabilities and environmental opportunities. But Andrews' outlook on strategy is retrospective; an observer can only discover strategy over a period of time, once a pattern of decisions about direction has been made by a company's executive elite. Moreover, this outlook does not take account of confrontation.

In his short rationale for strategic thinking, Henderson reflects a similar viewpoint: that strategy is concerned with avoiding competition. Henderson envisages firms creating alternative growth paths through differentiation, that is, so that the companies no longer compete. Again, the implied aim is harmonious avoidance of competition, rather than the development of ideas which would permit one entity to prevail over the other by competitive means. From this perspective, Adobe's aim would be to differentiate.

Based on these two widely influential sources, strategy is regrettably divorced from competition by ignoring the primary purpose of strategy which is to see off competitors. But others view purpose differently.

So far as the business press informs us, Adobe's strategic purpose is quite clear. The company has developed for its Acrobat software the ability to recognise and insert personal signatures in PDF documents from electronic personal identity cards. In marketing language, using this product, Adobe's aim is to revolutionise bureaucracy by reducing paper handling. However, Mr Bruce Chizen, chief executive of Adobe Systems, frames the company's purpose rather differently:

> Mr Chizen's brief is to win Adobe's shareholders, this time, a disproportionate share of the joy. That is why, he says, he spends most of his time thinking about three things: Microsoft, software platforms and workflow. . . . Microsoft, Mr Chizen says, is scary because 'PDF caught them by surprise'. As business enters a new phase, Microsoft may see an opportune moment to trample it. Mr Chizen, who in 1987 made the financially costly choice to leave a senior position at Microsoft to join a subsidiary of Apple, just as Microsoft began to clobber Apple (and others), knows what that usually leads to.[91]

The first priority of Adobe's chief executive is to secure the company's future. He anticipates success using the features of one of the company's products. Mr Chizen perceives that his firm has reached a strategic threshold: it is about to take a step which could well disrupt Microsoft's sense of order. His strategic purpose is to prevail in the oncoming competition.

Classic sources, in contrast to contemporary theorists, convey a very strong commitment to the importance of purpose when evolving a line of strategic thinking.

At the outset, Sun Tzu[92] emphasises the relevance of the study of strategy for the future of an enterprise. His view begins with fundamentals. The aim of a sovereign is to preserve his state. Competition with other sovereigns can bring about the destruction of a state, so the study of strategy must be thorough. Mr Chizen is well aware that his main competitor could wreak considerable damage.

Kautilya's[93] advice to the king has the same imperative: prevailing and preserving his kingdom in the face of inevitable competition from rivals is of highest priority. Any kingdom with a common border, according to

Kautilya, could reasonably be assumed to have designs on its neighbour; this is assumed as human nature. So the king's purpose is to maintain his state's wealth by preserving it against competitors.

It needs to be said that neither Sun Tzu nor Kautilya regard the corporate purpose of prevailing in competition and protecting sovereign interests from threat by rivals as the sole aim of an enterprise. Nor does Mr Chizen; he is also attending to the features of his product and its ability to serve the needs of his customers. For Sun Tzu and Kautilya, accumulation and maintenance of wealth for the benefit of stakeholders is implied. However, both agree that if competition, and therefore strategy, is disregarded, then the future of the enterprise is in jeopardy.

Von Clausewitz[94] and Machiavelli[95] agree. Both develop their ideas with preservation of the state as the primary goal, without which the enjoyment of wealth is at risk. This goal is what von Clausewitz calls the 'political objective'. It is the policy objective which is translated into strategic purpose, that is, discouraging competitors.

Now, a caution: opportunity as portrayed above could be interpreted as a motivation for confrontational action for its own sake, if an assessment of advantage was made. But Sun Tzu warns against rash action:

> If not in the interests of the state, do not act. If you cannot succeed, do not use (forces). If you are not in danger, do not fight. A sovereign cannot raise an army because he is enraged, nor can a general fight because he is resentful. For while a man may again be happy, and a resentful man again be pleased, a state that has perished cannot be restored, nor can the dead be brought back to life. Therefore, the enlightened ruler is prudent and the good general is warned against rash action. Thus the state is kept secure and the army preserved.[96]

It appears clear that strategy benefits from having a clearly defined aim. It also benefits, as we will see below, from an appreciation of the conditions under which competition takes place.

Competitive context

Up to a point, contemporary and classic sources of ideas about strategy agree on the significance of understanding the field and circumstances which contain competitive engagement. But once again, the two views diverge when rivalry is considered.

Consider the advertising industry and its field of competition. The four largest advertising groups, Publicis, WPP Group, Omnicom and Interpublic compete together in an arena where consumers are becoming harder to reach due to the effects of shifts away from traditional media, and clients are cautious about expenditure on advertising:[97]

> Snatching each other's business remains the way to grow, especially as the stakes can now be much higher. This is because some of the big multinationals have decided to stop using a roster of agencies but instead to hand all their business to one of the big holding groups to manage.[98]

Understanding competitive context for the advertising groups means an appreciation of the terms on which they compete: which clients lean towards using one agency, which still prefer dealing with different advertising agents; which media are offering leverage for which advertisers; where are the sources of creative talent . . . In essence, the key question for each advertising group is: which environment is favouring and which is working against each competitor?

Porter's Industry Analysis is well-known as a means for surveying the competitive environment of a commercial enterprise. The economic forces of suppliers and buyers, potential industry entrants and substitutes provide a framework for predicting the likely factors affecting financial returns in an industry. Rivalry in Porter's terms is a matter of degree rather than character.

For any firm these calculations provide an opportunity to decide whether returns are sufficient to warrant staying or leaving the industry. However, for enterprises comprising an industry, all these factors are experienced in common: Porter's five factor model affects all four main advertising groups. Therefore, they do not provide a basis for better understanding competition, except by seeking advantage through securing marginal benefits in the factors Porter identifies. Nevertheless, Porter's environmental understanding is a useful precursor to strategic thinking.

In their distillation of contemporary scholarship, Johnson, Scholes and Whittington[99] take a somewhat broader view, as would be expected in their encyclopaedic approach to business development. They view strategy as a question of deciding on overall corporate direction, and they support this endeavour by providing an executive with an array of relevant considerations to support such a choice. Analysis encompasses three main factors.

The first, appropriately, is acknowledgement of stakeholder expectations; these define the goal of the business direction. The second is the business environment including the state of the industry, the economic outlook and the market. Third is the state of the firm's corporate competencies and capabilities.

Notably, competitors and factors affecting rivalry are overlooked. Again, the business development perspective does not help in recognising the particular purpose of a specific firm; its analysis would yield a similar outcome for all four of the major advertising groups. Yet, as we have seen above, these advertising groups are firmly fixed in their competitive attention on each other.

In contrast with contemporary views, Sun Tzu's advice is concentrated directly on competition and he notes that strategic thinking should begin with estimates of the competitive situation. Like Porter, he identifies five relevant considerations. But divergence between these two points of view is sharp. Master Sun's estimates are comprehensive: moral influence, weather, terrain, command and doctrine. These would be estimates by Publicis, for instance, of the character of competition with each of WPP, Omnicom and Interpublic.

Moral influence concerns the degree of harmony between leaders and staff; if morale in one's own company is superior to that in the competitor's enterprise, then this would be a favourable competitive circumstance. Weather refers to the influence of natural forces. If surrounding conditions such as the state of the economic cycle favours one business against another, then the competitive initiative of the first would be assisted. Terrain is the character of the ground on which competition occurs; this might be paralleled with Porter's industry analysis. Command is analysis of the relative strengths of character of those who lead an enterprise and its competitor. Master Sun expects that if a firm is led by a person with wisdom, sincerity, humanity, courage and strictness, and the competitor is not so, then this firm would compete with disadvantage. Finally, doctrine is the quality of organisational support for a competitive enterprise. The rival with superior organisation, structure, control and logistics would compete from advantage.

Sun Tzu's estimates are far more comprehensive than those presented in contemporary advice.

But his recommendations do not stop here. This initial calculation of the likelihood of prevailing in competition with a rival signals whether strategic thinking should go further. If so, then more detailed considerations are called for. For instance, Master Sun requires additional careful study of the competitive terrain, noting whether circumstances offer benefit to either or both rivals. What for instance, for Publicis, is the balance of its advantage in internet advertising compared with WPP? This analysis is a preliminary step towards identifying a strategic course of action.

Knowledge of the place and circumstances under which competition takes place is clearly important. It provides insight into the possibility of favour naturally falling to one rival over the other. It also allows for analysis to secure a position of advantage, and avoid circumstantial disadvantage. However, a descent onto the Plane of Confrontation initiates further investigation: enquiry into the intentions and capabilities of rivals. This is the domain of competitive intelligence.

Competitive intelligence

Competitive intelligence is insight gained as a result of purposefully and stealthily gathering and interpreting information about a commercial competitor.[100] Its aim is to gain a pre-emptive understanding of the competitor's capabilities and intentions[101] and to avoid being caught by surprise.[102] Such intelligence is an essential component of strategic thinking.

The imperative for competitive intelligence is nowhere as compelling as it is in the pharmaceuticals industry. Large drug companies spend very large sums of money each year on development and protection of new products. Insight into the intentions and capabilities of competitors reassures and redefines business direction. For companies producing generic drugs, those for which patents have expired, rivalry is intense:

> In generics, success depends on being cheap enough to keep manufacturing and other costs down, big enough to dominate distribution channels to wholesalers, and fast enough to move in and out of markets as opportunity ebbs and flows. Staying ahead of the competition, particularly the various low-cost Indian firms with their sights on western markets, is a further challenge.[103]

Imagine this industry from the viewpoint of Sandoz, a Swiss generic drug maker, for instance. Here is a set of questions which its executives might well ask about any competitor: what is its manufacturing cost structure, how do its distribution channels function, how quickly can it respond to market opportunities? Answers to these questions would permit Sandoz executives to weigh up the capabilities and intentions of its rival, and consequently to use this insight while creating its own strategic line of thinking. Lines of enquiry such as these might well have been influential in strategic decisions made by Novartis, the owner of Sandoz, to acquire Hexal and Eon Labs, two direct competitors of Sandoz.

Sun Tzu's view clearly places great value on foreknowledge. An enlightened leader is able to overcome a rival through the availability of information about the opposition's movements and accomplishments:

> Now the reason the enlightened prince and the wise general conquer the enemy whenever they move and their achievements surpass those of ordinary men is foreknowledge.[104]

He is also clear about the sources of such knowledge:

> . . . Foreknowledge cannot be elicited from spirits, gods, analogy with past events, nor from calculations. It must be obtained from men who know the (rival's) situation.[105]

In Sun Tzu's view spies are essential:

> . . . only the enlightened sovereign and the worthy general who are able to use the most intelligent people as agents are certain to achieve great things. Secret operations are essential in war; upon them the army relies to make its every move.[106]

Knowledge of one's own readiness and that of a rival is essential to assessment of the likelihood of advantage in competition. Victory depends on knowledge of competitive circumstances.

Sun Tzu asserts that:

> . . . If I know that my (forces) are capable of striking the (rival), but do not know that he is vulnerable to attack; my chance of victory is (half)
> . . . If I know that my (rival) is vulnerable to attack, but do not know that my (forces) are incapable of striking; my chance of victory is (half)

> . . . If I know that the (rival) can be attacked and that my (forces) are
> capable of attacking, but do not realise that because of unsuitable terrain I
> should not attack, my chance of victory is (half).[107]

Like Sun Tzu, von Clausewitz refers to an assessment of the opposition's
power of resistance which includes the means at their disposal and their
strength of will. In relative terms opportunity is the availability of superior
strength to overwhelm a rival at a crucial point.

Knowledge is central to one's strategic capability; it is the foundation of
ideas and action. Von Clausewitz observes that knowledge must become
capability: it must be so absorbed into the mind that it almost ceases to exist
in separate objective form. Because of continual change of strategic circumstances a commander must carry the whole intellectual apparatus of his
knowledge within him, always ready to bring forth an appropriate decision.
Knowledge thus becomes a genuine capability.

With particular reference to important subtleties in knowledge of a rival,
von Clausewitz observes that the Moral Factors, matters of will, spirit,
morale, temperament and courage, cannot be subject to quantitative analysis. He suggests that seeds of wisdom in these elements derive from experience and from study of the past.

Referring to *Information in War*, von Clausewitz observes that the great
part of information in a competitive situation is contradictory, a greater part
is false, but the greatest part is unreliable. Uncertainty is an inevitable
hazard and in fact, contradictory information is a fortunate signal of low
reliability. Consistent information which is in error is much more dangerous
because it readily induces commitment and possibly also folly.

In order to accommodate this resulting high level of uncertainty, he
stresses the requirement for ability to discriminate. Such ability derives, he
argues, from a leader's knowledge of people, things and good judgement. It
must be anticipated that incoming information will contradict expectations
once a plan is being implemented. Accepting this reality, von Clausewitz
calls for a leader to remain firm in reliance on prior convictions.

Among contemporary views of strategic management, recognition for the
idea of competitive intelligence is not widespread. While Porter, Hamel and
Prahalad, and Henderson imply that their recommendations are a basis for
strategic thinking, it is remarkable that they overlook a process by which

a company learns about a rival's strategic intentions and capabilities. Competitor threats to the firm's business are apparently ignored and pre-emptive competitive opportunities are neglected.

Although the importance of competitive intelligence is overlooked in much of the contemporary strategy literature, there are some writers who are well aware of the strategic imperative of the link between strategy and competitive intelligence. Fahey, Gilad, Nolan and West are prominent among the enlightened.[108]

Summing up the classic insights, the strategic imperative for competitive intelligence was appreciated and documented thousands of years ago when the great dynasties of China and India evolved and survived on a foundation of such thinking. The survival of nations has always depended on an ability to reduce risk of disturbance by those who are willing and able to threaten wellbeing, wealth or way of life. Nations have gone into decline and disappeared through their unwillingness or inability to detect and address such threats.

The essence of this outlook is described succinctly by Sun Tzu:

> Know the enemy and know yourself; in a hundred battles you will never be in peril. When you are ignorant of the enemy but know yourself, your chances of winning or losing are equal. If ignorant of both your enemy and of yourself, you are certain in every battle to be in peril[109]

The following concept map, Figure 2.8, draws this chapter to a close. It offers a summary of main considerations comprising the Principle of Competition.

Reflection

Is successful strategy based on lessening corporate incapabilities?
Gathering competitive intelligence is surprisingly easy; equally so for a competitor.

Appendix 2: The practice of competitive intelligence

I turn now from ideas of strategy to the practice of competitive intelligence[110] with a brief digression into the nature of this field which is vital to strategic thinking.

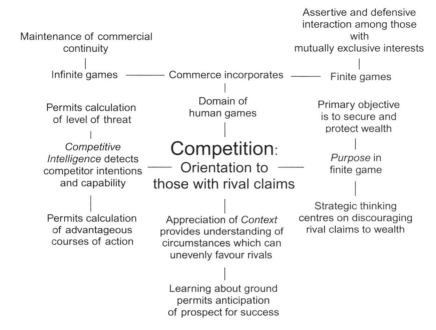

Figure 2.8 Concept map for Competition.

Competitor intelligence is derived from information gathered from sources close to a competitor which are reliable, credible, accurate, timely and relevant.[111] Patterns of expected competitor behaviour are pieced together from indicators which are interpreted as signals of capability and intent.

Whatever a competitor's activity, a stream of indicators will be emitted through its transactions with suppliers, contractors, distributors and customers among many others. Sets of indicators are considered in the context of their commercial circumstances. When competently collected and interpreted, these indicators reveal a pattern in the rival's intentions and capability. The main indicators which are typically publicly available are those found in statements of a competitor's staff, observable behaviour (or absence of it) and outcomes of marketplace strategy.

An assessment can be made of both the level of harm which could be delivered by a rival, and of opportunities revealed for the Focal Firm.[112] Analysis of threat has the highest priority.

Combined high levels of intent to cause harm and a coexisting capability to do harm to the Focal Firm comprise the most serious current threat. Deficiencies in such analysis can commonly be traced to the fact that competitor capability is more readily detected than intention. Capability is apparent in counting hardware; intention lies in the minds of a rival's decision-makers.

In the practice of competitive intelligence two main activities are crucial.[113]

Data collection and sources: It is a common misconception that competitive intelligence involves gathering information directly from a competitor. In the majority of situations, the information needed to construct a model of a competitor's activity system is available from people within the Focal Firm, and from contacts among associated industries. The community of suppliers, distributors and customers, which is common to both the Focal Firm and the competitor, are likely to be well-informed about indicators of a competitor's capabilities and intentions. Often, all that is required is to ask . . .

An essential insight in information gathering is to anticipate which person or body would gather intelligence-relevant information for purposes of their own. The aim then is to identify and source the required dispersed items of information which will form meaning as intelligence. It is common knowledge in the competitive intelligence community that a very high proportion of information needed to construct a valid picture of a competitor's capabilities and intentions is readily available without even approaching the competitor's firm.

Selection of sources and utilisation of their yield needs to take into account source evaluation. Two main criteria are employed: Reliability and Credibility. Both criteria involve cross-reference to other information. Reliability is a comparative measure of whether this source can be relied upon, from previous experience with this source, to give true and accurate information. Credibility requires cross-reference to other sources: is this source believable in relation to other sources?

Master Sun is emphatic about the best sources for gathering competitive intelligence. In particular, he says that it is unwise to rely on secondary or tertiary sources. Rather, he stresses the importance of gathering information about a competitor from people with firsthand knowledge.

Analysis and Interpretation: A diverse array of indicators of competitor capability and intention are displayed through its beliefs (statements and assumptions), action (activities and interactions) and change. The competitive intelligence puzzle is to interpret the pattern of these indicators. This can never be reduced to a routine or procedure; it is always a product of human imagination, logical rigour and situational experience.

The task of competitive intelligence is most often one of assembling many small pieces of information and constructing a puzzle which reveals the competitor's situation. Rarely will it be possible, or even desirable, to learn much from few sources. Stealth involves contentment and confidence in the value of accumulating small unobtrusively gathered fragments.

Interpretation of competitor mindset is the most difficult analytical task because indicators are often obscure. However, a competitor's strategic thinking process should be consistent with all the indicators, plausible in the competitor's context, comprising the only reasonable interpretation of the data, and matching information gathered through time; in other words, it should be holistically coherent. Simply put, a valid interpretation of competitor thinking should make sense from the competitor's point of view.

Inference is based on human perception. Interpretation and inference will always, therefore, be dependent on the analyst's mindset. Pattern recognition imposes structure on ambiguous data and is susceptible to bias. Analytical procedures should therefore be detached and logically structured to reduce the possibility of bias and misinterpretation.

Circumstances offer advantage to the degree that one has an accurate assessment of capabilities of oneself and rivals and knowledge of the competitive terrain. Ignorance of any one will diminish the likelihood of competitive accomplishment. Opportunities are created then from this conjunction of knowledge.

Strategy depends on foreknowledge of a competitor; but the relationship is symmetrical. It is in the interests of competitors to generate competitive intelligence on each other. Both sides are vulnerable to strategic initiative of rivals, reduction of liberty and potential loss of wealth unless adequate countermeasures are taken to prevent information leakage.

Counterintelligence involves two activities. One is finding out what a rival knows about a Focal Firm's commercial activities. The other is using a rival's sources of intelligence to deliberately spread misinformation that will distract the competitor.

In both cases, it is important to deny a rival knowledge that such counterintelligence has occurred. *Better for a rival not to know what we know that they know about us.* If they think that they know and, furthermore, believe that we do not know that they know, then they would use their information freely. In so doing they will expect their insight to translate into more disadvantage for us than will be practically the case because of our unfathomable cautions.

Effort should be spent to conceal as much of the firm's activities as possible. The priority in defensive counterintelligence should be in protecting those aspects of the firm's assets and activities that would be of most competitive value to a rival.

Securing corporate wealth and protecting freedom of future strategic initiatives requires consideration of the possibility that unscrupulous competitors might be willing and able to do harm based on access to sensitive information from the Focal Firm. Risk management depends on being able to view strategic interests as if one was taking the perspective of a potentially harmful competitor. There is a saying: to anticipate theft, *one should think like a thief*.[114]

Winkler[115] refers to counterintelligence through the following expression describing risk:

$$Risk = \frac{Threat \times Vulnerability}{Countermeasures} \times Value$$

Value = the worth to the Focal Firm of its information, noting that it makes no sense to spend more money protecting information of lesser value (e.g. list of Focal Firm's customers could be of considerable value to a competitor intent on poaching).

Threat = the level of motivation of those inside and outside the Focal Firm who want to obtain information about the firm's intentions and capabilities (e.g. the importance of knowing the Focal Firm's clients to create opportunities for competitor's rapid growth).

Vulnerability = openings to exploitation; the Focal Firm's weaknesses which can be exploited by threat (e.g. lists of customers left on a sales counter).

Countermeasures = steps, devices, procedures that are installed to address specific vulnerabilities (e.g. protective barrier to prevent public from seeing sales work space).

Information held by a Focal Firm carries different kinds of value. It has functional value for conduct of the firm's business. This can be assessed in terms of the cost of replacement and performance deficiencies resulting from its loss or loss of integrity.

In counterintelligence, a more critical assessment of value is the strategic loss to a Focal Firm arising from it being available to the competitor and used by them to the Focal Firm's disadvantage. To make this assessment it is essential to consider the value of information from the viewpoint of its benefit to a competitor.

The objective of implementation of countermeasures is to reduce the level of risk of loss of strategically important information.[116] At least, the aim is to make it very difficult for a competitor to piece together the meaning of small pieces of information to solve the puzzle of the Focal Firm's strategy.

One of the most important countermeasures to a competitor's attempts to gather information from a Focal Firm is to undertake a programme of education to raise security consciousness. Losses will decline to the degree that staff realise the consequences of information leakage. It is a fact that leakage often occurs inadvertently through actions of those who simply did not know the value of their information to a competitor.

In addition to raising awareness, organisational learning depends on detection and reporting leaks. Only when security violations occur can new areas of vulnerability be addressed with appropriate measures.

Misinformation is a programme for attempting to distract or misguide a competitor as to a Focal Firm's true strategic direction. Such a tactic needs to be attempted only with great caution, and when it is most likely to influence only the competitor's comprehension of the Focal Firm. The information channel to the competitor must be direct and reliable. The danger is that the Focal Firm's clients and stakeholders might also become misguided to the Focal Firm's commercial disadvantage.

3

Assessment

Principle of Assessment: Strategy ensures that the enterprise creates a compelling and logical argument for choice of direction to achieve aims.

Assessment involves two components: design, which is the formulation of a logical argument for action; and evaluation, the estimation of relative value of alternative courses of action. Recommendations reached through Strategic Assessment form the framework for planning tactical action.

The growth of Body Shop as a business and as an idea is one of the most impressive stories in recent corporate history.[1] From very modest beginnings it grew into an outstanding worldwide enterprise in body care, social justice and business ethics. Its strategy was clearly more than just to 'grow the business', although this was a necessary element. Body Shop did grow very successfully worldwide, first in Britain and then in Europe.

It grew through a series of strategic thresholds comprising important questions about competitive direction for the various strands of the business. At each of these points an assessment would have been made of objectives, current circumstances, future prospects and alternative courses of action. At most thresholds a fruitful course of action was chosen and success followed; the expansion into the United States in 1988 was an unfortunate exception. Why?

To explain why the venture in the United States almost brought the company to its knees it is first necessary to explain Strategic Assessment as a method for logically and systematically deciding a strategic direction.

A Strategic Assessment is a stock-take of a firm's current circumstances and prospects for the future. It simply represents a sequence of linked ideas and steps which can highlight important matters needing attention now, soon, or in the future. The appraisal could be conducted by an insider or a consultant, but the focus of the report is the same; 'What are the main things that require this firm's attention?'

Details will vary by firm, industry and circumstances. And, of course, the assessment will also reflect the quantity and quality of information available to the analyst. Furthermore, an assessment can only be regarded as a basis for continuing discussion and debate; there can be no final Strategic Assessment since circumstances change constantly.

Briefly, Strategic Assessment recognises the environment in which the Focal Firm operates, now and in conceivable futures. Examination of both the current business model, which is the commercial engine of a firm, and also likely activities of competitors, leads to identification of relevant questions or issues facing the company. These might be problems that need to be addressed or benefits to be reinforced. Next, steps should be identified, as part of the development of the argument for the Strategic Assessment, to address the issues identified. The requirements of the alternative courses of action are that they are practical, pertinent and plausible. Evaluation follows. In this final stage of the assessment a recommendation is made, based on argument involving reasons advanced in favour of the recommended course of action, and reasons against those alternatives which are dismissed.

Table 3.1 is a diagrammatic representation of the intent of the Principle of Assessment, taking account of the posture of both an assertive and

Table 3.1 *Interactions among design and evaluation.*

Assessment: Logical rationale for action	Design	Evaluation
Design	Identification of strategic issues in context of appraisal of current circumstances	*Issues arising from appraisal highlight threats to value needing action to circumvent rival action*
Evaluation	**Issues arising from appraisal highlight opportunities for value by exploiting rival vulnerabilities**	Comparison of alternative courses of action for recommendation based on value

Assertive strategic posture
Defensive strategic posture

defensive competitor. It shows Assessment in an holistic sense in which neither design nor evaluation overwhelms the other.

Strategic assessment

Strategic Assessment is a well informed and logically structured appraisal of a firm's business in its context of current and future competitive circumstances. Such an appraisal identifies issues likely to affect future prospects. Alternative courses of action are recognised and recommendations are argued for tactical direction.

A Strategic Assessment is intended to be a compact and concise document which attracts and holds the attention of its reader, drawing them to the vital aspects of the situation at hand. Such an assessment can be conducted at any time. However such an assessment is vital at a *Strategic threshold* where a choice of strategic direction is imperative.

A Strategic Assessment comprises four components:

1. *Appraisal*: An appraisal is the foundation for an assessment. It assembles the context comprising the firm's past and present circumstances, as well as anticipating future relevant events. Most importantly, this appraisal is a statement of the firm's competitive position in its commercial environment.

2. *Issues*: Issues arise directly from the appraisal. These can be visualised as the highest priority matters that need attention, in view of current and anticipated circumstances.

3. *Alternative courses of action* comprise the basis for strategic decision-making. Each issue can be addressed with at least two alternative options: do something and do nothing are the very least.

4. *Recommendation*: The strategic argument is drawn to a conclusion with a persuasive case for one of the alternative courses of action identified in the previous step. The recommendation weighs up the alternatives and shows a judgement in favour of one. It also recognises contingencies in implementation.

To illustrate, Kodak is a firm with a longstanding reputation. Events have brought the firm to a strategic threshold.[2] This circumstance in recent corporate history forms the basis for a Strategic Assessment for Kodak (Table 3.2), which the reader will find useful in following the discussion about the purpose, form and design of a Strategic Assessment.

In practical terms, the form of a Strategic Assessment reflects its purpose; it should be written in two pages at most, sufficient for a preoccupied executive to absorb its main point while walking from one meeting to another.

Design

Strategic appraisal

The appraisal takes its aim from Policy objectives. Based on this direction for the enterprise, the initial survey in Strategic Assessment weighs up relevant factors that influence consideration of possible changes in direction. It encompasses the aspirations of all who are involved as stakeholders, an appreciation of the firm's history of accomplishment to date and available resource capabilities; all in view of circumstances give full recognition to purposes, capabilities and activities of competitors. All these considerations will influence strategic thinking.

An appraisal comprises at least four elements: a statement of corporate purpose, a specification of the Focal Firm's current business model, identification of competitor profiles and anticipation of future trends.

Corporate purpose: Strategic thinking requires a specification of purpose. What is to be accomplished? What is the enterprise aiming to achieve? Corporate purpose is a crystallisation of the aim of the company; it is a statement of commercial intent: specific, descriptive and deliberately simple.

It is not a Mission Statement which is most often a vague and meaningless assertion akin to wishful thinking. Neither is it an ambitious propaganda statement made to impress the general public or indeed internal stakeholders.

The following are examples of statements of corporate purpose. Each takes the form of a statement of Policy:

* *To reduce the firm's current dependence on local geographic markets.*
   Note that this statement of purpose does not specify particular future directions: that is the task of strategic thinking.

Table 3.2 *Strategic Assessment for* Kodak.

Appraisal
Company Profile: US based international firm with long history in photographics

Corporate Purpose: To double revenue from digital business to 60% in 3 years[a]

Business Model: Transition from one business model to another[b]

Film Business Model – **Distinctive Capability** in photographic chemicals manufacture. Historically, **Competitive Advantage** is its globally recognised brand, appealing to **Customer Value** for reliability.[c] Customer base is drifting to digital photography, greatly reducing returns leaving no **Financial Surplus** to support film technology. **Stakeholder** returns shrinking.

Digital Business Model – Aiming to secure **Distinctive Capability** in equipment design which will create **Competitive Advantage** in comparatively low product price or superior performance. **Customer Value** is based on ability to store high quality images on computer for low price. Camera sales are yielding revenue, insufficient as yet to support required investment to create **Distinctive Capability**. Dividends are being withheld from **Stakeholders** to acquire design and manufacture capability.

Competitor Profile: Canon is a leader in digital imaging worldwide, growing rapidly in the US market where it is 3rd behind Sony and Kodak in camera sales.[d]
Industry Trends: Digital photography eclipsing film technology in developed world.
Scenarios: Most Likely: Canon will rapidly increase its influence in the industry.
    Most Threatening: Canon will join with Sony to eliminate Kodak.

Issues (Listed in priority order)

1. How to rapidly switch main revenue stream from film to digital?

Kodak's Film business model is not sustainable in the light of clear drift in customer value towards digital imaging. This trend is apparent worldwide. Kodak is developing a digital business model which is not yet self-supporting; Distinctive capability has not yet been established. It is clear that market indicates far greater potential in digital imaging than in film. Several well established companies in a variety of industries are capitalising on this trend, including Canon which is the most likely threat to Kodak. By itself, or allied with others, Canon has the most potential to deny Kodak its objective. Kodak's digital business model needs Distinctive Capability which equals or surpasses Canon's in technical capability. That technological capability will be needed very quickly.[e]

2. How to maintain stakeholder support?

Kodak shareholders are being deprived of dividends to fund the development of the digital business model. They will be dismayed by the speed of eclipse of the traditional film business. Some might be likely to withdraw their support for the business during this inevitably costly transition

Table 3.2 *Continued*

Alternative Courses of Action (for Issue 1)

A. Dispose of Film Business
A shift towards creating a revenue base derived from digital imaging can be accelerated by disposing of the traditional business of film, paper and chemicals. A buyer would be sought with an interest in capitalizing on the very substantial assets and capability developed by Kodak over the past century. Consequently Kodak's business would centre almost entirely on digital imaging.[f]

B. Acquire Digital Businesses
A rapid and substantial step towards concentration on Kodak's digital imaging business model would be achieved by acquiring the Distinctive Competencies of one or more firms who are already well advanced in this field. Olympus and Nikon are obvious targets, both with sound reputations in digital imaging and photographics.

C. Divert Internal Priorities from Film to Digital Business
Redirect internal resources towards the digital business model.[g]

Recommendation

Alternative	Benefits	Limitations

Dispose of Film (A)	Rapid break
	Cash to invest in digital
		Few likely buyers
		Low price in
		  declining
		  industry

Acquire Digital (B)	Rapid increase in
	  available expertise
		Targets not industry
		  leaders
		Acquisition
		  expensive

Shift Internal Priorities (C)	Internal funding Maintains Kodak ethos	Transition inevitably slow

Comparison of Benefits: Acquisition and consolidation of the industry leading technical expertise to create a Distinctive Capability is most likely in a timely manner through (A). Yet, (B) does not exclude this path once Film has been sold. Benefits of (C) are relatively weak.[h]

Comparison of Limitations: A struggle is likely in looking for a buyer for Film (A); Chinese and Indian interest is possible but unlikely when the alternative is digital. Option (C) risks achieving objective on time. Expensive investment in lesser then leading technical expertise is a weaker limitation than the alternatives.

Recommendation: Acquire digital businesses to quickly develop digital capability.[i]
Contingency Alternative: Dispose of the company's assets.[j]

[a] This statement of purpose contains a specific and measurable end state; preferable to the more general and ambiguous 'secure a digital future for Kodak'.
[b] This is a rather unusual situation where a strategic assessment requires reference to 2 business models. More typically, the elements of one model would be described here. Note that the approach of this assessment might have been repositioned by taking a higher level view of the firm's business, where there would be only one business model.

ᶜ Shaded elements refer to information not found in the articles from *The Economist*.
ᵈ This competitor is selected for profile because it apparently has the greatest potential capability to threaten Kodak's purpose. This assessment is based on its size in the US market, its growth rate in the US and its competitive stature worldwide.
ᵉ This statement of issue draws together the main threads presented in the appraisal. No new information should be presented here, rather, the survey conducted in the appraisal is focused and concentrated for the reader's benefit.
ᶠ Each of the alternatives is described in this section, not evaluated. The aim here is to show that the option is realistic and a feasible alternative with which the corporate purpose can be achieved, and the primary issue addressed.
ᵍ This third option is essentially a status quo alternative. It should be included to provide a realistic basis for comparison with new initiatives.
ʰ This comparison is a consideration of benefits across the three options, a different analysis from the listing of benefits and limitations for each option.
ⁱ The recommendation can be relatively brief because the balancing of benefits against limitations will have been achieved in the previous steps.
ʲ This course of action is a prepared response for the possibility that unanticipated circumstances prevent implementation of the recommendation.

- *To increase profit from the current business by 10% within the next two years.*

  Compare this specific objective with a more vague ambition such as 'To increase profit'. The indefinite alternative needs clarification in Policy.

- *To establish a more secure position in the current business to support future growth.*

  This example is a conditional statement of purpose with two steps: security in the near term, growth in the future. Strategic thinking which follows will have two time horizons.

- *To increase the firm's share of domestic business.*

  Such a purpose is stated in relative terms and therefore aims for a position of advantage compared with specific competitors. Note the difference between this statement of purpose and the vague and indefinite 'Be the best at customer service'.

Focal Firm profile: The aim of the business profile is to briefly summarise the main elements of the firm's development to date. This includes main accomplishments and turning points, as well as the primary lines of business products and services.

This is a context setting item which ensures that the culture and history of the competitor are not overlooked in weighing up future possibilities.

Items included in the business profile include a brief overview of structure and capabilities. Structure includes internal and external organisation; grouping of responsibilities and the network of alliances and partnerships. Capabilities recognise available assets, comprising human, financial, physical and information wherewithal. Abilities are also included among capabilities, comprising technology, skill sets, capacity for change and other means for leveraging assets.

Business model: The business model is a statement of the Focal Firm's current activity. In its simplest form it is a causal statement comprising a theoretically self-reinforcing set of interrelated concepts identifying commercial aspects of the firm's operations which support a healthy, profitable and stable enterprise.

Van der Heijden explores the foundation of this model in some detail. He[3] uses the term 'business idea' to capture the same concept. A particularly useful aspect of his analysis is the construction of cause maps which explain the rationale for the Focal Firm's business. Construction of such maps is a valuable method for thinking through dynamic aspects of the business. Not only does it yield a crystallisation of the current state of the business as described in the following diagram, it also offers a basis for scenario building.

The following diagram of a business model Figure 3.1 shows self-reinforcing relationships among key concepts which comprise the engine of a healthy business.

The theoretical structure of the business model rests on the following argument: customers purchase the Focal Firm's product or service because they *value* pertinent attributes over and above the offerings of competitors. The proceeds of sales generate a *surplus* which is available both to *stakeholders* and to invest in maintenance of the Focal Firm's *distinctive capabilities*. It is these distinctive competencies which are the foundation for producing the Focal Firm's *competitive advantage* relative to commercial rivals.

The model also needs to make sense by following the argument backwards through the causal loop: customers *value* certain attributes of the Focal Firm's product or service in comparison with that offered by competitors. The Focal Firm sustains an *advantage* over commercial rivals through some aspect of their business. This advantage is based on the Focal Firm's

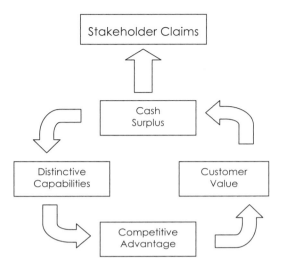

Figure 3.1 Structure of a business model.

maintenance of *capabilities* which are distinctive and difficult for competitors to replicate. These special competencies are protected through the firm's investment from *surplus* on sales.

Customer value is assessed from the viewpoint of customers themselves. Most importantly, it is not what the Focal Firm thinks customers value.

Competitive advantage is a statement of the Focal Firm's relative position in offering customer value, relative, that is, to commercial rivals. Simply speaking, a Focal Firm is able to deliver value to customers because they offer different product attributes, because they price on the basis of a cost advantage, or else they serve a particular target group of customers particularly well. In Porter's[4] terms the three generic types of competitive advantage are differentiation, cost leadership and focus.

Distinctive capabilities are the assets and capabilities available to the Focal Firm which generate competitive advantage. They are distinctive because they are rare, difficult to replicate by competitors or else very costly for others to acquire. Human, physical, financial, informational assets and capabilities are included. Van der Heijden makes the important point that distinctive competencies in human resources are those which cannot be easily replicated or acquired, that is, human resource systems; not individual people.

Cash surplus assumes that there is money left over from the proceeds of sales after the expenses of running the firm have been paid. This does not mean that all surplus is invested in maintaining distinctive capabilities, simply that there is sufficient to maintain distinctive competencies in good order.

Stakeholder claims refer to the dividends required by the owners and share-holders of the firm.

Competitor profiles: This section of the Strategic Assessment identifies past, current and possible future competitors. A profile is produced for each. It refers to:

- principals, staff and organisational structure, now and intended, including a history of financial performance including future expectations, debt levels, financial assets and credit ratings;
- products, production, services, research and development, including future trends;
- upstream supply chains including supplier alliances and contracts, now and expected in the future;
- marketing methods, price, promotional methods, target markets, distribution channels; now and in future; and
- apparent strategic intent; short, medium and long term.

Scenarios: This is a crucial part of the Strategic Assessment. It involves visualising the way in which critical elements of the Focal Firm's business environment will affect it in the future.

Scenarios are well informed, logical and imaginative lines of thinking about how circumstances might evolve.[5] Note that it is based on knowledge about trends, it is a rationally structured and persuasive line of reasoning, and it is a creative product: nobody ever knows for certain how circumstances will evolve.

It is useful to think of a scenario as a line of reasoning that can take two forms. It can start from a pattern of current events and project them forward in an extension of cause and effect reasoning. Alternatively, it can begin with an assumed state of affairs sometime in the future, and reason backwards to see whether and how this might have come about.

Scenarios can be derived from causal maps by considering the implications of the possible combinations of conditions arising from different variable states.

Schwartz[6] identifies three main factors interacting in scenarios:

1. The Focal Firm and its future intentions and capabilities;
2. Competitors, present and future, and their intentions and capabilities;
3. The economic, social, political, technological environment in which all competitors, including the Focal Firm, aspire to succeed.

Scenarios are most useful for mid-range thinking about the future. By comparison, in the short term it might be possible to calculate trends based on statistical patterns. Long term futures are most uncertain, and here scenarios might lie beyond the scope of imagination.

Strategic issues

This, the second phase of preparation of a Strategic Assessment, builds on the foundation established in the appraisal prepared above. Its aim is to identify the most important matters the Focal Firm must attend to in the short, medium and long term.

The list of issues, which should be assembled in priority order, is a combination of risks to be managed, and opportunities to be harnessed. Based on the appraisal, this analytical phase investigates the pattern of relationships among the elements addressed above. Issues arise from any one of the items in the appraisal, or any combination of them.

Typical sources of strategic issues for a Focal Firm are the following:

- This firm has no clear Corporate Purpose. The Focal Firm clearly needs to address the question of its overall direction if Purpose is not well defined. Remember, this is the real aim of the firm, not the version designed for public consumption.

- The Business Model is not self-sustaining because
  - one or a combination of Customer Value, Competitive Advantage, Distinctive Competencies, or Surplus are not present; or
  - links between elements of the Business Model are not present.
- The Business Model is not consistent with Corporate Purpose
- The Business Model is not sufficiently robust to be sustained in plausible scenarios of future trends for change, either
  - among competitors; or
  - within the industry.
- The Business Model is not sufficiently flexible to cope with future surprises

A flawed business model is a source of concern. If the current way of doing business is unsustainable, or is likely to become so in the future, then steps need to be taken to correct it. Business models can be threatened by internal deficiency or external rivalry. Whichever is the case, the firm's business model will need to be modified to reduce risk.

Issues might just as well be opportunities as they are risks. An important issue might arise from the question of how to maintain a robust business model in foreseeable future circumstances.

It helps to phrase an Issue in terms of a simple question:

How should we . . . ?

In sum, the issues address the likely future of the company; the most important is the threshold issue. This is a question of whether the firm is currently prospering, and whether this is likely to continue. Some call this a question of 'resilience'.[7] At any one time, there should be three or four issues current at most. If the analysis concludes that there are a larger number of issues, then it is likely that the analytical view taken is too detailed. Remember, strategic issues, as distinct from tactical matters, are concentrated on matters that involve very substantial resources, a view to the long term, and action taken at a strategic level will be difficult and costly to reverse.

Alternative courses of action

For each issue a set of feasible and plausible courses of action needs to be identified,[8] as shown in Table 3.3. These options should be described in sufficient detail to show that each is a realistic method for either addressing the risk identified, or for realising the potential benefits from the opportunity recognised.

Contemporary discussions of choice among corporate directions distinguish between alternatives available for creation of advantage for portfolios of businesses, and for business units themselves.

Table 3.3 *Links between issues and courses of action.*

Issue	Course of Action
This firm has no clear Corporate Purpose	*A clear and unambiguous statement of end state which defines Corporate Purpose needs to be established*
The Business Model is not self-sustaining. Either:	*A flawed Business Model is not self-sustaining. This issue requires identification of the nature of the flaws to prevent deterioration of the essential source of business prosperity*
(a) One or a combination of Customer Value, Competitive Advantage, Distinctive Competencies, or Surplus are not present, or	*Shortcomings or absence of critical elements of the firm's Business Model requires steps to be taken to correct deficiencies: restore customer value, present customers with advantage in comparison with other competitors, establish and reinforce systemic and unique capabilities, and ensure that surplus is sufficient to sustain these capabilities.*
(b) Links between elements of the Business Model are not present	*Elements of the Business Model must be complementary with one another; action needs to be taken if this is not so to restore a positive self-reinforcing cycle of relationships.*
The Business Model is not consistent with Corporate Purpose	*Here there are two alternative courses open: adjust the Business Model to bring it in line with Corporate Purpose, or redefine Corporate Purpose to match the existing Business Model.*
The Business Model is not sufficiently robust to be sustained in plausible scenarios of future trends for change Among competitors Within the industry	*While the current Business Model is suited to current competitive and industry conditions, changes need to be made to elements of the Model, and their relationships, to enable it to be expected to cope productively with future anticipated circumstances.*
The Business Model is not sufficiently flexible to cope with future surprises	*Preparation for a future beyond the realm of forecasts and scenarios is problematic. Courses of action associated with this issue are based on creating flexibility in the business model to enable the possibility of productive response.*

Corporate level direction: managing portfolios of businesses

Contemporary thinking, distilled by writers such as Johnson, Scholes and Whittington,[9] refers to the wealth-creation function of corporate centres which oversee and manage businesses of varied diversity. Consideration of the courses of action open to the 'centre' is based on a rationale for benefits from maintaining a variety of businesses, and for maintaining the level of diversity which is retained.

One of the main questions addressed at the corporate level is: what degree of diversification is desirable, and what alternatives are available to achieve this degree of diversification? This is clearly a matter of the extent and benefits of backward, horizontal and forward integration. It is also a question of assembly of a portfolio of businesses with any level of relationship among them; related and unrelated diversification.

Commonly, the corporate centre is referred to as the 'corporate parent' with responsibilities to add value to the focal firm by managing resource allocation to the 'children', exploiting opportunities for synergy, and for intervening for developmental purposes.

Specific roles which follow from this line of reasoning are:

- *Portfolio Manager*: acts to maintain the overall balance of the firm's business assets through activating the cycle of business development described by the BCG Portfolio; including eventually divesting unproductive Dogs (and children?).
- *Restructurer*: intervenes to transform the performance of business units for their commercial environments through investment of appropriate resources including application of specialised expertise.
- *Synergy Manager*: seeks benefits by transferring resources and skills between businesses to enhance prospects for advantage.
- *Parental Developer*: applies central control and lending experience to help individual businesses.

Business level direction: managing sources of competitive advantage

Johnson, Scholes and Whittington, among others, reflect on the bases on which business units might achieve competitive advantage in their own markets. Much of this thinking centres on two main sources of advantage:

through the management of cost and through differentiation of product or service. The various combinations derived from these two axes are illustrated below in Table 3.4 derived from that found in Johnson, Scholes and Whittington.[10]

One of the key competitive concerns flowing from this representation of alternative courses of action is how to sustain advantage once it has been achieved. Sustaining a low price advantage requires, as Michael Porter recognises, conducting a business in such a way as to be *the lowest cost producer*; not to keep costs low, but to be the *lowest*. This is a challenging prospect.

Differentiation is not *being different*. Differentiation can only be sustained if, in the eyes of customers, products or services remain distinguishable from alternatives over time. This is also a demanding task for a business.

Four categories of development are envisaged in contemporary literature, comprising alternative courses of action to enhance business opportunities.

1. *Protect and build on current position* comprises consolidation or increased penetration of current markets.
2. *Market development* involves expansion into new segments or territories, developing new uses for products or services.
3. *Product development* is extension of business activity into new products.
4. *Diversification* builds on current capabilities to move into new products and markets.

A further categorisation of business development is the choice between internal development based on the firm's own abilities and assets, and alternatively, through mergers, alliances and acquisitions.

To summarise, at this point in the production of a Strategic Assessment, a survey has been conducted of current circumstances, including the state of health of the business itself. Matters needing attention have been recognised and acceptable courses of action have been identified in response. Linking back to the situation of Body Shop, this is the stage of analysis in which, with European competitors beginning to materialise, the company would have been considering whether to reduce the impact of rivals on future growth by either further consolidation in Europe,

Table 3.4 *Sources of competitive advantage.*[11]

PERCEIVED BENEFITS	PRICE		
	Low		High
High	**Low Price** Need to be cost leader – risk of price war and low margins	**Hybrid** Low cost base and reinvestment in low price and differentiation	**Differentiation** Perceived added value with price premium	**Focused Differentiation** Perceived added value to particular segment	**Failure Mode** Risk of losing market share
Low		**'No Frills'** Segment specific	**Failure Mode** Loss of market share	**Failure Mode** Only feasible in monopoly	

or establishing the business in the United States. How to evaluate the alternatives?

Evaluation

Effort in identifying courses of action designed to address corporate purpose is an activity in synthesis. Evaluation, the basis for choice among alternatives, is on the other hand, an analytical phase of Strategic Assessment. It should be guided, as we will see in subsequent chapters, by principles: Integrity, Security, Feasibility and Morality. In this section I will explain how these three principles can be shown to derive from a combination of contemporary and classic approaches to weighing up the benefits and limitations of alternative strategic options.

Choice of a course of direction is a logical argument, a story or narrative, derived from an appraisal of conditions and a survey and evaluation of perceived available options. But, however compelling a chosen course of action might be at an intuitive level, it is important to employ a set of criteria which will increase confidence in the ability of this direction to move the odds substantially in the competitive direction of the Focal Firm.

Technical criteria will be used to test the viability of the strategy story. These will ensure that the recommendations are consistent with financial, marketing, production and human resource principles. The logical structure of the strategic story will be based on these foundations, ensuring the argument is sound. It also needs to be appealing. Therefore, the ethical and aesthetic aspects of the story need to be recognised.

In the comparison between contemporary and classical views on evaluation which follows, the reader will find it helpful to refer to the accompanying portion of a Strategic Assessment for Fiat Auto shown in Table 3.5.

Contemporary criteria

Rumelt's[12] set of four criteria for evaluation of business strategy is perhaps the most well known. He refers to Consistency, Consonance, Feasibility and Advantage. Consider Rumelt's criteria in the case, for instance, of Fiat Auto[13] as they apply to the three alternative courses of action identified in the table below.

Table 3.5 *Strategic Assessment for* Fiat Auto.

Appraisal
Company Profile: Italian manufacturer of motor cars and other industrial products

Corporate Purpose: To reduce debt and return to profitability

Business Model: Business model is in decline

Firm Business Model – **Competitive Advantage** has been lost through reduction in perceived product quality and variety. **Customer Value** has subsequently drifted to attractive competitive offerings. Revenue is shrinking, leaving little **Financial Surplus** available to support heavy fixed costs and investment in **Distinctive Capability** which has been eroded through distraction and neglect. **Stakeholders** depend on profits from other Fiat Group businesses to maintain Fiat Auto and its high level of debt.

Competitor Profile:
Volkswagen is the largest European manufacturer by market share, with benefits in production efficiency and substantial investment in product development.

Kia Motors, a South Korean division of Hyundai, is investing heavily and rapidly installing production capability in Europe with the apparent intention of building strength in market influence.

Industry Trends: Excess manufacturing capacity exists in Europe. New capacity is being installed in Central Europe to gain cost advantages. Manufacturers worldwide are seeking efficiencies through subcontracting.

Scenarios: Most Likely: Kia will grow aggressively in small, stylish, economical cars
Most Threatening: Volkswagen will directly threaten Fiat's recovery effort

Issues (Listed in priority order)

1. How to create revenue growth?

Fiat Auto's business model is unable to sustain the business and it needs to be reconstructed. The company is heavily in debt and it depends on funds from elsewhere in the Fiat group to maintain itself. Unless Fiat can generate substantial revenue it will be unable to invest in facilities required to secure its survival, even in the near term. It no longer has distinctive capabilities and consequently, it is losing market to competitors in Europe. Fiat Auto's market share is vulnerable to both ambitious newcomers such as Kia, and the prescient domination of Volkswagen. Growth will need to be vigorous and quick to anticipate Volkswagen's likely attempt to seek control of this ailing firm.

2. How to competitively reconfigure production capability?

Fiat's manufacturing capability has clearly slipped well behind steps taken by its European competitors. Volkswagen has successfully recovered its competitive position through substantial investment in new product development and improvements in production efficiency. And the industry is rapidly reconfiguring itself worldwide. Fiat is burdened by outdated technology and excess capacity by industry standards.

Table 3.5 *Continued*

Alternative Courses of Action (for Issue 1)
A. Sell Fiat Auto The burden of debt is unsustainable. Dependence on other more profitable areas of the Fiat group for funds would be eliminated and debt reduction could be achieved by selling the Auto business. Intense competition in Europe, and indeed worldwide, would motivate any number of firms to purchase Fiat to reduce industrial production capacity through acquisition.
B. Invest in New Products Fiat Auto can borrow further from within the Fiat group to fund reconstruction of the business model. The new business would replicate the successful formula found elsewhere in Europe, that of investing in a sequence of new product introductions. Appealing, high quality vehicles will improve market share and raise production efficiency. Debt reduction and profitability will follow.
C. Status Quo Maintain current direction based on incremental improvement.

Consistency: Is the degree to which goals or policies reinforce each other. Inconsistency arises from contradictory action (e.g. success in one function such as production is associated with failure in another such as marketing).

Fiat is investing in new manufacturing capacity in Central Europe, indicating an intention to take advantage of lower production costs. This, together with the historical support the Fiat group has provided for Fiat Auto, suggests that there is every intention of maintaining the motor car business. The idea of selling Fiat Auto is a course of action which would clearly be inconsistent with this policy. Both investment in new production and support for the status quo are consistent with this direction.

Consonance: Is the degree to which strategy represents adaptive response to external environment: both matching trends and patterns, and also competing with other firms attempting to adapt and employing distinctive competitive positions, skills and resources to advantage.

Status quo for Fiat Auto is apparently not consonant with an adaptive response to the firm's environment. Market expectations are for more frequent offering of new products than Fiat is producing. The company's competitors are moving with this trend and at the same time developing production efficiencies. Fiat Auto is not achieving this benefit and there seems to be non-alignment with its business environment.

Sale of Fiat Auto would be a step consonant with the industry's consolidation, provided it generated a sufficient return to the firm. A move towards more frequent new product offerings would also present a direction consonant with environmental trends.

Advantage: Is provision for creation and/or maintenance of competitive advantage, while emphasising the importance of striving for differentiating features that are most telling, enduring and difficult to duplicate.

As demonstrated in the declining business model for Fiat Auto, there has been insufficient investment in developing and maintaining distinctive capabilities. Simply put, the company has lost its basis for competition with other motor car manufacturers. Selling Fiat Auto would at last acknowledge this fact, recognising that the business model could only be reconstructed with substantial further investment and with sufficient time. However, competitiveness has been lost.

Maintenance of the status quo is a course of action which does not offer competitive advantage since it involves no effort to create a basis for differentiation or cost reduction.

The new product route is designed to catch up with the market trends which are currently matched by Fiat Auto's competitors. This is not, therefore, the creation of a foundation for differentiation at a competitive level.

Feasibility: An acceptable and practical course of action does not cause long term damage to financial, physical, human resources and is congruent with stakeholder expectations.

Detailed technical analysis is needed to demonstrate the feasibility of alternative courses of action. Two questions are posed: is this course of action possible, and if it is possible, will it put unacceptable strains on resources?

To illustrate at the broadest financial level,[14] selling Fiat Auto will be a feasible course of action if there is a buyer willing to purchase the company and all its constituents, and if the purchase price exceeds the cost of sale by an acceptable margin. If the yield is sufficient, then the objective of eliminating the debt of Fiat Auto should be achieved. This will assist the Fiat group's profitability. But this will conflict with the strong expectations of internal and external stakeholders who do not want to lose control of Fiat Auto.

The status quo option is apparently funded from within Fiat Auto. It depends on internal reorganisation to create the efficiencies which would bring a return to prosperity.

Overall, Rumelt's criteria call for consideration of important grounds for comparing alternative courses of action. But are they sufficient? Are they complete in scope and detail? Alternative sets of evaluation criteria presented in the literature (Table 3.6) cover similar ground to those offered by Rumelt, in some places using different labels, but with additional points of detail.

As the reader will see, the main point in common is the feasibility criterion. All four sets of criteria call for consideration of the practicality of a course of action. This involves both ensuring the availability of the necessary wherewithal to achieve the action, and avoidance of overtaxing those resources. Industry context is considered, as is the availability of time to plan and to act.

Suitability is a label used with two meanings: whether the course of action anticipates future environmental developments, and alignment with corporate objectives. Both these ideas contain a similar sense to Rumelt's consistency and consonance.

Acceptability refers to a concept which is not included as a consideration for Rumelt. Johnson, Scholes, Mitchell[15] call for consideration of risk associated with a course of action: whether in view of probable benefits and costs, the level of risk is tolerable.

A further three criteria are offered. Appropriateness refers to the question of whether the course of action builds on corporate strengths and opportunities. Desirability reinforces the aim of goal achievement. Mitchell's term, distinguishability, ensures that a course of action is clearly distinct and different from alternatives under consideration.

The following is a distilled set of criteria which largely encapsulates the essence of the criteria surveyed above.

Effectiveness: whether the course of action is likely to achieve its strategic objective and contribute to accomplishment of corporate purpose.

Feasibility: whether the course of action is practically possible within environmental circumstances, time and corporate capability.

Risk: whether the course of action is tolerable in terms of probable risk and cost/benefit.

Table 3.6 *Contemporary criteria for evaluation of strategy.*

Rumelt[16]	Tiles[17], Hofer & Schendel[18]	Johnson & Scholes[19]	Mitchell[20]
Consistency Degree to which strategy is internally aligned with all goals and policies			
Consonance Degree to which strategy is an adaptive response to relevant aspects of the environment			
Advantage Degree to which strategy creates or maintains competitive advantage			
Feasibility Degree to which strategy avoids overtaxing resources or creating unsolvable problems	**Feasibility** ... Whether strategy can be implemented effectively to achieve desired objectives ... Whether industry success factors can be met ... Whether strategy creates or sustains competitive advantage ... Whether sufficient time is available to plan effectively and act decisively	**Feasibility** Whether strategy is practically possible in terms of resources and strategic capability	**Feasibility** ... Whether time is sufficient to execute envisaged action ... Whether environmental conditions including space, territory or marketplace are capable of sustaining envisaged action ... Whether resources are sufficient or can be reasonably expected to sustain envisaged action

Suitability Whether envisaged action is aligned with corporate purpose and policy	**Suitability** Whether strategy addresses circumstances: fit with future trends and environmental changes, and degree to which it exploits core competencies
Acceptability Whether envisaged action is tolerable in terms of probable risk and cost, against anticipated benefits in achieving purpose	**Acceptability** Expected performance outcomes (return or risk) and whether these are consistent with expectations
	Appropriateness Whether strategy meets its objectives, building on current strengths and opportunities, consistent with available capabilities, and in a way that can be simply conveyed to implementers.
Distinguishability Whether this envisaged action is unique in comparison with alternative courses of action	
	Desirability . . . Whether strategy meets objectives . . . Whether strategy is likely to produce acceptable returns with reasonable risk, and meet stakeholder expectations

We turn now to a question of perspective. Has there been anything over-looked? Are there criteria which are worthy of consideration in addition to those listed above? Classic sources of strategic thinking raise other ideas which bear consideration in choosing a course of action at a strategic threshold.

Classic criteria

Although Sun Tzu and von Clausewitz would no doubt see value in a sys-tematic approach to strategic choice, for them the greatest challenges lie in the subtle interplay between the strategist and the situation. This is engage-ment with a turbulent world of contradictions, paradox and uncertainty.

Meticulous assessment of circumstances lies at the heart of Sun Tzu's approach to strategic choice. Preparation requires careful assembly of infor-mation giving consideration to one's opponents, natural forces and terrain, all allowing calculation of appropriate size of force and its most appropriate attributes. Only with the results of such calculation is it possible to decide when to divide or concentrate, and when to engage or disengage.

Calculations at the heart of the Fiat Auto choice of course of action would, in Sun Tzu's terms, concentrate more focused attention on the inten-tions and behaviour of competitors than is revealed through contemporary evaluation criteria. This is not surprising in view of our encounter with competition in the previous chapter. But more so than simply weighing competitive intelligence, Sun Tzu calls for consideration of the character of the strategist himself.[21]

As to the choice of general or strategist, Sun Tzu advocates wisdom, sincerity, humanity, courage and strictness. He cautions against recklessness, cowardice, impulsiveness, together with excess in pride, and compassion. The inference is that a choice-maker's own attributes will influence de-cisions. This, the selection of generals, is among all aspects of strategic choice, a matter for the ruler or sovereign.

A firm entering a competitive phase without clearly identified senior leadership will, in Sun Tzu's terms, be vulnerable to its opponents.

To elaborate, Fiat Auto has encountered difficulties recently at the top of its organisation. Master Sun would count this as a very serious concern with implications for the likely success of any chosen course of action in the competitive circumstances.

The corporate context in which a campaign takes place is an important matter in Sun Tzu's view. For a general to be successful in a struggle it is essential that he have the full support of his sovereign or patron. After all, the campaign is to be carried out to support the sovereign's interests. Choice of strategy is integral with matters of political sponsorship.

For Fiat the Agnelli family has been the major shareholder throughout its history. Fiat's sovereign interests have been those of this family. Crucially for Fiat, the guidance of Gianni Agnelli has recently been lost through his death: the sovereign is dead. It is to be expected that some time will be needed to secure political confidence in his successor. In such uncertain times, Sun Tzu might well be cautioning against a competitive campaign.

While sponsorship is essential, so also is a sovereign's restraint. Strategic choice is the domain of the sovereign's general. For a campaign to be successful the sovereign must not interfere once policy direction has been established and the competitive endeavour is under way.

Consequences of the ruler's inappropriate intervention in an ongoing campaign will almost inevitably result in confusion, uncertainty and demoralisation, so resulting in misfortune and placing the enterprise at risk. Specifically, a ruler is likely to bring about these threats to the success of a campaign by ordering advance when there should be none, by ordering retreat when there should be none, by perplexing staff through ignorant participation in administration of the confrontation, and by creating doubt among staff through sharing competitive responsibilities in ignorance.

The general must be permitted to control the progress of the struggle and choose appropriate strategic courses of subsequent action at his or her own discretion. Strategic decision making must therefore be constrained by policy direction but without further limitation from above.

Sun Tzu also appreciates the significance of a general's careful attention not only to an opponent's disposition of force, but details of his or her own organisation will need to be taken account of in strategic choice. He refers to means of control, to assignment of staff roles and to supply of provisions as fundamental factors for reflection in strategy.

Furthermore, he places considerable emphasis on morale as a key factor influencing strategic choice. It is this moral influence which causes people to be in harmony with their leaders, and to accompany them to danger without fear of peril. A general will be conscious of building and maintaining morale and his or her choice of campaign strategy will be influenced by an estimate of the harmony among opponents.

Master Sun is, of course, referring to the military goal of building fighting morale sufficient to face an aggressive opponent. However, there is no doubt a commercial parallel, even though the nature and intensity of competition is not as compelling as in war.

One of the very important issues facing Fiat Auto is the state of morale of its workforce. The declining business model of the company has resulted in loss of performance which will no doubt affect the confidence working staff have in themselves, their work and their company. This will be a serious obstacle in considering what courses of action are feasible for the firm.

Von Clausewitz is very clear in arguing that no engagement or campaign should be commenced without first seeking an answer to the question: 'What is to be attained . . . ?'

This viewpoint carries a caution about the sources of strategic direction which require consideration of the whole circumstances. Although there is no doubt about the preliminary decision to enter a campaign being based on a rational analysis of the available information, the final choice will always rest on judgement.

Choice of strategy should therefore be focused on specific objectives which will guide accomplishment. Moreover, these policy objectives will be deduced from political considerations; the campaign will not form an end in itself.

And what is the role of the military in evolving such policy? Von Clausewitz argues that policy must not be based on military opinion; it must derive from a political agenda rather than a military one. Similarly in business.

The policy objective for Fiat Auto is twofold: to reduce debt and return to profitability. It is apparent that policy is formulated for the benefit of the entire Fiat group and these objectives are designed to ensure that the contribution of Fiat Auto is no longer a drain on group performance.

One particular consideration which will require judgement is the state of morale or spirit among one's own forces and those of an opponent. This is an obvious point of concurrence with Sun Tzu. Von Clausewitz regards this as a matter of relationship of an army with its leaders. Moral force is among the most important; it forms the spirit which permeates competition. Such force needs to be recognised in full value and always taken into account, despite the difficulty in describing and analysing it. In von Clausewitz's view, a spirit of willingness, including maintenance of confidence and respect for leaders is derived from success in campaigns and through staff activity, sometimes carried out to its highest pitch.

Again, the misfortunes of Fiat Auto over the past years have no doubt eroded worker morale. Furthermore, talk in the press about selling the firm will add job security concerns to an already worried work-force. These are not circumstances in which it can be expected that great commitment to a new cause can be asked of staff.

Following the decision to proceed, the next phase of strategic choice involves consideration of how resources are to be applied to the venture. There is no doubt for von Clausewitz that force should be concentrated. Overpowering strength is required, applied at the decisive time and place. Application of this force should be concentrated, not divided. Von Clausewitz views the policy objective as accomplished when force is sufficient to achieve the following:

- decisive victory in competition;
- follow up which prevents opponent from regaining balance; and
- a result which does not motivate a rival's allies to intervene and secure the rival's recovery.

A focus on competitive success for Fiat Auto would involve securing advantage over one or more of its rivals. Von Clausewitz expects that the feasibility of a course of action designed to prevail in such a competition would take account of these three aspects of an end state.

Having once decided on direction and force, action should be pre-emptive. Offensive must be made in the shortest possible time; speedily and with persistence.

From this point further choice of direction raises even greater challenges. As the campaign unfolds confusion and uncertainty are inevitable. Information received about competitive circumstances becomes doubtful at best, inducing reservations about plans and tempting indecision. As von Clausewitz points out, strategy, compared with tactics, goes slowly, leaving much scope for remonstrance, objections, apprehension and regrets. Inherent conjecture and doubt about assumptions leads to the likelihood of weak conviction and bewildering, immobilising doubt and a temptation to continually return to analysis, sometimes called *analysis paralysis*.[22] A general must counteract this hesitation.

Circumstances will be constantly found different from expectation with insufficient time for full review. Uncertainty increases the tendency to hesitate while waiting for further confirmation of revised expectations. But typically plans do not require complete revision; they only need a change of assumption or premise.

Not all uncertainty will derive from the turmoil of the competitive engagement. Von Clausewitz warns a general in strategic choice to anticipate *friction from the machine*. Even with an unambiguous objective, steps towards its execution are typically inhibited by 'natural inertia', that is, friction of the organisation's parts resulting from inevitable inconsistency, vagueness and hesitation (or timidity) of the human mind. While surprise, tricks, deception and reserve are crucial to tactical operations, they will therefore rarely be of benefit to strategy because of their tendency to contradict the principle of concentration and their contribution to inevitable friction in large scale implementation in space and time.

The aspects of strategic choice referred to above offer considerable challenges to campaign leaders. A number of special abilities are called for to complement the choice process:

- will of the commander to counteract demoralisation;
- resolution to remove the torment of doubt;
- experience and judgement to overcome unanticipated barriers;
- perseverance to maintain control despite inevitable friction and error; and
- discrimination between the significant and irrelevant to counteract distraction.

Summarising the views of these classic strategy theorists, it is clear that considerable emphasis is placed on the role of leadership, its attributes, its responsibilities and its obligations. Choice itself is an essential function of leadership; challenging, demanding and no doubt rewarding.

The process of choice is one which calls for the highest levels of judgement and experience. The success of the competitive enterprise depends on it; success not so much in the application of logic, but in persistence and unhesitating commitment to the campaign.

It is noteworthy that both Sun Tzu and von Clausewitz refer to the vital relationship between the campaign commander and the sovereign's Cabinet. Policy making and execution to accomplish its objectives are separated. Moreover, von Clausewitz recommends that commanders should not become involved in leading the formulation of policy: this is a political problem, one for the state or sovereign.

Table 3.7 brings together Assessment criteria derived from contemporary and classic sources, indicating how they combine in the Principles of Strategy.

Evaluation of a course of action is a complex and demanding activity. As the discussion above has shown, it can be considered at a number of levels. As a choice of direction it needs to pass the test of reason; the argument for a particular activity, rather than another, must be coherent. It needs to demonstrate likelihood of accomplishing objectives, based on present and future capability, and within tolerable risk. It also makes demands on those leading the competitive enterprise, ensuring that the course of direction secures dynamic control and psychological dominance over a rival, employing superior strategic capability and building confidence in a morally justified cause.

Table 3.7 *Criteria for evaluation and principles of strategy.*

Contemporary Criteria	Classic Criteria	Principles
Effectiveness: *whether the course of action is likely to achieve its strategic objective and contribute to accomplishment of corporate purpose*	Holism: *whether the line of strategic thinking developed is holistic and comprehensive in its scope and purpose*	Integrity: *Strategy ensures that the enterprise maintains unity of thinking which integrates progressive enhancement of competitive advantage*
Risk: *whether the course of action is tolerable in terms of probable risk and cost over benefit*	Dominance: *whether the line of strategic thinking builds and sustains confidence*	Security: *Strategy ensures that the enterprise secures its position from a condition of psychological strength and stability*
Feasibility: *whether the course of action is practically possible within environmental circumstances, time and corporate capability*	Feasibility: *whether the line of strategic thinking flows from competent corporate leadership*	Feasibility: *Strategy ensures that the enterprise acquires and maintains sufficient capability to accomplish aims*

Metaphorically, strategy is a compelling story, told to those who will be charged with implementing it at a tactical level. Its timing is important; the story needs to be heard when it will have most impact. Its language is important; a story will be compelling if it is heard in a familiar tongue. Most of all, the story needs to be convincing through being interpretable within the mental maps of the implementors; it needs to make sense and relate to practical reality.

Returning to the question of Body Shop, where this discussion of Strategic Assessment began, the question can be restated: why did Body Shop's progress falter when the decision was made to enter the United States market? Was there a flaw in Strategic Assessment?

In 1988 something went wrong. Until this time the development of the Body Shop business had been faultless. As Anita Roddick explained, there were indications that expansion into the United States would succeed from the viewpoint of potential product demand. It was a logical course of business development. Hesitant to move too far too quickly, Body Shop decided first to establish one of its own stores in New York to test the market before launching its usual franchise-based method of growth.

The one single element of the Strategic Assessment which was overlooked in the appraisal was potential competition. Without taking account of the speed with which large rivals would materialise once Body Shop moved into the American shopping malls, the newcomer was surprised and badly thrown off balance. Suddenly Body Shop was surrounded by firms such as Bath and Bodyworks offering similar products. Balance was lost, initiative evaporated, confidence wavered and large sums of money were lost. Recovery took some time. It was a sobering experience, from which the company learned.

The following concept map summarises the form and function of a Strategic Assessment.

Reflection

Can strategic thinking, and therefore Strategic Assessment be a collective activity among executives or is thinking something only one person can do?

Is evaluation a choice among criteria for choice?

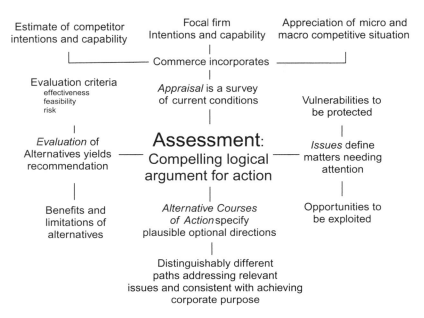

Figure 3.2 Concept map for Assessment.

Appendix 3: The look of a Strategic Assessment

In practice, the format of a Strategic Assessment should allow the presentation to be easily accessible to its audience:

The Strategic Assessment should be two pages long; no more. And it should be professionally presented and easy to read. Some object to the apparently arbitrary restriction. Let it be an exercise in disciplined crafting of an argument.

The Assessment contains the four sections explained above, with approximately equal space allocated to each, that is, half a page. This ensures that the presentation is balanced and no portion of the Assessment overwhelms the others. The greatest trap is allowing the appraisal to become too long.

Each section should contain all the elements included in the discussion above, and in the order presented. That is, for instance, the appraisal should contain Company Profile, Corporate Purpose, Business Model, . . . and so on, in that order. The template offered here is intended to provide a foundation which depends on a reasoned flow of information leading towards a conclusion; all the elements are necessary.

The argument should be developed logically, starting with the appraisal as the foundation. Issues must only refer to information in the appraisal. Alternative courses of action must clearly be means of addressing the main Issue. These are evaluated in the Recommendations. Logical flaws include: breaks in causal reasoning, introduction of irrelevancies, unsound deductions, resort to rhetorical language, ambiguity, circular reasoning, confusing language, use of red herrings and straw men.

A Strategic Assessment is, after all, a summary. It does depend on supporting information which cannot be included in the document itself because of limits on space. It is recommended that the audience be provided with an appendix in which supporting information, as well as the listing of assumptions, and conduct of analysis, is systematically collated.

4

Integrity

Principle of Integrity: Strategy ensures that the enterprise maintains unity of thinking which concentrates on progressive enhancement of competitive advantage.

Strategic thinking is unified through building and maintaining competitive momentum, by flexibly adapting to changing circumstances, and by maintaining competitive readiness.

In May 1940 the German army attacked France in such circumstances and with such momentum, that the French had no choice but to surrender their sovereignty very soon afterwards. A great military accomplishment on one side was matched by a great military catastrophe on the other.

Putting aside the question of Germany's Policy purpose in invading, and whatever reservations one might have about contemplating the idea of warfare, there are lessons for a strategist in commerce to learn from events in 1940.

As we look back on the history of the French invasion[1] there is a very clear contrast between the *integrity* of German thinking which formed the basis for the attack, and the obvious lack of such unity of thought among the French.

German intelligence indicated that the French defensive capability in the Ardennes in North Eastern France was weak. This was brought about by French military thinking which had been governed by two considerations.

First, German manoeuvring had led the French to believe that the main attack would take place in a thrust through Belgium. French and British Expeditionary forces had therefore been positioned to resist. And second, the enormous investment in construction of the Maginot fortification by the French after World War I had led to the belief that its *world best practice* in forts would discourage Germany from any attack in that quarter.

German military thinking aimed to capitalise on the opportunity which was presented. The offensive involved a commanding initiative comprising a strong and sudden attack on the French through the Ardennes. As circumstances changed through the attack, so the Germans were prepared to adapt to their advantage. Building on the success of the initial thrust, the advancing German army maintained its balance, almost overstretching itself in its rapid rate of forward movement, but not quite. The offensive can be concisely described in three words: initiative, flexibility and balance.

On the French side, competitive thinking was severely limited by a complete absence of political will. Deep divisions in society, bitter conflict between political factions and, perhaps, an element of complacency based on previous success in the fight with Germany in World War I, all contributed to a Policy vacuum. The French military leadership was sadly unsupported; what was needed was a determined and purposeful French government. There was none.

The resulting loss for the French was almost inevitable. Aims were unclear. There was no clear anticipation of German intention or capability. Defensive manoeuvre was superficial and ineffective. Contingencies were limited. And responsiveness was unbalanced. Furthermore, these deficiencies almost ensured that when an attack came, losses would be demoralising and immobilising, thus compounding the advantages to the opposition. And so it happened.

This book is not about military history. But if the thinking processes are considered on both sides of this particular dramatic confrontation, the implications are revealing for strategy in any field of human competition, including commerce.

The principle of integrity guides strategic thinking to consider an orientation towards competition with a mindset fixed on achieving objectives with an understanding that important considerations should be considered together, in a unified way, rather than separately. In this chapter three ideas

Table 4.1 *Interactions among initiative, flexibility and balance.*

Integrity: Unity of thinking for competitive advantage	Initiative	Flexibility	Balance
Initiative	Build and sustain competitive momentum by forward thrust to seize advantage	*Undermine competitor's momentum by adaptively disrupting rival's focus*	*Destabilise rival's momentum by drawing competitor into state of loss of balance*
Flexibility	**Maintain momentum while capitalising on opportunities and circumventing obstacles as they arise**	Adapt to changing circumstances for persistent concentration on advantage	*Cultivate rival's loss of balance through continuous movement and balanced repositioning*
Balance	**Capitalise on competitive momentum with continuous readiness to seize advantage without overreaching**	**Move to adapt to circumstances within range of readiness and without loss of stability**	Maintain a state of fitness and readiness to build and sustain momentum

Assertive strategic posture
Defensive strategic posture

are explored: initiative, flexibility and balance. Integrity calls for them to be thought about in combination as a basis for strategic thinking; a sketch of such relationships is illustrated in Table 4.1.

The Table helps to interpret the strategy of the rivals in the invasion of France. On the German side, as we have seen, the invasion was designed as a thrust to accomplish advantage, moving forward quickly, taking advantage of circumstances and well placed to maintain motion with stability. For the French, there was no capacity to respond through building moral dominance; the flow of advantage was against them. Stability was lost and any ability to regain it was undermined by loss of flexibility.

How did initiative, flexibility and balance combine? The cells below the northwest to southeast diagonal describe the German assertive posture which comprised close interdependence between the three concepts: momentum was sustained by readiness to adapt and maintenance of balance.

What was required of the French if they were to discourage the German advance? The cells above the diagonal describe a *defensive* posture. Through a combination of initiative, flexibility and balance, the French would have succeeded in defence if they had caused the German advance to trip and falter. A counterattack on the exposed left flank of the German advance, as it turned west to race for the English Channel after crossing the Ardennes, would have disrupted the advance. For the French this would have called for a combination of their own ability to seize the moment of German vulnerability, and adapting to the situation turning in their favour from a position of readiness and stability. Its effect would have been to cause distraction and loss of focus, a threat to stability and loss of freedom of movement.

The way has been prepared now for a more detailed discussion of the three concepts of initiative, flexibility and balance, ideas which the reader will now realise form a combination in strategic thinking.

Initiative

Above all, initiative is important in maintaining moral dominance in a competitive situation. As we have seen in the opening illustration about the invasion of France, the idea of initiative provides a powerful explanation as a contributor to competitive success, initiative is also readily seen as those movements in sport which are designed to overwhelm rivals through a surging effort to direct the flow of the game.

I choose to maintain a military orientation here for a short while longer to visualise and more fully explain Initiative in this context before moving on to its application in commercial competition. I trust the reader will understand that this is not an indulgence in military history, but rather an effort to secure clarity.

Military thinking is geared towards prevailing in what might be called the ultimate competition. All military organisations around the world employ a set of principles which are used to evaluate strategic thinking. The number of principles varies from one military organisation to another, ranging from 8 to 12. However, the idea of initiative is found in all lists of guidelines for assessing strategy.

In Australian military circles, this element is included under the heading of 'surprise':

Surprise is a most powerful influence in operations. Every endeavour must be made to surprise the enemy and to guard against being surprised. Surprise can produce results out of all proportion to the effort expended. When other factors are unfavourable, surprise may be essential to the success of an operation. It may be achieved through skilled use of new doctrine, intelligence, secrecy, concealment, deception, simplicity, originality, audacity, timing, speed of action and technology. The use of surprise by friendly forces enhances their morale and serves to lower the morale of the enemy.[2]

Among examples of the application of initiative in military history, Lord Nelson's naval manoeuvres in Napoleonic Europe stand out as excellent illustrations of tactical initiative.[3]

Lord Nelson is one of the greatest of heroes of British naval history. His place in history was truly sealed at the Battle of Trafalgar in 1805 where he led the British to a victory over a much larger Franco-Spanish fleet. This brought to an end Napoleon's ambition of invading England. Nelson was killed during the sea battle.

His final success at Trafalgar was a tactical rather than a strategic victory. He was a great naval tactician. As his career progressed he created a powerful impression as one who was prepared to take unexpected initiatives to unbalance his naval rivals. More often than not, these resulted in important tactical victories for Nelson and his fleet.

His tactical initiative is best demonstrated on three particular occasions: at the battle of Cape St Vincent, at Aboukir Bay near the entrance to the Nile River and at the Battle of Copenhagen. In each of these cases, Nelson took a calculated risk and surprised his rival by taking an unexpected move which left them disadvantaged through loss of balance.

- *Cape St Vincent*: While engaged with a fleet in a surprise action against the Spanish, Napoleon's ally, in 1797 off Spain, Nelson recognised that the Spanish fleet was about to move to consolidate its position to the British disadvantage. So, on his own initiative, he drew his ship out of the line of attack and moved to pre-empt the enemy. In doing so, he achieved fame by capturing two Spanish warships, one considerably larger than his own.
- *Aboukir Bay*: After chasing Napoleon's Egypt fleet back and forth across the Mediterranean in the summer of 1798, Nelson finally found the French fleet at anchor in Aboukir Bay in the late afternoon of 1 August.

Rather than wait, he immediately and unexpectedly took advantage of a narrow stretch of navigable water and destroyed the unprepared French fleet. For this Nelson was called 'The hero of the Nile'.

• *Copenhagen*: In an attempt to persuade the Danish to withdraw from Napoleon's blockade of Britain's vital supplies from the Baltic, Nelson challenged the Danish fleet at anchor at Copenhagen in April 1802. Ignoring orders to withdraw, Nelson proceeded to fight until achieving the truce which was his goal.

Considering these three events together, common themes are apparent and these help to define a meaning for initiative,[4] showing also its contribution to competitive success.

• calculation of risk and likely benefit;
• feasibility in terms of accurate assessment of available capability;
• surprise by anticipating rival's competitive mindset and acting outside expectations;
• rapid judgement and quick action;
• ability to follow through and bring the initiative to a successful resolution.

Initiative applies the benefits of clear intention, flexibility based on balanced assets and abilities, and an accurate and reliable assessment of the capabilities and intentions of a competitor. It involves a full understanding of the mindset of a competitor. It also involves an appreciation of the value of speed, time and timing.

Creating momentum

The aim of initiative is to unbalance a competitor, most particularly in disrupting its strategist's ability to think clearly and to organise a response. Initiative is designed to secure a position which at the same time avoids vulnerability to the unbalancing initiatives of others.

Nestlé is a company which has demonstrated exceptional performance over a long time.[5] Its success is no doubt due, in part, to a long sequence of successful strategic initiatives which have kept its major competitors guessing about its next moves.

By contrast Barclays, a British bank, also has a very long history.[6] But in recent times it has apparently lost its initiative on many occasions; it has lost the ability to present its competitors with an unexpected move which has produced a benefit for it. Perhaps Barclays has lost its focus on competitors and become preoccupied with internal issues of organisation and structure.

Initiative is a vital element of strategic thinking, according to classic sources. Based on his extensive study of military strategy, Liddell Hart[7] refers in particular, to competitive advantage achieved by initiative in terms of its effects on both a rival's physical and psychological dislocation.

- Physical dislocation: upsetting and scattering resources, endangering supplies, menacing logistics.
- Psychological dislocation: impression left on commander's mind of sudden disadvantage and inability to counter move – the sense of being trapped.

These effects are precisely those which Sun Tzu aims for in his advice to a strategist. Sun Tzu likens the effects of initiative to the creation of momentum which can become an unstoppable force which overwhelms a competitor:

> When the enemy presents an opportunity, speedily take advantage of it. . . . Therefore at first be shy as a maiden. When the enemy gives you an opening be swift as a hare and he will be unable to withstand you.[8]

> When torrential water tosses boulders, it is because of its momentum; When the strike of a hawk breaks the body of its prey, it is because of timing. Thus the momentum of one skilled in war is overwhelming and his attack precisely regulated.[9]

According to von Clausewitz, strategic initiative is more likely to be successful than not, when a properly prepared Focal Firm takes action against a vulnerable competitor. Competitors most prone to the disabling effects of strategic initiative are likely to be those with the following attributes:

- resource deficiency;
- absence of direction: absence of motion or purpose (flatfooted);

- structural deficiency;
- deficient competitive intelligence;
- lack of balance;
- inflexibility;
- dislocation of policy-strategy-tactics.

Proper preparation involves anticipation of a competitor's retaliatory action. Von Clausewitz identifies the following requirements for initiative:[10]

- a primary objective: to unbalance competitor and secure advantage;
- simultaneous defensive support to secure assets;
- anticipation of tempo;
- sustained advance to the extent of preventing competitor's recovery;
- replacement of consumed assets;
- superior moral and material strength.

Von Clausewitz respects the great strategic value which can be achieved with initiative, but he cautions the strategist about the greater risks that are associated with greater and bolder ambition:

> The more boldness lends wings to the mind, . . . so much further they will reach in their flight, so much more comprehensive will be the view, the more exact the result, but certainly always only in the sense that with greater objects greater dangers are connected.[11]

In commerce, the primary objective of initiative is to act at a time and in a way that finds a competitor unprepared; to take them by surprise.[12] This involves bringing together the full range of elements of strategic thinking which is designed to unbalance the rival's strategic thinking processes. As a result of such loss of balance they will suffer a consequent loss of flexibility and find themselves, at least temporarily, unable to respond. Their capability to take initiative will be lost and an opportunity will then be available for advantage to be taken.

Among the very few contemporary scholars of business competition who discuss the concept of initiative, MacMillan[13] refers to the application of strategic initiative under various competitive conditions. He points out that initiative designed to unbalance and unsettle a competitor should be selected based on a well-informed foundation of product, market and competitor intelligence.

Strategic initiatives will be most effective, Macmillan explains, when this aspect of strategic thinking is matched to a company's purpose, in its market. Strategic thinking should be concentrated on clearly identified target companies. It should include what MacMillan calls *counterpunch planning*, that is, planning the series of moves which will follow the initial step, should the competitor retaliate.

Examples he offers of strategic initiatives to achieve pre-emption include securing control over main suppliers and distributors, contracting key customers, pre-emption through first entry to new market segments, and establishing benchmark production capacity. From their seven-year study of competitive behaviour in 41 industries, Smith, Ferrier and Grimm[14] identify strategic initiatives which have been successful in 'dethroning' market leaders. Their results show that successful challengers are more aggressive in taking action; they carry out a more complex repertoire of actions, are unpredictable in the timing and location of attack and are able to delay the reaction of industry leaders.

In recent corporate history two examples illustrate the importance of initiative in commercial competition. One is offered by Lynn[15] who describes the action taken by Airbus to secure for itself a position among American buyers of civil aircraft.

Airbus was anxious to make an impression in the American market with its A300 Airbus. However, Boeing was a powerful competitor and the American airlines were cautious about buying from Airbus. In 1977 Eastern Airlines was looking to re-equip its fleet with a large order of new aircraft. But it was in financial difficulties. The strategic initiative Airbus took was to offer Eastern some very favourable financial engineering, a step the American airlines would not have expected: airlines buy aircraft, manufacturers sell them. Airbus was taking a position as a financier as well as an aircraft manufacturer. Boeing was set back on its competitive heels. Its European competitor had suddenly secured a large order in its territory. It took some time for Boeing to recover; perhaps it never did. And Airbus received a competitive boost; which it never lost.

In a second example, more recently, turbulence in the mobile telephone industry brought about conditions where the unexpected occurred.[16]

Ericsson, one of the major competitors in the industry, lost ground due to its concentration on electronics and engineering, rather than on the product preferences of the customer. Opportunistically, Sony, a small participant in the mobile phone industry, but a worldwide giant in electronics, took a strategic initiative involving the acquisition of a controlling interest in Ericsson. Nokia, the leader in the field, now has a very influential competitor to contend with.

Before concluding this discussion on strategic initiative, one more point needs to be made. Time is an important concept for helping to further understand strategic initiative. The theme developed so far is that strategic initiative is designed to meet short term objectives: action to dislocate a competitor's strategic thinking. But a rival might recover in due course and regain its stability; the initiator's action might have short-lived effects. On the other hand, a company's successful initiatives, over a long period of times, might no longer hold the element of surprise.

The objective of strategic initiative is to influence a competitor's strategic thinking: action designed to encourage a competitor not to enter a market (by raising barriers to entry), prompting them to limit the scope of their objectives (restricting their access to key assets or customers), or encouraging them to leave the market (lowering costs of departure).

Such thinking imposes important leadership expectations, as we shall see when we later consider the principle of feasibility: specification of purpose and policy, maintenance of morale, provision of appropriate assets and abilities, and definition of goals. But that is to jump ahead; first there are other ideas to discuss in relation to Integrity.

Flexibility

Flexibility contributes to initiative through perception of changing situations from a standpoint of balance, and responding to circumstances for competitive advantage by capitalising on opportunities and circumventing obstacles.

Pernod Ricard, a French firm, approached the point of purchasing Allied Domecq, British and another global spirits firm, after having manoeuvred through a period in which it has grown rapidly by acquisition.[17] Its acquisition of Allied was likely to double its size and thus place it squarely in competition with Diageo which is the global market leader. Reflecting on its recent history, Pernod has absorbed Seagrams in 2001, partnered with Fortune Brands, and rationalised its portfolio of spirits brands. Through this path Pernod's bid for control of Allied was unopposed by other possible rivals including Bacardi, Brown-Forman, Constellation Brands. As a demonstration of the strategic thinking of Pernod's chief executive, Patrick Ricard, it is impressive in its display of flexibility.

How then can we explain the elements of flexibility?

Flexibility is the intelligent ability to adapt in a responsive and productive way to altering circumstances. It is characterised as a thinking process which engages with the psychology of a competitor. Strategy is flexible when such thinking responds to the changing actions, character, perceptions, intentions, beliefs and assumptions of a rival. As a competitor's strategic thinking shifts, Focal Firm strategy needs to adapt so as to maintain the initiative. Strategic flexibility is thinking again and thinking differently.

By comparison, Tactical flexibility is an issue of organisational change. Responsive, within the scope of strategic direction, the orchestrated deployment of assets and abilities allows for adaptation to unexpected initiatives by a rival and opportunities arising from a competitor's emerging vulnerability. Tactical flexibility is adaptive rearrangement and redeployment of assets and abilities.

At an operational level, flexibility in use of assets and employment of abilities allows changes to be made effectively and economically when facing shifting transactional circumstances. Operational flexibility is effective multiple function of assets.

It is almost inconceivable that any business enterprise would be blind to changes in its commercial circumstances. Marketing is based on awareness of trends in customer preferences and the making of efforts to provide for these changes. Flexibility is therefore found in common intelligent adaptation to business circumstances.

This is the view of flexibility which is found in the contemporary thinking of Andrews, and Hamel and Prahalad. Andrews refers to strategy as the flexible matching of environmental opportunities to corporate resources. Hamel and Prahalad call for a commitment among executives to create new rules for the way business is conducted so that future advantage can be assured. The common theme from these scholars is the need to adapt to circumstances to create situational advantage.

Adapting to circumstances

Inevitably, the circumstances of any competition vary with time and with the effects of competitive interaction. This was no doubt so in the view of Patrick Ricard as he surveyed the spirits industry in which his firm was located. It is important, therefore, to be able to clearly detect and understand these changes, and alter course accordingly as the situation permits. In strategic terms, flexibility aims to enhance corporate capacity to adapt as situations change. Not an end in itself, it supports a competitive ability to prevail in competition through circumventing obstacles and capturing opportunities while launching initiatives to create advantageous momentum.

From a purely competitive perspective, Sun Tzu's view of responsiveness to circumstances envisages an attempt to create relative advantage based on competitive intelligence:

> If I am able to determine the enemy's dispositions while at the same time I conceal my own then I can concentrate and he must divide. And if I concentrate while he divides, I can use my entire strength to attack a fraction of his. There I will be numerically stronger. . . . the enemy must not know where I intend to give battle. For if he does not know where I intend to give battle he must prepare in a great many places. And when he prepares in a great many places, those I have to fight in any one place will be few. . . . the ultimate in disposing one's troops is to be without ascertainable shape. Then the most penetrating spies cannot pry in nor can the wise lay plans against you.[18]

Because strategy concentrates on the long term, with large asset commitments and decisions can only be reversed with difficulty, future uncertainty will bear heavily on strategic thinking. Circumstances will always change and flexibility is a mindset which is designed to cope with the unforeseen.

Raynor[19] observes that a common contemporary recommendation for remaining competitive in a turbulent environment is to simply develop the corporate capability to swiftly reorganise, restructure and develop new competitive skills. Ansoff[20] classifies this type of flexibility as 'after-the-fact' response to strategic surprise. Learning and the ability to grow are desirable, but continuous quick change will interfere with direction through its creation of dysfunctional corporate instability.

Quick, continuous, responsive action is antithetical to the long term requirements for a firm's commitment to investment in essential assets and abilities. This calls for reasonable certainty about future events. But forecasts are notoriously unreliable, and surprise is inevitable. Or is it?

What to do? Ansoff offers a useful analytical method for thinking through possible futures and configuring alternative responses. He calls this 'strategic issue analysis'; continuous consideration of possible discontinuities and feasible responses. This approach provides a foundation for a method advanced by Courtney, Kirkland and Viguerie[21] who recognise that future uncertainty is not all of one type: they envisage four levels involving discrete outcomes, possible outcomes, a range of possibilities and ambiguity.

Raynor proposes a view of flexibility which is adaptive to environmental shifts, yet its basis is a firm commitment to activities which are essential to future prospects, whatever future change is encountered. The process he recommends begins with defining a series of plausible scenarios within which policy objectives can be accomplished. Assessments are made of required resources and organisation for each scenario, common, or 'core', elements are identified and commitments are made to these features of all scenarios. Thus a primary level of uncertainty is reduced.

Next, contingencies are considered for the different scenarios and investment is made to the minimum level in each, sufficient to be successfully built upon, if over time, a particular forecast begins to materialise. Courtney, et al.[22] refer to this as 'reserving the right to play', a position from which a decision can be made either to advance by increasing commitment, or by withdrawing.

There is, however, another view which cuts across this idea of flexibility. It is found in Porter's article 'What is Strategy?'[23] Here Porter presents an argument for inflexible commitment to unique activity systems within a firm, as his rationale for securing and maintaining competitive advantage. Long term benefit will ensue, he says, from concentrating efforts on developing unique capabilities which distinguish one firm from another. As one considers the situation of Pernod's acquisition of Allied again, this idea would surely apply to such operational matters as management of supply chain: not a strategic issue at all.

Interestingly, the combination of calls among contemporary commentators, for both flexibility and inflexibility, is made without direct reference to competition. On one hand there is a need for adaptation to the market and industry environment. On the other, reinforcement of unique assets and abilities will yield business advantage as an act of faith.

The kinds of adjustments Sun Tzu calls for require a balance. On one hand, taking account of competitive circumstances designed to anticipate favourable terms for achieving an overall objective, and on the other, avoiding engagement if necessary to avoid premature disadvantage:

> ... do not engage an enemy advancing with well ordered banners nor one whose formations are in impressive array. ... when the enemy occupies high ground, do not confront him; with his back resting on hills, do not oppose him. When he pretends to flee, do not pursue. Do not attack his elite troops. Do not gobble proffered baits. Do not thwart an enemy returning homewards. To surround an enemy you must leave a way of escape.[24]

At the time Machiavelli wrote *The Prince*, his aim was concentrated on preventing his Florentine heritage from being destroyed by invaders and by civil war. To prevent destruction and preserve culture itself, Machiavelli was prepared to advocate a kind of flexibility which is judged in some quarters as morally indefensible: simply, that preservation of supreme value requires whatever means are available and effective:

> ... there are two ways of fighting: by law or by force. ... But as the first way often proves inadequate one needs have recourse to the second ... So as a prince is forced to know how to act like a beast, he must learn from the fox and the lion; because the lion is defenceless against traps and a fox is defenceless against wolves. Therefore one must be a fox in order to recognise traps, and a lion to frighten off wolves. Those who simply act like lions are stupid. So it follows that a prudent ruler cannot, must not, honour his word when it places him at a disadvantage and when the reasons for which he made his promise no longer exist. If all men were good, this precept would no longer exist; but because men are wretched creatures who would not keep their word to you, you need not keep your word to them.[25]

This flexibility designed to prevail over what Machiavelli observes as the failings of human nature, lies in contrast with his recommendation that *The Prince* take an inflexible stance, avoiding a neutral position when others are in conflict:

> A prince also wins prestige for being a true friend or a true enemy, that is, for revealing himself without any reservation in favour of one side against another.

This policy is always more advantageous than neutrality. For instance if the powers neighbouring on you come to blows, either they are such that if one of them conquers, you will be in danger, or they are not. In either case it will always be to your advantage to declare yourself and to wage a vigorous war; because, in the first case, if you do not declare yourself you will always be at the mercy of the conqueror, . . . The conqueror does not want doubtful friends who do not help him when he is in difficulties; the loser repudiates you because you were unwilling to go, arms in hand, and throw in your lot with him.[26]

Adaptive responses to changing circumstances need to be deliberate and measured; to bend without breaking. Pernod's path of rapid growth towards direct confrontation of Diageo would need to be thought through so as not to advance in such a way as to place the outcome in jeopardy. Changes will inevitably need to be brought about to capitalise on opportunities and circumvent obstacles, all the time aimed at accomplishing predefined aims. But shifts in direction can run the risk of misfortune if they do not take account of the limits to which corporate wherewithal can be bent to achieve ultimate goals. Flexibility therefore accommodates a calculation of what is feasible and what is not when changes are made to corporate direction.

Sun Tzu urges a strategist to minimise the costs of success in competition, ensuring also that opportunities for success are not lost by adapting the form of confrontation to a rival's relative strength:

Those skilled in war subdue the enemy's army without battle. They capture his cities without assaulting them and overthrow his state without protracted operations. Your aim must be to take All-under-Heaven intact. Thus your troops are not worn out and your gains will be complete. This is the art of offensive strategy.

. . . the art of using troops is this:
When ten to the enemy's one, surround him;
When five times his strength, attack him;
If double his strength; divide him;
If equally matched you may engage him;
If weaker numerically, be capable of withdrawing;
And if in all respects unequal, be capable of eluding him, for a smaller force is but booty for one more powerful.[27]

A distinction might also be made between what Mintzberg and Waters[28] call deliberate and emergent strategy. Flexible adaptation occurs, as they observe, when intended strategy accommodates integration of new ideas, capabilities and opportunities which inevitably arise as time passes. Flexible strategy permits emergence, entrepreneurship and internal corporate process to intervene, in contrast to inflexibly imposed and rigidly maintained plans.

Restated in Master Sun's terms:

> Now an army may be likened to water, for just as flowing water avoids the heights and hastens to the lowlands, so an army avoids strength and strikes weakness. And as water shapes its flow in accordance with the ground, so an army manages its victory in accordance with the situation of the enemy. And as water has no constant form, there are in war no constant conditions. . . . thus (be) able to gain victory by modifying . . . tactics in accordance with the enemy situation.[29]

If strategy rests on strategic thinking, then flexible thinking means: not rigid and not pliable. Paul Raimond,[30] in his contribution to an edited book on strategic flexibility, takes an unconventional stand which offers a way of considering strategy at a cognitive level.

Raimond asks where strategy comes from, and he speaks of the benefits of contemplating the assumptions and unspoken beliefs which might underpin a prevailing strategic outlook. He argues for flexibility; flexibility in the way executives think about strategy. He calls for an ability to think about strategy, to think strategically, and to think again. In his discussion about the differences between strategic thinking and strategic planning, Mintzberg[31] offers a similar viewpoint.

In my opinion, the ability to think again, that is, to reconsider a line of strategic argument is a vital ability which supports strategic flexibility.

Under pressure of responsibility which often accompanies strategic thinking, the ability to apply judgement and to properly seek and evaluate relevant information can become limited. In extreme circumstances where time is perceived as short and the stakes are very high, limitations in cognitive processing can bring about suboptimal decisions.

Holsti[32] advances a number of propositions which help to explain limitations in cognitive performance under conditions of crisis. As a result of perception of surprise, heightened threat and short decision time, a stressful response contributes to narrowed span of attention, cognitive rigidity and diminished time perspective.

Applying such insights to policy decisions, Janis[33] identifies four dysfunctional decision-making phenomena associated with emotional stress arising from decision dilemmas; the first two are characterised by pliability, the second two by rigidity in thinking:

- *Unconflicted change*: Willingness to change direction based on little search for alternatives or evaluation;
- *Hypervigilance*: Panic; impulsive action aimed at escaping from the problem as quickly as possible;
- *Unconflicted inertia*: Recommitment to existing course of action, with little consideration given to change;
- *Defensive avoidance*: Under pressure of circumstances, procrastination or simply avoiding thinking about the problem.

Rather than taking action based on incomplete search for alternative courses of action, superficial evaluation and poor contingency planning, flexible strategic thinking is based on what Janis calls 'vigilance'. Emotional responses to critical situations are displaced by a vigilant rational formulation of the problem encountered and a systematic and thorough evaluation of alternatives and their consequences.

Master Sun also refers to cognitive aspects of strategy, including knowledge of one's own capabilities. Flexibility in strategic thinking encompasses understanding different situations with appropriate versatile responses. Among those situations in which Sun Tzu predicts a general's victory:

> He who knows when he can fight and when he cannot will be victorious. He who understands how to use both large and small forces will be victorious.[34]

Application of creativity and imagination are essential elements of strategic thinking, in Sun Tzu's view. Benefits derive from their translation into practice:

> That the army is certain to sustain the enemy's attack without suffering defeat is due to operations of the extraordinary and the normal forces. . . . Generally, in battle, use the normal force to engage; use the extraordinary to win. . . . in

battle there are only the normal and extraordinary forces, but their combinations are limitless; none can comprehend them all. For these forces are mutually reproductive; their interaction as endless as that of interlocked rings.[35]

Surprising to some, Sun Tzu also calls for creativity in avoiding repetition of successful competitive action, so denying a competitor with perception of a predictable pattern in initiative:

... when I have won a victory I do not repeat my tactics but respond to circumstances in an infinite variety of ways.[36]

At a strategic level, flexibility offers considerable competitive benefits:

- capability multiplication through surprise;
- swift capitalisation on opportunities;
- articulation of alertness to shifting circumstances;
- promotion of interchangeability in application of elements of capability.

Limitations also arise from flexibility when it is not understood as an integral part of corporate culture:

- economic efficiency sacrificed through non-dedicated resources;
- risk arising from misinterpreting flexibility for indecisiveness;
- misinterpretation of flexibility for pliability and unassertive submission;
- potential loss of purpose through readiness for multiple objectives.

Balance

Contemporary scholarship, as we shall see below, offers some diverse views about balance and its associations with strategy. These are of interest since they reflect on current prescriptions; however as has been observed earlier, with the exception of Chen's[37] thinking, they convey little interest in actual competition.

Balance in the BCG product portfolio

This analytical device was the first of a series of variations on the strategic theme: choice of investment among diversified businesses. The idea of utilising a concept more traditionally used in the management of financial portfolios is derived from the work by Henderson and his colleagues at the Boston Consulting Group. The essence of the portfolio idea is that a firm that operates a range of businesses (strategic business units), or at least intends to, will be faced with investment decisions within the company requiring evaluation of cash flow between the businesses. The objective is to manage risk among the diversified businesses in such a way as to increase returns to the company.

The portfolio framework concentrates on two dimensions that specify characteristics of business units: product market growth rate and the firm's market share. In its most basic representation this form is a four cell matrix.

Two propositions underlie the portfolio idea. One is that a firm needs business activities that generate cash. The other is that this cash must be invested with an expectation of positive return.

Business units with high market share in low growth markets will generate access cash over and above that required to maintain market share. No further investment is required therefore in this business. A business with these features has been called a Cash Cow.

The BCG argument then is that cash from such a business should be directed towards investment in new businesses in high growth markets that have hope of a future return. In its early stages such a business is a Question Mark which will require more cash than it generates, investing to increase its relative market share.

If this is successful and market share does indeed increase, the new status of the business would be that of a Star: a business unit with the high market share in high growth market.

Over time, almost inevitably, market growth will decline and business will achieve its payoff, becoming a Cash Cow which should be 'milked' of cash to fund new businesses. Once yields decline, the business moves on to the right in the matrix to become a Dog on its way to divestment.[38]

The main theme of this analysis is to construct and maintain a balanced business portfolio.

Balance in meaning – content and process of strategy

Markides[39] and Mintzberg et al.[40] survey contemporary scholarship on strategic management and remark on the diverse range of views and opinions presented. While such diversity contributes to scholarly controversy, these authors note that much of the claim and counterclaim by the protagonists is pointless in practice. There are, indeed, different points of view about strategy, but these simply reflect particular, but not exclusive, angles of observation.

Mintzberg and his co-authors survey points of view about strategy in a variety of schools of thought. Markides remarks on confusion that is generated by debates about strategy process and content. One is simply how strategic thinking is conducted and the other is what is thought about; neither should prevail in practice as the main issue, whereas it might in scholarship.

Markides also comments on the question of whether strategy is analysis or creativity; surely it is both. And is strategy ahistoric? Again, surely not. Its frame of reference is past, present and future.

Both Mintzberg and Markides call for a balance: 'and' not 'either-or'.

A balance between thinking and planning

Mintzberg[41] expresses concern about what he perceives as a bias towards strategic planning, to the detriment of strategic thinking. He refers to strategic planning as the analysis of logical possibilities for action. Strategic thinking, on the other hand, is the synthesis of possibilities which define advantage.

The dilemma which Mintzberg draws attention to is that organisation, logic, efficiency and routine are desirable corporate attributes which favour planning. He argues that if taken too far, strategic thinking, which is more difficult to organise since it relies on imagination and creativity, will be displaced. The result is that more of the same will be performed ever more efficiently, without addressing the question of whether strategy should take a new direction.

While Mintzberg attempts to discourage what he sees as a worrisome trend by downplaying the importance of strategic planning, it is clear that both strategic planning and strategic thinking are necessary; in balance. This parallels a balance which Langley[42] refers to as lying between *paralysis by analysis* and *extinction by instinct*.

Balance among stakeholder claims on strategy

A further view on balance emerges from Freeman's[43] so-called Stakeholder Approach to strategy. Simply put, Freeman argues that an essential ingredient to strategy is a thorough and systematic analysis of influences of stakeholders on development of corporate direction. Aspirations and expectations of internal and external constituencies need to be recognised and politically merged to determine and combine vectors of support for positions and goals.

Accommodation of stakeholder objectives is in essence a matter of political balance.

Maintaining stability

Initiative springs from a state of balance; a stable distribution of assets and abilities in space and time, matched to circumstances and poised to contribute to potential for creating and maintaining competitive momentum. This is clearly revealed in Pernod's recent corporate progress.

Now imagine a field team sport such as hockey. One team is positioned to take an initiative which is designed to push back its opponent and create a competitive advantage. The aim of this initiative is to reduce the opponent's psychological and physical balance. Catching a rival 'wrong-footed' is an apt term to describe an unfortunate opponent's being thrust back upon its metaphoric heels and unable to recover before being completely thrown off balance by the attacker.

The purpose of initiative is to unbalance a rival, while simultaneously maintaining the focal firm's own strategic balance.

A critical review of Hewlett-Packard's recent position[44] provides an illustration of lost balance. Since completing its controversial takeover of Compaq, Hewlett-Packard performed poorly, at least relative to two major competitors: Dell and IBM. If HP were a person, one would see it being disconcerted about its aims, confused and possibly disoriented. Its loss of balance might have been brought about by some of its own activities, as much as by responses to the initiatives of its main competitors, but the result, just the same, was a movement of competitive advantage in favour of Dell and IBM.

It is clear in considering this commercial example that the achievement and maintenance of balance pervades strategic thinking. Consider, for instance the following internal tensions which needed to be balanced within Hewlett-Packard to attain a position of 'sure-footedness':

Diversify the business	Concentrate on specialities
Work on new products	Priority to existing products
Investment in innovation	Invest in consolidation and efficiency
Pursue many new business initiatives	Concentrate on few new ventures
Aim for rapid evolution	Anticipate steady growth
Adopt structural change	Maintain a stable structure
Improvise	Commit
Future orientation	Focus on the present
Build new capabilities	Concentrate on current capabilities
Concentrate on one competitor	Keep many competitors in view

Few would argue that these issues are not *either-or*, but rather, *and-to-some-degree*. This is the essence of balance; awareness and creation of constructive unity within the tensions.

Carly Fiorina's position as Chief Executive of Hewlett-Packard was extremely demanding. Foremost were the intellectual demands required to maintain balance among the competing tensions such as those identified above. She was obliged to ready her company in every way needed for its competitive fitness, and concentrate the minds of her executives on HP's strategic objectives.

All the while ambiguities, challenges, performance imperatives, uncertainties, forecasts and unknowables filled her information space. Let us not underestimate the scale of intellectual performance needed to balance judgement in coping with these pressures and at the same time maintain direction.

Carl von Clausewitz reminds us of the intensity of these demands by comparison with the expectations of the role of a general in Napoleonic Europe:

> Many intelligence reports in War are contradictory; even more are false, and most are uncertain. What one can reasonably ask of an officer is that he should possess a standard of judgement, which he can gain only from knowledge of men and affairs and from common sense. . . . The commander must trust his judgement and stand like a rock on which the waves break in vain. It is not an easy thing to do. If he does not have a buoyant disposition, if experience of war has not trained him and matured his judgement, he had better make it a rule to suppress his personal convictions, and give his hopes

and not his fears the benefit of the doubt. Only thus can he preserve a proper balance.[45]

Loss of balance in a competitor is the aim of strategic initiative. It dramatically reduces a rival's ability to respond due to demoralisation, confusion, limited scope of action, reduced flexibility and time demand for recovery.

Liddell Hart refers to such an experience in its psychological terms within a military context:

> In the psychological sphere, dislocation is the result of the impression on the commander's mind of the physical effects of (unexpected interference with supply, communications, equilibrium of dispositions or line of retreat). The impression is strongly accentuated if his realisation of his being at a disadvantage is sudden, and if he feels that he is unable to counter the enemy's move. Psychological dislocation fundamentally springs from his sense of being trapped. . . . An army, like a man, cannot properly defend its back from a blow without turning round to use its arms in a new direction. 'Turning' temporarily unbalances an army as it does a man, and with the former the period of instability is inevitably much longer. In consequence, the brain is much more sensitive to any menace to its back.[46]

Further insight into the nature of balance is offered by Colin Gray[47] who writes about requirements for effective joint action of naval forces. He discusses the demands for bringing otherwise disparate military capabilities together to act in unison. Although his particular interest is different from that facing Hewlett-Packard in its experience of lost balance, his arguments for relevant considerations are valuable.

Gray proposes five meanings for the concept of balance:

Instrumentality: Capabilities need to be balanced for their external strategic integrity rather than their internal beauty. Wonderful clockwork efficiency can be achieved among internal elements of an organisation, but this serves for nothing if it does not contribute towards strategic, that is, competitive objectives.

To recover its balance in this sense, Hewlett-Packard would be less concerned with the achievement of efficiencies and structural refinements, than with bringing collective capabilities to bear on competitive objectives.

Sustainability: Separate capabilities need to be balanced in the sense of working together as one. They need to be co-ordinated and co-operative so that together corporate goals and strategic initiatives can be accomplished.

Balance in HP's terms would comprise, among other considerations, the integration of plans and activities of the separate businesses so that they operate together, rather than as individuals.

Specialisation: Collective capability requires balance against the variety of demands which could be made of it. Competitive circumstances will arise in different kinds and forms and it is essential that balance is maintained to enable effective response.

Competitive behaviour of its main rivals is consolidating advantage against Hewlett-Packard, and no doubt Dell and IBM continue to take new initiatives. HP needed to develop balance to cope with anticipated variety of new competitive demands.

Compatibility: Capabilities need to be balanced for a tolerable fit with tradition and historical modes of performance. Although viewed as a possibly conservative requirement, the risks of venturing from customary norms need to be calculated when much is at stake in competition.

Hewlett-Packard has traditionally been guided by the principle embodied in 'The HP Way'. Much of its historical growth and competitive advantage has originated in cultural dimensions which flowed from this. Now, after the Compaq merger, cultures have been combined in some manner, possibly neutralising the power of HP traditions. A balance was needed to combine subtle sources of cultural foundation for competitive behaviour by the new Hewlett-Packard.

Complementarity: Investment in development and maintenance of separate capabilities needs to be balanced against the required performance of the whole for strategic purposes. Arithmetic or budgetary balance should be subordinate to the balance based on needs for accomplishment of strategic objectives.

How much should be invested in the separate business capabilities in Hewlett-Packard? In reality such decisions are inevitably influenced by the relative political power of HP divisions. Rather than being based on politics, investment decisions within the company should be balanced with anticipated contribution to achievement of strategic objectives.

From a competitive viewpoint, balance is one of the most important features of combined assets and abilities. It has both a relational and dynamic character.

Balance in configuration refers to a match between essential assets at any particular moment. It derives from an understanding of complementarity: certain combinations and relative proportions of assets are of benefit in competitive terms. Each matches the other to bring about competitive advantage.

Static equilibrium comprises the combination of elements at a moment incorporating static counteracting forces.

The following are among factors which might be evaluated in considering *structural balance* across businesses:

- difference in growth potential;
- differences in assets and abilities;
- differences in authority in relation to the centre;
- differences in independence in relation to the other businesses.

Dynamic balance is the second strategically important aspect of balance. This refers to a corporate ability to move forward, flexibly maintaining initiative and renewing action that continues to dislocate a competitive rival. Dynamic balance involves ensuring that assets are ready and readily used from moment to moment, not only in one transaction. Dynamic equilibrium combines elements in motion across time, again incorporating dynamically counteracting forces.

Among considerations affecting judgement of *dynamic balance* are the following:

- intensity of competition;
- availability of valid competitive intelligence;
- mounting counterintelligence activity;
- time and speed of development;
- consolidation of gains.

A loss of either configurational or dynamic balance is disabling to strategic thinking. Simultaneously moving forward and standing still is problematic; in sport this is called *flatfootedness*. And through metaphor, this is exactly the strategic effect sought in the mind of a rival.

To conclude, from the perspective of the Focal Firm, balance is a state of readiness. Its elements are the following:

- to commence a competitive initiative;
- to respond to a competitor's countermeasures;
- to circumvent obstacles encountered;
- to capitalise on competitive opportunities.

Balance is at the same time, characterised by:

- poise, that is being stable, fit, united and co-ordinated;
- capability in terms of availability and maintenance of appropriate assets and abilities;
- support through logistics and morale;
- mindfulness; being well-informed and with clear purpose.

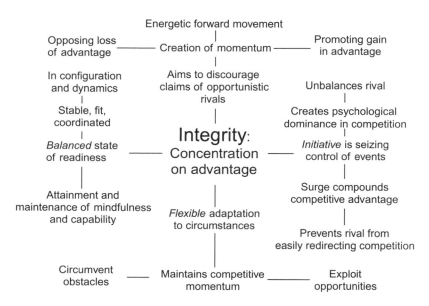

Figure 4.1 Concept map for Integrity.

The concept map above draws together the ideas of initiative, flexibility and balance within its summary of the Principle of Integrity.

Reflection

Initiative can achieve its effect, even if it is poorly executed; it is the aim that is most important.

What are the limits of flexibility?

How best to assess the availability of balance?

5

Security

Principle of Security: Strategy ensures that the enterprise secures its position from a condition of psychological strength and stability.

A temporal frame for thinking and action needs to be maintained so that time in all its aspects is central to strategy. Efforts to shape rivals' perceptions and their consequent choice among courses of action should be designed to restrict competitive freedom of movement. Such influence is designed to increase a rival's perception of perceived dependence.

Napoleon Bonaparte regarded the campaign which culminated in his victory over the Russians and Austrians at Austerlitz in December 1805 as his finest.[1] His strategic thinking was simple, clear and purposeful. Having put aside his ambitions to cross the Channel from Boulogne to invade England, his objective was to eliminate the threat from Austria and Russia. His intelligence told him the allies were building strength to the east, and he aimed to discourage their forces before the Prussians joined them. This he did on the Pratzen Heights on 2 December.

While the objective was achieved, Napoleon's means for accomplishing this victory are of particular interest because they demonstrate the significance of the psychological interplay between the competitors. Napoleon's method embodied a level of psychological security which emboldened his army and its success was almost a forgone conclusion at the outset. His rivals were repeatedly thrown off psychological balance; their security was uncertain.

Napoleon's *Grande Armée* comprised self-contained divisions which were capable of fighting separately or in combination. They were usually dispersed, yet no more than a day's march from each other. As Bonaparte's aim turned east he ordered his divisions from their separate locations to move by different routes to approach the Bavarian city of Ulm which was occupied by the Austrian army under the leadership of General Mack. The *Grande Armée* divisions were preceded by cavalry which moved as a cloud back and forth across the path of the direction of advance. This manoeuvre was designed to confuse the enemy by obscuring the actual direction of overall movement.

And confuse General Mack it did. From his viewpoint, he was aware that Napoleon's army was on the move but all he knew was that he was facing probing advances by one of the French divisions from his west through the Black Forest. Napoleon had succeeded in fixing Mack's attention on this false offensive, while his many other divisions approached in a clockwise spiralling pattern, eventually converging on Ulm from the opposite direction, the east. When it finally became clear to him that he had been tricked, Mack was forced to surrender his army of 60000 without resistance. Napoleon had prevailed.

General Kutuzov, Mack's Russian ally, had failed to reach and support the Austrians before Bonaparte's arrival. Poor co-ordination is blamed. But perhaps the fact that the allies were using different calendars, the Austrians using the Gregorian calendar and the Russians the Julian, with a ten-day difference between the two, also contributed to their confusion. Perhaps also, Napoleon was aware of this and capitalised on the anticipated confusion.

After taking General Mack's surrender, Napoleon chased the retreating Russian Army through Vienna where he took advantage of its stock of military supplies. *La Grande Armée* was tiring and its communication lines were stretched so a decisive confrontation with the Russians and the remaining Austrians became urgent.

Bonaparte manoeuvred for a battle on terrain near the Czech town of Austerlitz. He could see this would suit him. He needed reinforcements to support his outnumbered army so he waited, luring his enemy into complacency by giving the false impression that his forces were weak, vulnerable and in disarray. Meanwhile, on the night before the intended battle, his reinforcements arrived. Hidden in fog, which Napoleon rightly expected to settle at this time of the year, the additional soldiers took the Allies by surprise in the morning as the Russians and Austrians moved into the trap Bonaparte had set for them.

For the French the result was an impressive victory; for the Allies it was a disastrous and humiliating defeat. In time, Napoleon was tamed after dominating Europe for 20 years, and the Russians and Austrians were eventually able to regain their pride.

Napoleon's reputation as a military strategist places him among the best, if not the best, in Western history. His broader ambitions will always remain controversial, but at his military best, as he was before Austerlitz, his competitive method is instructive for strategic thinking.

Three considerations were brought together in aesthetic combination, revealing Napoleon's thinking as his army began to move under his orders from Boulogne. The first was time. It would take time for *La Grande Armée* to reach Ulm; meanwhile he was successful in inducing General Mack to wait. This was a psychological game of hypnotically luring Mack into using time to prepare for just the right opportunity to fight the French who were repeatedly threatening from the west.

The second was psychological deception; a trick in impression management. Bonaparte succeeded in creating for Mack the illusion that a weak French attack would come from the west. He masked the actual movement of most of his army, revealing only one alluring opportunity for the Austrians. When reality replaced illusion, Mack's surprise left him unbalanced and unable to effectively respond.

Third, the result was a matter of power. Mack perceived complete dependence on the action of Napoleon's army; this was what Bonaparte intended. The Austrian army surrendered, laying down its weapons. This illustrates Napoleon's exercise of power in its psychological dimensions.

Napoleon's tactics supporting his strategic aim of eliminating a threat to his east reveal a combination of lines of thinking which secured his strategic objective. For the reader to imagine the differences in what one would perceive, think and feel if one happened to be placed among staff close to Bonaparte and Mack will be sufficient to show the importance of security viewed from the psychological perspectives of time, deception and power.

Before taking the next step, which is to consider these three elements in turn, an impression of both assertive and defensive postures is provided in

Table 5.1 *Interactions among time, deception and power.*

Security: Psychological strength and stability	Time	Deception	Power
Time	Psychological impression of moment and duration	*Anticipate rival's capability to think and act quickly and study time-related cues*	*Anticipate and accurately estimate level of changing dependence*
Deception	**Create complacency in mind of rival through a false impression of timeliness and time sufficiency**	Psychological impression of prevailing state of reality	*Anticipate rival's efforts to influence perceptions of dependence and check for validity*
Power	**Accelerate and enhance rival's perception of dependence**	**Create and magnify false impression of dependence in the mind of rival**	Psychological impression of perceived dependence

Assertive strategic posture
Defensive strategic posture

Table 5.1. This illustrates how interactions among time, deception and power might be envisaged within a Principle of Security.

Napoleon's genius was to create in the mind of his rival a false impression of psychological security. The cells below the northwest-southeast diagonal in Table 5.1 show how this was achieved. Through his influence on a combination of time, deception and power, General Mack's mind was in Napoleon's grasp. The French advance through the Black Forest, to the west of Ulm, was tentative and hesitant. Its impression was one of French unassertive reluctance and perhaps weakness. It gave Mack the idea that he had time to prepare. However, his confidence was shattered all at once when the larger scope of the French initiative was clear. At this time his experience of dependence must have been sadly profound.

How might General Mack, an able and experienced soldier, have acted to avoid this humiliating surrender? What strategic thinking might have saved him and his army? The cells above Table 5.1's diagonal outline securely *defensive* strategic thinking. Although it might sound like an oversimplification, what Mack lacked, at least momentarily, was an alert and uneasy mind. Effective defensive thinking would have anticipated the possibilities of Napoleon's position, his ability to move faster than usual, his ability to appear to be in several places at once, his ability to control a movement of dispersal and concentration in a very large army. Not only would these have come to mind as possibilities, alternatives would need to have been ruled out only with reliable and credible intelligence. In short, Mack would have needed the benefit of placing himself in Napoleon's mind to consider his own points of vulnerability in strategic thinking.

The reader will now have a glimpse of the combination of insights into ways in which time, deception and power contribute to a concept of psychological security in strategic thinking. To further appreciate the subtlety of this combination, I explore the three ideas separately in the sections which follow.

Time

Time is a concept of great and enduring fascination. It relates to every aspect of human affairs. Time has occupied the interests of scholars in philosophy, science, theology, psychology and beyond.[2]

Time has a physical dimension measured by convention in years, days and hours. Time is also a psychological, social and cultural construct which has a bearing on strategy through its inherent opportunities for disorder, ambiguity and deception. But this is jumping ahead; first let us consider what we find in contemporary literature about business strategy.

Since Johnson, Scholes and·Whittington[3] take a business development, rather than a competitive perspective, their references to time do not recognise the significance of this concept for framing competitive relationships between rivals. It is not surprising, therefore, to find that their references to time are linked to either matters of marketing, or to considerations of internal organisation.

Adopting a marketing perspective, they refer to the importance of time in terms of rate of product innovation, pointing out its particular relevance for synchronisation with changes in customer preferences, a central point made also by Eisenhardt and Brown,[4] for instance.

Johnson and associates also refer to time for its relevance to implementation of strategy. Effective change management needs to be orchestrated to a time-based agenda so that required shifts in activity are productive. This involves managing staff expectations in a timely fashion and building on psychologically significant moments to promote change.

In their best selling book, *Competing for the Future*, Hamel and Prahalad[5] observe that in practice senior management typically spends very little time considering the future. Their book is aimed at bringing this to attention and urging a comprehensive shift in thinking towards a continuous debate about the shape of the future, and how this future can be adapted to a firm's advantage:

- How do we want the industry to be shaped in 5–10 years?
- What must be done to ensure that the industry evolves to our advantage?
- What skills and competencies need we build for future benefit?

Hamel and Prahalad confine their view of time to time horizons, that is, to moments in the future when a judgement can be made that an industry has been shaped to the firm's advantage. This involves developing insight into developmental trends among customer preferences, technology and corporate capability. They refer to 'competition for industry foresight and intellectual leadership':

> This is competition to gain a deeper understanding than competitors of the trends and discontinuities – technological, demographic, regulatory, or lifestyle – that could be used to transform industry boundaries and create new competitive space.[6]

Competitors do not figure in their *competition for the future*, yet somehow on judgement day in 5 or 10 years hence, the aim is to have achieved competitive advantage. In competitive terms, this outlook is strategy based only on hope.

In view of these apparent shortcomings among contemporary conceptions of strategy it is of considerable interest to note a small number of voices of difference. One is a study of competition in the American airline industry by Chen and Hambrick.[7] Their research is primarily concentrated on similarities and differences among the competitive behaviour of large and small firms. They find that

The small airlines more actively initiated competitive challenges and were speedy but low-key, even secretive, in executing their actions. They were also less likely and slower to respond when attacked and, contrary to expectations, their responses were more visible than those of their larger opponents.

The distinction made by Carse[8] between finite and infinite games has embedded within it a concept of time. Finite games, as defined, are played over a particular duration agreed beforehand by the participants. During this time the rules do not change. A finite game also starts and concludes at particular agreed times. Infinite games, on the other hand, persist indefinitely. The game is played by its participants, purely for the purpose of maintaining play. Here time is of no relevance.

The question of whether commercial competition is a finite or infinite game has been discussed earlier. However, the practical realities of business show that time is a vital consideration in this form of competition.

Consider the situation of LG Philips.[9] This joint venture has as its competitive aim to challenge Samsung-Sony for control of production of LCD screens. In this industry decisions to commit to investment in large and expensive production facilities are balanced against events in the near and far future; supply and demand are cyclical. From a competitive viewpoint, therefore, LG Philips is taking an initiative which is timed to influence its position relative to Samsung-Sony, creating circumstances in which its rival will now need to reconsider its own investment plans. Interlocking strategic thinking of both competitors will occur in view of increasing but uncertain demand.

More generally speaking, a competitor chooses a course of action, taking account of the circumstances presented in the commercial context: state of the economy, stage of the business cycle, prevailing market demand and so on. These circumstances change in time. So the choice of a course of action is time dependent in the sense that the same course of action will be appropriate at one time and not at the next, because of change in circumstances and regardless of the behaviour of the competitor. By analogy, tactics in the game of cricket take account of the available light at the time of day, and the state of the playing surface.

Outcomes vary with time. If both competitors in an imaginary two-player competition select the same courses of action, the results as these actions interact will be different from one episode to another. This will come

about, not least because there has been opportunity for each of the competitors to learn about what happens when a combination of rival actions
intersect.

A Focal Firm therefore approaches a choice of course of action with a set
of particular considerations in mind. Each of these is time dependent. The
example of competitive manoeuvre by Finmeccanica, a helicopter manufacturer, is a suitable illustration.[10]

In 2002, a new chief executive, Pierfancesco Guarguaglini, was appointed
to Italy's largest defence group. He quickly acquired control of AugustaWest-
land, with which it had a joint venture, with a speed that caught his rival,
EADS the Eurocopter manufacturer, by surprise. Subsequently, with equal
haste, Guarguaglini formed a relationship with Bell and Lockheed to help
Finmeccanica move to a position of strength in the American market ahead
of EADS.

Impressions of time

Time is a significant framing concept for strategic thinking. Strategy is future
oriented; it relates to actions which are planned to take effect over a period
of time, beginning at a moment which is yet to arrive, to create corporate
advantage which will endure for some time afterwards.

Competitive action is chosen to create the possibility of enhancing
temporal space, creating time in which to plan and manoeuvre. The effect
of chosen action is designed, if possible, to be unanticipated by a rival; it
should take them by surprise, at a moment they are least expecting it, and
their time will be short as they take time to recover.

Although time and timing are critical to strategic thinking, their significance is largely overlooked among contemporary views about strategy. Ges-
tures are made in the direction of seeking benefits through long term
advantage; however, it is most common to regard time as primarily a tactical
matter of scheduling.

Among classic strategy theorists, the outlook on time is much more compelling. Master Sun points to the importance of speed, momentum and timing
in gaining control of a competitive situation. Machiavelli regards time as a
variable in the calculation of power. Von Clausewitz reveals the contradictions implied by time: strategy develops relatively slowly, yet there are

demands for instant judgement. Strategic thinking is psychologically demanding for the strategist.

Time is woven inextricably through Sun Tzu's thinking about strategy. For him it is a crucial consideration for a general who rightly concentrates on bringing a speedy resolution to an episode of competition.

Time is required for analysis, first and foremost analysis of prevailing conditions and their suitability for engaging in a war. If there is no alternative, preparations and planning take time while capability is assembled and competitive intelligence is gathered about the sovereign's rival.

Several issues of time and timing are central to strategic thinking:

- A purposeful Focal Firm will deliberately enhance capabilities to improve the likelihood of securing advantage. Such change in capabilities will require *time*. Furthermore, intentions are best cloaked so that a competitor is ignorant for as *long as possible* about a Focal Firm's anticipated direction. Such cloaking is likely to be effective and of assistance for a *limited period of time* while an able rival conducts competitive intelligence.
- Competition relates to relative advantage to the participants: advantage when in *time*, and for what *duration*?
- Participants employ capabilities to enhance value and opportunities are *time* dependent: *when* are capabilities ready to be employed, *when* are capabilities employed, at what *pace*, for most effect in value creation?
- Vigilance yields insight into the capabilities and intentions of rivals: rival capabilities *change over time*, as do intentions; what are their intentions *now* and in the *future*, and *when* in the *future*?
- Willingness and ability to protect interests is a defensive posture: *when* will this posture be prepared for threats to interests, and for *how long* can this posture be sustained?

Learning about a rival's dispositions and responsiveness is vital in creating advantage, as Master Sun observes, when preparing for a competitive engagement; and it takes time to learn:

> ... victory can be created ... Agitate him and ascertain the pattern of his movement. Determine his dispositions and so ascertain the field of battle. Probe him and learn where his strength is abundant and where deficient.[11]

Learning about a competitor's intentions and capabilities is not an instantaneous and once and for all event. Rather, it takes place over a period of time, progressively.

And when the appropriate moment arrives, striking with speed:

> When the enemy presents an opportunity, speedily take advantage of it. . . .
> Therefore at first be shy as a maiden. When the enemy gives you an opening be swift as a hare and he will be unable to withstand you.[12]

. . . and overwhelming the rival with skilful application of timing:

> When torrential water tosses boulders, it is because of its momentum;
> When the strike of a hawk breaks the body of its prey, it is because of timing.
> Thus the momentum of one skilled in war is overwhelming and his attack precisely regulated.[13]

The importance of time in strategy culminates in consideration of interlocking competitor decision cycles. Figure 5.1 illustrates the elements of a competitive decision cycle.[14] It comprises a sequence of logical steps, as identified earlier in Chapter 3's Strategic Assessment, each leading to action.

Decision cycles require time: each step builds on the previous one and must be completed before the next can logically and productively follow (time T1, T3, T5, T7 and T9). And there might well be a delay between each step (T2, T4, T6, T8, and T10). The duration of a decision cycle is the sum of time periods from T1 to T10.

Competitor decision cycles interlock because each step in a rival's cycle creates a situation requiring appraisal by their competitor. Each competitor then decides on a course of action aimed at outwitting its rival.

Advantage flows from an ability of one competitor to complete its decision cycle faster than its rival. This is called *acting inside a rival's decision cycle*. It occurs when the Focal Firm decides on a course of action and implements it before its competitor has completed the steps leading to action.

The consequence is that the Focal Firm will have intervened to alter the situation which the competitor has appraised, and before its action phase has begun. This places the Focal Form in an advantageous pos-

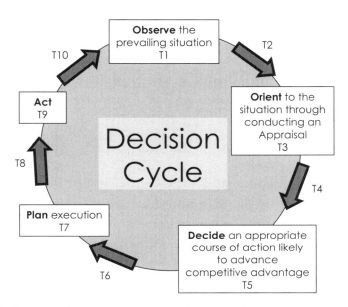

Figure 5.1 Sequence of steps in a competitive decision cycle.

ition where it dictates situations to which the competitor responds to its own benefit, rather than having terms of competition dictated by a competitor.

As I will show below, deception is just such an attempt to induce a rival to believe that competitive circumstances are different from reality, so that they will be tricked into acting against their own interests. Inevitably surprise will follow. Time is an integral part of deception.

Reflecting again on the situation of competition between Finmeccanica and EADS, it is clear that Pierfrancesco Guarguaglini took decisions to strengthen his helicopter group by initiating an acquisition before his rival was prepared to offer its own bid. Finmeccanica acted inside the EADS decision cycle.

In his chapter on Strategy, von Clausewitz refers to the demands that are made on the strategist, greater as they are than those experienced by those involved with tactics and operations. The problem for a strategist is that often time passes relatively slowly:

> . . . more strength of will is required to make an important decision in Strategy than in Tactics. (In tactics) we are hurried along by the moment. Strategy

... goes on at a slower rate ... there is more room for apprehensions, regrets and bewildering doubts.[15]

Von Clausewitz recognises that those who excel in war have personal attributes which he classes as 'Genius for War'. One of these is imagination:

Imagination permits one to find one's place in time and space ... enables events to be pictured immediately leading to quick and confident decisions.[16]

Imagination is directly linked with a deep appreciation of time, as von Clausewitz shows, and this permits a strategist to quickly apprehend his or her competitive circumstances.

He also highlights further traits of strategic genius, all of which reveal further deep appreciation of the significance of time in competition:

- penetrating mind: to be able to see through circumstances to appreciate their essence;
- rapid judgement (coup d'oeil): to be able to take a decision quickly based on assessment at a glance;
- resolution: to be willing and able to sustain a judgement with resolve;
- presence of mind: to be alert to circumstances and priorities.

A deeper analysis of the relationships between strategy and time in *The Art of War* and *On War* reveals both further similarities and differences. Paquette[17] notes that in von Clausewitz's view strategy involves instant conception, prolonged engagements, restricted flexibility and foreknowledge, emphasis on tactics over strategy and surprise as an obstacle. By comparison, Sun Tzu refers to the conception of strategy over a longer period of time and constantly revised, engagements are quick when they are absolutely unavoidable, advantage is gained through surprise, flexibility and fore knowledge are critical, and strategy itself is emphasised over tactics. Paquette concludes that the conception of time is different in each work, attributing divergence, at least in part, to sociocultural factors embedding the authors.

What can happen if time is overlooked in strategy? Rational competitive considerations are put aside and integrity of strategic thinking is lost if time is disregarded. The following are likely implications:

- If corporate purpose is assumed constant then strategy will be simply misdirected and thus flawed if changes in direction have been introduced. Unchanging strategy will become misaligned with Policy and advantage will be lost.
- A strategic assessment which relies on an assumption that competitive circumstances are fixed, and on a belief that a rival's intentions and capabilities are unchanging, will be flawed or at least very risky.
- Implementation of a strategic course of action without allowance for sufficient time to plan and prepare, and possibly to enhance capability, risks stalling for lack of readiness.
- Once a course of action is initiated, it will require time to have its competitive effect resulting in anticipated benefit. Premature evaluation of outcomes would risk disadvantage from selection of a new course of action before the previous course had achieved its effect.
- Sun Tzu warns that if victory is long delayed then morale will suffer and it will be all the more difficult to press home a favourable result. Offensive capability will become blunted.

Finally, modern times are often perceived as almost impossibly dynamic and turbulent; change is rapid beyond comprehension as impressions of time duration are compressed. Demands on those who are responsible for building and maintaining businesses are therefore almost crushing: too much needs to be known about too many considerations in too little time.

It is a sobering thought to consider the possibility that perhaps it has always been thus. In the year 1014 Wulfstan, the Archbishop of York made a speech which began:

> Beloved men, recognise what the truth is: the world is in haste and it is drawing near the end, and therefore the longer it is the worse it will get in the world.[18]

Nearly a thousand years ago the pace of change was almost intolerable. Is it even more so today . . . or is change a matter of how events are perceived within a mindset of the meaning of time?

Deception

The idea of a feint or false move is a common element of competition in sport. The aim of this tactic is to create an impression of weakness or false intention in the mind of the competitor, then to act in an altogether different and unexpected manner. The effect is to create a momentary advantage.

A typical element of such deception is for the perpetrator to move in such a way as to convince the competitor that certain events will follow, and for the rival to consequently commit to a particular response. Once this commitment is made, and the weight of the competitor's body is swung out of balance to meet an expected initiative, and it is impossible to return to equilibrium, then the perpetrator shifts direction.

A clearly visible example is a tactic seen from time to time in hockey when the goal is attacked from a short corner penalty. One player blocks the ball and positions it for a second player to strike. This player makes a false stroke at the ball, encouraging the goal keeper to dive to anticipate the ball's arrival. However, the ball passes through to a third player who actually strikes the ball in a slightly different direction to the one being blocked by the falling goal keeper. Once committed to their defensive move, it is almost impossible for the goalkeeper to move their weight to block the ball taking the new direction.

Deception, when performed successfully, creates the impression that circumstances are different from their reality. The person who is the target of the deception attempt then acts according to their belief in their perceived reality. Consequently, at some later time, they face a surprising dislocation and possibly confusion when what they thought was true is shown to be false.

In competition, a period of disability and confusion in the mind of the target gives advantage and relative freedom of movement to the initiator of deception.

In commerce there are a number of famous examples of competitive activity which remain controversial because benefits and losses are attributed to perceived tricks.

Some of the most prominent examples have arisen through deception found in the history of event promotion. Brewer's[19] article refers to ambush marketing as a method for gaining disproportionately large promotional benefits from major events to the direct disadvantage of advertising competitors. He discusses rivalry between American Express and Visa, Fuji and Kodak, Nike and Adidas; all of whom depended on investment in promotion at world class events, and one of whom in each pair claimed that the other gained unfair advantage through underhanded and deceptive practices. More recently, similar claims and counterclaims have appeared in promotion of the 2000 Olympics[20] and in World Cup Football.[21]

Of course, the tricks are challenged as dirty, unfair, underhanded and morally wrong by the disadvantaged. On the other hand, the winners merely say they are looking after their shareholders and they have done nothing wrong.

Impressions of reality

At a strategic level, competition is essentially rivalry between the thinking processes of competitors. This is a subtle interaction among perceptions of all aspects of the competition. Note that the accompanying state of mind of the rivals is invisible. Tactics and operations often reveal the drama of competition, at least for onlookers, more readily than is apparent in strategy.

Competitors will be drawn to decide on directions and actions based on impressions and perceptions of circumstances. Deception is an element of strategy which aims to interfere with a rival's perception of reality. Advantage might be accomplished, even with modest resources, by leading a rival to believe that their circumstances are different from reality.

It is not necessarily a destructive or damaging process, except insofar as deceptive actions lead to a competitor's state of confusion and imbalance, rendering them unable to bring clear thinking to their judgement. Surprise, unexpected action, ambiguous movement, and misleading indicators of action can all contribute to a rival's psychological disorientation.

Master Sun's emphasis on the psychological dimension of competition is revealed in his views about deception. He values efforts made to interfere with a rival's view of reality; he encourages the creation of false impression, the kind that will leave a competitor confused and uncoordinated when disadvantaged by false perceptions:

> Now war is based on deception. Move when it is advantageous and create changes in the situation by dispersal and concentration of forces.[22]

And again:

All warfare is based on deception. Therefore, when capable, feign incapacity; when active, inactivity. When near, make it appear that you are far away; when far away, that you are near. Offer the enemy a bait to lure him; feign disorder and strike him.[23]

Discussion of issues of deception in international relations, military, intelligence and counterintelligence[24] emphasises the importance of psychology, and in particular the nature of human perception applied to the practice of deception. Whaley[25] bases his presentation on a classification scheme for perception which concentrates on a typology of 'misperception'. Within his taxonomic structure he distinguishes among several elements of deception.

Deception is the distortion of the perceived reality; its task is to profess the false in the face of the real. Magicians call this 'magic' or a 'trick'. Every deception is comprised of only two parts:

- dissimulation, hiding the real by masking, repackaging or dazzling; and
- simulation, showing the false by mimicking, inventing or decoying.

Whaley identifies a series of steps in this process of deception:

1. Identify a strategic goal: what is to be achieved by the deception.
2. Choose how the planner wants his target to react to the situation.
3. Decide what the planner wants the target to think about the facts or event, precisely what it is they should perceive.
4. Decide what is to be hidden about those facts or impending events, and what is to be shown in their stead.
5. Analyse the pattern of the real thing to be hidden so as to identify its distinguishing characteristics, specifically which of these characteristics must be deleted or added to give another pattern that suitably masks, repackages or dazzles.
6. Do the same for the false thing to be shown to give another pattern that plausibly mimics, invents or decoys.
7. Having designed the desired effect and its hidden method, the next step is to explore the means for presenting this effect to the target.
8. Operational phase begins.

9. Channels through which false characteristics are communicated must be open to the target's sensors.

10. Target must accept the effect, perceiving it as an illusion.

Whaley's explanation of the process of deception is applicable in general, and also specifically to goal oriented deception in commerce. Here the aim is to create sufficient psychological dislocation in the rival to allow the perpetrator a competitive advantage.

To create the impression in a competitor's mind that a Focal Firm is more interested in rivalry elsewhere can possibly induce behaviour which creates later vulnerability. Consider an example in the world of commerce.

Deception offers a plausible interpretation of one aspect of the so called *Cola Wars* of the 1980s.[26] New entrants threatened the beverage empires of Coca Cola and Pepsi. President's Choice, a new Canadian brand, accumulated a substantial proportion of its home market. Doug Nichols, the CEO, was pleased to have cost the national brands 'millions and millions of dollars while they ignored the growth of President's Choice'.

Perhaps Coke and Pepsi were drawing Nichols into a commitment from which he could not withdraw. Production, marketing, distribution and maybe even debt would have committed him to pursuing his product's future. At this point President's Choice became vulnerable. Coke and Pepsi promptly reduced their prices dramatically, below a level their competitor could sustain. This left Doug Nichols 'just this side of oblivion'.

The art of deception is an art in creative thinking. Master Sun calls for application of creative thinking to create circumstances which will interfere with a rival's perception of reality. He refers to this as the use of 'normal' and 'extraordinary' forces:

> That the army is certain to sustain the enemy's attack without suffering defeat is due to operation of the extraordinary and normal forces. . . . Generally, in battle, use the normal force to engage; use the extraordinary to win . . . These two forces are mutually reproductive; their interaction as endless as that of interlocking rings. Who can determine where one ends and the other begins?[27]

Viewed from a rival's perspective, the competition is commenced with a Focal Firm's engagement with what appears to be the main source of confrontation. Master Sun's deception is that while creating this appearance, and moving to ensure that it is reinforced in the mind of the rival, the main source of attack is designed to come from an altogether unexpected or 'extraordinary' direction.

Interestingly, Sun Tzu bases his reasoning for success in the application of deception on his belief in a strategist's unlimited capacity for creativity:

> Now the resources of those skilled in the use of extraordinary forces are as infinite as the heavens and earth; as inexhaustible as the flow of the great rivers . . . The musical notes are only five in number but their melodies are so numerous that one cannot hear them all . . . The primary colours are only five in number but their combinations are so infinite that one cannot visualize them all.[28]

Creation of a deceptive element in strategic thinking is not enough; Master Sun appreciates the demands of operational execution:

> Apparent confusion is the product of good order; apparent cowardice, of courage; apparent weakness, of strength . . . Order or disorder depends on organisation; courage or cowardice on circumstances; strength or weakness on dispositions.[29]

How, then, might these ideas about deception be applied in a commercial context?

Consider the following example of a successful deception where a company found itself lured into a sense of false security by deceptive manoeuvring.[30] This story is one of a powerful American cycle manufacturer, Schwinn, being temporarily disabled by short term industrial difficulties. The company approached Giant, an Asian cycle producer, to help it bridge production shortfalls. Schwinn was later surprised to find that it had lost control of important aspects of its design and technology, a surprise brought about by Giant's management of Schwinn's impressions of its intentions and capabilities. Schwinn cried 'unfair' without realising that its vulnerability was a psychological state, self-constructed.

Finally, the following six steps adapt Whaley's explanation to competition between businesses in which a Focal Firm seeks at least temporary dislocation in a competitor:

1. Focal Firm conducts research to determine the competitor's world view, that is, to build an understanding of what the competitor believes and understands are the ways in which business is done. This will include its appreciation of its history, what has proven successful and what has led to shortcomings.

2. Focal Firm behaves consistently with the competitor's model of reality.

3. Focal Firm checks to ensure that the competitor is noticing its behaviour and that the competitor is responding within its understanding of commercial reality.

4. Focal Firm maintains its behaviour consistent with competitor's expectations for a period of time sufficient to ensure that the Focal Firm's behaviour is ordinary in the competitor's terms.

5. Without warning, Focal Firm behaves outside the competitor's range of normality.

6. Focal Firm notes the competitor's difficulty in interpreting this extraordinary behaviour and while the competitor struggles to make sense of events and to find ways to respond, the Focal Firm capitalises on the competitor's dislocation.

Power

Intuitively, power carries with it images of force and forcefulness, even coercion. It is a contest of assets, ability and will: the strongest, the most skilful and the most determined will win.

In many fields of competition this image holds true. Yet, if this is the only formula for power, then weaker and less able competitors are doomed to fail. Yet, common observation shows that smaller competitors can succeed, but the supporting strategy relies on a different calculus of power.

Social psychology provides an explanation of power which offers a more general interpretation than one relying on brute force. It places the experience of dependence at the centre of this idea of power: one is more powerful than another to the extent that the second perceives dependence on the first.

In competition, perceptions are therefore critical: power is created and dissolved through perceived dependence.

Powerful behaviour can be viewed from two perspectives: one is by prevailing through the ability to induce a change in behaviour of a rival; the other is to be positioned so that one's own behaviour is not vulnerable to an overbearing rival.

Application of forceful constraint

The powerful are commonly regarded as those who exert their will on others, inducing them to act in ways other than they would normally choose. Power brings to mind capabilities of the powerful to force compliance.

The powerful in commerce are typically conceived as those companies which are rich enough and influential enough in the right quarters to arrange business affairs to their own advantage.

This view of power regards its essence as existing in the capabilities of the powerful: a company is powerful because it has overwhelming assets and abilities. Coca Cola Company, Microsoft, and Nestlé come easily to mind as companies with enormous financial and marketing might.

One of the features of Napoleonic campaigning which von Clausewitz found most compelling was the French Emperor's purpose in bringing about a resolution to a military contest. Napoleon aimed for an undisputed result, a win to the French.

This idea of achieving a definite outcome from a conflict became one of the foundations for von Clausewitz's theory of war, and in particular the objective of a battle. He reduced the objective of a confrontation to one which could be recognised as successful if three criteria were met:

1. That the enemy was defeated in battle
2. That they were rendered incapable of recovery and therefore unable to regroup and fight back, and
3. That the defeat was so convincing that it discouraged any possible ally who might be tempted to come to the enemy's assistance.

Power in von Clausewitz's terms is therefore a sufficiency of force to end a rival's ability to threaten. This can be interpreted as brute force.

But von Clausewitz is also acutely aware of the importance of morale in winning or losing battles. In fact, he regards this as more decisive in bringing about success than he does the capability to apply force. A second theme in his concept of power therefore emerges: power to eliminate a rival's will to fight.

Avoiding dependence

Consider an alternative outlook on power. Centre the essence of power in the perceptions of the influenced, rather than in the assets or abilities of the powerful.

Drawing from social psychology,[31] power might be defined as prevailing in a relationship between two social entities, for instance between person A and person B. When the following conditions are met:

1. If entity A wants to influence entity B, and
2. If entity B perceives dependence on entity A through A's ability to reward or punish, and
3. If entity A perceives entity B's increased desire to comply with the wishes of A, B's decreased desire not to comply,

then, entity A has power over B.

The example used here illustrates this definition of power in the relationship between two people. It allows us to consider subtle aspects of power which extend beyond brute force.

To illustrate this idea, consider the relationships between McDonalds and its suppliers. McDonalds is powerful in these relationships because its suppliers are only permitted to supply to McDonalds; they cannot provide product to anyone else. McDonalds is powerful, therefore, because it is able to dictate these terms of business.

From a supplier's perspective, McDonalds is also powerful because the supplier perceives dependence on McDonalds. This aspect of power resides in the mind of the supplier.

The most useful features of this definition are that power does not exist in absolute form, and most importantly, because of its basis in perception, one is only powerful to the degree that another perceives their dependence. Consequently, power can only be accumulated through the perceptually based willingness of its target. Hence, a paradox: the more power one attempts to accumulate, the less one becomes powerful because among human beings dependence will be resisted with counter dependence, at least in perception.

There is no doubt that power in strategy can be reduced to the degree with which one firm can apply irresistible pressure, or force, on a commercial rival.

But a company does have free will, at least to the degree that its executives are able to choose its course of action. Therefore, 'irresistible pressure' requires a psychological interpretation, in addition to one associated purely with the application of physical force.

Power as perceived dependence is clear to see in the relationships between companies and their dependent suppliers. Yet the future of a company might be dictated by its customers or clients: customers are powerful to the extent that a company perceives dependence on them.

What then does power mean in a relationship between competitors? From the discussion above, one company is more powerful than another to the degree that it can dictate terms of competitive behaviour; such is the case in establishing product standards. This might be regarded as 'irresistible force' in commercial strategy.

However, there is another perspective, and this is the manifestation of power in the perception of dependence of one competitor on another. This is the form of power which permits a small firm to compete effectively on its own terms by perceiving little dependence, regardless of its rival's application of what it considers to be irresistible commercial force. The rise of low cost airlines in a highly competitive travel industry is a case in point.[32]

Another example is presented in the American coffin industry. Costco, a warehouse retailer, sells cut-price coffins, thus reducing the power of the dominant funeral homes on which it perceives little dependence.[33]

While a distinction has been made here between power as force, and power as perceived dependence, a case can be made for strategic initiative bringing about a combination of the two. MacMillan[34] presents a range of actions which a Focal Firm might take with the purpose of securing a relative advantage with its competitor. If successful the momentum created through initiative will both induce behaviour otherwise unlikely to be chosen, and bring about a state of perceived dependence associated with dislocation.

Forcefulness and perceived independence are useful descriptions for the game once it has begun. However, power can also be viewed from the perspective of shaping the form of competition itself.

Competitors who rival each other in more than one market are likely to select initiatives and counter initiatives with the aim of influencing the overall state of competitive relationship, rather than dealing with rivals in one market at a time. The low-cost airline industry is an example; in the United States, JetBlue, Frontier, AirTran and Southwest were among the most vigorous competitors across a large number of travel markets.[35] MacMillan, van Putten and McGrath[36] explain the relationship between competitors across markets in terms of three characteristics:

1. Competitor's propensity to react to a Focal Firm's initiative in a market, based on incentives such as existing market share, profitability and financial contribution
2. The attractiveness of the market to the Focal Firm, and therefore its likely initiative, based on estimated market share, profitability and financial contribution
3. Relative capability of the Focal Firm and competitor to either sustain an initiative or repel such a move based on assets such as technology and abilities such as means of distribution.

This three-dimensional representation of relative power indicates that both the competitive context and characteristics of participants contribute to what MacMillan *et al.* call a situation of strategic interdependence.

A Focal Firm has six alternatives available for conducting a campaign for control of a market as defined above:

1. Direct attack designed to force rival's retreat through application of overwhelming resources where a competitor has little capability to sustain a response.

2. Contest carefully chosen markets where a judgement is made that the Focal Firm will prevail through a choice of initiative which cannot be easily matched by the rival.

3. Guerrilla campaign is conducted in a field of competitor's strength using focused and progressive growth in areas which are narrower than the rival is prepared to consider. MacMillan[37] elaborates.

4. Feint: an initiative designed to distract a competitor away from an area which is particularly valuable to the Focal Firm.

5. Gambit as occurs in chess: the Focal Firm creates an opportunity for initiative in an area it values by sacrificing its position ready to attack elsewhere.

6. Harvesting takes place when both competitors play an end game reaping whatever rewards are available for little investment in an area which is judged of little future value.

The calculus of power employed by MacMillan *et al.* is a Focal Firm's ability to achieve three things: to sustain its own dominance in its own highly valued markets, to eject a competitor from markets which it favours for future development and to shape its competitors' views of the attractiveness of the markets it considers.

Impressions of dependence

Power comes naturally to mind when considering strategy. Apple appears to command a powerful position in the market for hard-disk-based music players and for legally downloadable music.[38] Power implies an ability to lead others in the specification of product features and price. Such a position is even referred to as 'dominance'.

The commonsense idea of strategy is to construct plans to achieve a goal under conditions of opposition from arrival. This achievement is so much easier if one holds the balance of power.

Although power is closely associated with strategy and strategic thinking, its significance for competitive outcomes is more subtle than it first appears. The problem is one of paradox: the more power one has a less powerful one is. The enormous influence which is brought to bear by Microsoft is also vulnerable to open source software.[39]

This is illustrated again in the situation of Apple introduced above. Apple's pre-eminence in hard-disk-music-players naturally draws interest from potential rivals; the more powerful, the more likely others will seek their own advantage. RealNetworks sought Apple's assistance in allowing those with access to its music library to download music to Apple's iPod. Apple refused so, almost inevitably, RealNetworks found a way to achieve downloads anyway. And this could be just the beginning of efforts by others, such as Microsoft, to undermine Apple's position.

One of the themes in contemporary thinking about strategy is the various ways in which those who have an interest in a company can influence its direction.[40] Maps of stakeholder influence typically recognise the economic, physical, information, moral and social claims which should be recognised by a company in its corporate and cultural context.

Analysis which follows on from such mapping attempts to gauge the degree to which corporate direction should align with external expectations. This influence is a measure of the power exerted by stakeholders.

This perspective on strategy presents it as the creation of corporate direction through a political resolution resulting from the sum of stakeholder vectors of influence.

Kautilya's[41] recommendation to the king for managing competitive relationships with neighbouring sovereign states also carries a political theme. His theory for managing a kingdom's relationships with neighbouring states is based on a form of power centred on diplomacy. The king's representatives and ambassadors spend much time in neighbouring states, observing capabilities closely and listening and prying to elicit a neighbour's intentions. Efforts are also made to form alliances based on mutual interests.

When states become rivals, Kautilya advocates building on the structural friendship of 'my enemy's enemies'. Power, in Kautilya's terms, is therefore the ability to engage *friends* to distract a competitor into dealing with threats from several directions. Kautilya's theory for managing relationships between competing states is based on structural principles as portrayed in his *Circle of States*. Power arises from a state's ability to persuade a *friend* to distract a rival while the king attacks from the rear.

Note that if this attack is successful and the king occupies the rival's kingdom, the structural pattern of allies and enemies shifts: former friends become structural enemies.

Sun Tzu[42] lays considerable emphasis on a general's ability to manoeuvre his army into a position of competitive advantage. Taking advantage of his assessment of a rival's intentions and capabilities, and of prevailing circumstances, Sun Tzu's general positions his army to attack his rival's point of weakness.

MacMillan[43] takes a long term outlook as he discusses the dynamics of taking control through a sequence of competitive initiatives and counterattacks. The argument he makes is that a strategic initiative needs to be complemented by planning which anticipates a rival's possible reactions to this competitive move. Sustaining the power to maintain competitive momentum requires a mindset that assumes that advantages are provisional and have limited duration.

For the following examples of sources of strategic initiative, MacMillan reminds the reader of preparations for sustaining initial advantage.

Anticipating and securing access to the industry's critical materials and components, especially if they are expected to be in short supply, needs to be complemented by steps which must be taken to maintain this advantage once a competitor begins to looks to circumvent this disadvantage. The situation of de Beers, the diamond trader, is a good illustration of this point.[44]

In manufacturing, the initiative of producing a very successful new product which sells well, to the disadvantage of a competitor, should be complemented by the parallel design of its replacement for the inevitable release of a competitor's copy of the first item. This is an argument for Apple following its iPod product with the next generation of music technology.[45]

As MacMillan also points out, imaginative (rather than merely expensive) advertising and promotion campaigns also have the potential for creating strategically valuable initiative. These need to be followed by further generations of creative ideas to counteract competitor attempts to neutralise initial marketing efforts.

Sustaining initiative calls for corporate capability to resist sources of inertia which have the potential for undermining power which flows from initiative. Countervailing corporate power is the ability to overcome resistance to invest in new initiatives before counteraction by a rival occurs, and when many will view it as unnecessary. It requires, as MacMillan observes, circumventing bureaucratic obstacles such as are likely to arise from structural, procedural and planning systems. Stakeholders also need to be prevented from adding inertia which slows or prevents follow-up to successful initiative.

Two interpretations of a concept of power are evident in this line of thinking. One is perhaps the obvious, power consisting of the application of overwhelming force at a critical point of weakness from which a rival will be unlikely to recover.

The other, more subtle, is the power inherent in the thinking process which conceives of this method of attack. This is the analytical power which weighs all the relevant circumstances and reaches the rational conclusion that a course of action will achieve the general's objective. This might be termed 'powerful strategic thinking'.

Strategic thinking is an intellectual activity of synthesis. It depends on judgement, intuition and imagination; it rests on creative insight.[46] However, pure intellectualisation is unproductive since it needs to be transformed into systematic action to achieve competitive advantage. Because of the benefits of efficiency and orderliness in action, the trend will always be towards formalising the strategic thinking process.

As Mintzberg[47] points out, formalisation involves the imposition of structure onto the thinking process. It becomes regulated through the application of conventional categories for concepts and employment of standard analytical techniques. These often well-intentioned attempts at assisting refinement of thinking will actually suppress creativity and judgement that are essential to strategic thinking.

If this is so, then, power is lost in strategic thinking if it is limited and constrained by imposed structure. Yet, structure imposes discipline in thinking which enhances the creative clarity of strategic thinking. Herein sits the paradox of strategic thinking: power for strategic thinking relies on discipline and order, and discipline and order undermines the power of strategic thinking.

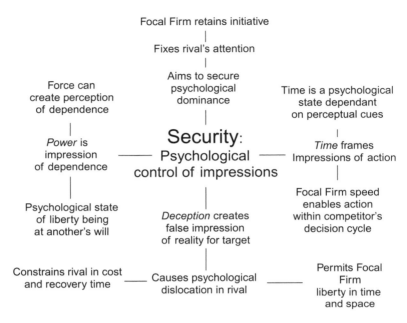

Figure 5.2 Concept map for Security.

Security is a state of mind. The Principle explored here proposes that psychological security is a source of strength with which to capitalise on an opportunity. If, alternatively, one becomes thus psychologically disadvantaged, then a rival will be in a position to secure relative advantage. Understanding the influences of time, deception and power are therefore important, as much from a defensive posture as in considering the prospect of commercial benefit through assertiveness.

Reflection

What part does rhythm play in strategic thinking?
Deception is wrong.
What are the ethics of creating perceived dependence?

6

Feasibility

Principle of Feasibility: Strategy ensures that the enterprise acquires and maintains sufficient capability to accomplish aims.

The necessary assets and abilities to act need to be acquired to enable accomplishment of aims. Alliances will support strategy to the degree that they are satellites which extend competitive influence.

Julius Caesar, a dominant figure in shaping European history, was a military strategist of limited capability. But his ambition had little to do with leading the Roman army. Caesar's political and military accomplishments, which included the conquest of Gaul, were designed merely as theatre to impress Romans. For Caesar, these achievements were incidental, except insofar as they were a means to leading Rome.[1]

Caesar's primary aim, his Policy objective, was purely personal: to control the Roman Empire from Rome. And this he achieved. For strategists, his achievements are of interest because we ask, from the viewpoint of strategic thinking: what was it that allowed him to accomplish his objective; why was it feasible?

Born of a family of minor nobility, Caesar set about the task of securing influence at an early age. He met the normal administrative and political expectations by progressing through Rome's governing apparatus. As he did so, he married into a prominent family and procured the support of influential figures. By so doing, he placed himself in substantial financial debt. He also invested in his own abilities, learning the arts of oratory, debate and rhetoric, skills which helped him sway opinion in the Senate and further consolidate his interpersonal influence. All the while, his aim was fixed: to eventually control Rome.

In 60 BC Caesar was appointed to a provincial governorship, a step which soon brought him back to Rome where he formed an alliance with two key people; Pompey who was Rome's most successful general, and Crassus, Rome's wealthiest man. This support was sufficient for Caesar to secure election to the post of consul, at the same time intimidating his co-consul, Bibulus into simply staying away for the year of the appointment.

This achievement was substantial, but Caesar wanted more. He wanted to rule Rome indefinitely. So he took steps to further that aim. Counterintuitively, these steps actually took him away from Rome, to the post of governor of provinces at Rome's boundary with Gaul. These steps also gave him control of an army. Caesar now had the ingredients to enable him to manoeuvre towards his greater objective.

Caesar's alliance with his soldiers was an arrangement of mutual benefit. Caesar gained the ability to force issues with his opponents, and the army gained the support of a governor who would secure their welfare and reward them well.

Proximity to Gaul gave Caesar an opportunity to invade and eventually secure control of this new province. But it was not simple control of further provinces that Caesar wanted; what was most important was winning battles which would be admired by Romans. Some of these were nearly catastrophes; some were utter disasters, such as the so-called invasion of Britain in 55 BC. But the formidable ability of the army allowed him to succeed, despite deficiencies in his military leadership. Needless to say, Caesar wrote his own reports of these heroic and courageous adventures, and these were the reports which were publicised in Rome.[2] Romans thought about Caesar's accomplishments in the way he wanted them to. In a relatively short time the Senate was afraid to obstruct him and Caesar returned to Rome at the head of his army. Rome was finally in his hands.

If feasibility is a vital element of strategic thinking, Caesar's history shows that turning an objective into reality depends, at least, on understanding what assets are critical to this accomplishment; acquiring them and then maintaining them. Caesar developed his personal assets: physical and financial, not to mention dependence on him by Romans. He developed and maintained key abilities, notably his own ability to influence others. And Caesar demonstrated the vital importance of extending his own influence through alliances with others, in particular with prominent political figures, but most importantly of all, with soldiers. For Caesar, alliances were fostered so long as they served his objectives; when they were no longer useful, such ties were cut.

Caesar's tenure as emperor was cut short by his assassination. He had created many enemies on his way to the top. However, his accomplishment is impressive all the same. Through his determination, single-mindedness and acquisition of the necessary assets and abilities, combined with captive allies, Caesar made feasible what would otherwise have remained a dream.

Action designed for competitive advantage flows from strategic thinking as a combination of assets, that is, corporate wherewithal, and also ability, that is, the facility to transform assets into productive results. A holistic sense of the relationships among assets, ability and alliances is offered in Table 6.1 to show integration among the ideas which follow.

Table 6.1 helps to summarise and explain how Caesar's strategic capability involved interactions among his assets, abilities and allies. His **assertive** posture rested on his acquisition of the necessary combination of his own skills and ability to overcome his rivals in Rome. Caesar's alliance with the army was one of dependence; the soldiers depended on him for their own success and well-being, and they were at the same time an extension of Caesar's own skill and ability. Caesar's formidable strategic capability derived from this combination of assets, ability and alliances.

Could Caesar's progress to control Rome have been blunted? What *defensive* strategic capability would his rivals have needed? The essential requirement would have been anticipation of Caesar's purpose and then the assembly and control of assets and ability which at least matched Caesar's. This capability would have been further secured if dependence on allies was unnecessary.

The quest for understanding the concept of feasibility in strategic thinking will concentrate first on strategic capability. Discussions of assets and abilities will follow. Alliances as we shall see, extend that discussion, rather than add a new variable in strategic thinking.

Table 6.1 *Interactions among assets, ability and allies.*

Feasibility: Acquisition and maintenance of sufficient capability	Assets	Ability	Allies
Assets	Wherewithal for accomplishment of strategic objectives	*Acquire assets and ability to anticipate rival's capability for initiative and retain balance*	*Avoid dependence on allied assets*
Ability	**Acquire assets and ability to create and sustain sufficient capability to seize initiative over rival**	Accomplishment of transformations needed to reach strategic objectives	*Avoid dependence on allied ability*
Allies	**Acquire control of allied assets to enhance strategic capability**	**Acquire control of allied ability to enhance strategic capability**	Assets and abilities of an associate, harnessed to reach strategic objectives

Assertive strategic posture
Defensive strategic posture

Capability proposition

I believe it is a reasonable proposition to assert that strategic capability is the ability to transform one situation or state of affairs into another, by employing available assets.

Consider a recent unexpected announcement by EADS (European Aeronautic Defence and Space) the parent of Airbus.[3] The company said it was planning to increase its aircraft production from 307 to 385 between 2004 and 2005–2006. This statement would have been a worrying plan for Boeing, its ailing competitor. It suggested that Airbus was in a position to move even further forward in aircraft sales than its recent history of success indicated, and clearly to the intended disadvantage of Boeing. The plan had the elements of a strategic initiative.

Its feasibility required that Airbus had both the assets, that is the wherewithal to take such a step, and the ability, that is the facility to act to apply those assets to achieve the performance outcomes planned.

For Airbus this required a definition of where the firm was and where it wanted to be in a competitive sense. Its requisite energy or effort lay in the production and sale of aircraft, the capacity to increase production and to successfully sell them to clients. To achieve the required end state (and not some other outcome), required a means for controlling effort, in other words the ability to apply corporate focus on the required outcome and to install the necessary control systems to achieve it. A means for knowing when and whether the end state had been reached provides guidance; a relatively simple matter if counted in numbers of aircraft manufactured and sold; but not always so obvious. Finally, residual capability was expected in anticipation of a longer term future; the outcome would be a false gain if it disabled the company in the process and Airbus destroyed itself in the effort to achieve this particular outcome. Capability needs to anticipate further strategic goals.

The capability proposition I propose rests on five requirements:

1. Ability to identify beginning and end states.
2. Assets providing requisite energy to transform beginning state into end state.
3. Ability to control the direction of energy towards the end state.
4. Ability to assess progress towards the end state.
5. Capability to undertake subsequent strategic initiative once end state is reached.

At the conclusion of this chapter, I will return to these propositions to show how they link with the ideas of assets, abilities and alliances. But first these three ideas require further discussion.

Assets

In contemporary scholarship, assets are discussed in several guises: resources, competencies and capabilities which are described as threshold, unique or core.[4] One of the most influential theoretical lines of thinking in this academic strand is the so-called 'resource-based view'.

Resource-based view

More than a decade ago a so-called 'resource-based theory' emerged through the scholarship of Wernerfelt, Barney, Grant[5] and others. The main theme of this line of thinking is that a firm's likelihood of outperforming its commercial rivals depends on its resources.[6] Strategy, according to this view, stems first from analysis of a firm's resource base, which leads to an appraisal of its capabilities and their profit-earning potential. Resource gaps are filled and investment is made in replenishing, augmenting and upgrading the firm's resource base.

As Grant[7] points out, this approach takes its origin from a corporate decision about the identity and purpose of the firm. Rather than find a match with the external environment to fulfil this aim, the alternative is to build on internal resources. Capability follows; it refers to what a firm '. . . can do as a result of teams of resources working together'. These teams involve complex patterns of co-ordination among and between people and other resources. This, Grant refers to as 'routines'. Routines are to the organisation what skills are to a person.

From a competitive perspective, Grant proceeds by proposing that a firm will maintain relative advantage so long as its capability is protected. Capability therefore needs to be durable, assured against depreciation or obsolescence. It needs to be opaque to competitors, preventing the possibility of imitation for as long as possible. Capability should be difficult to transfer from one firm to another owing to location, imperfect information, firm-specific resources and immobility of routines. Capability should be difficult to replicate through control of unique resources.

The thrust of the resource-based theory is echoed in Porter's article 'What is Strategy?'[8] He argues that sustainable competitive advantage derives from a firm's ability to deepen the distinctiveness of unique and systemic methods and processes.

The reader will note the inward looking orientation towards creation of competitive advantage in resource-based thinking. While capitalisation on a firm's assets is an essential foundation for creating and maintaining relative advantage, if considered alone it is *myopic*.

The view of assets which I propose here takes a more outward orientation in its view of competitiveness. Assets are a fundamental aspect of capability since they are the means available for action. Certain action is possible only if particular assets are readily available and organised in productive ways. Such questions of availability and fit are central, for instance, in Rupert Murdoch's assembly of assets for the strategic purposes of News Corporation.[9] This very large media company comprises assets including a broadcast network, studios, television stations, cable networks and satellite distribution. How should assets be assessed? It is an appropriate example with which to contemplate important questions about corporate assets.[10]

Which assets are available? The audit here involves an assessment of the stock of material, human and financial resources. It also weighs up their level of utilisation in terms of efficiency, that is how well assets are applied, and effectiveness which recognises what is accomplished through application of assets. A further feature of asset availability is the employment of controls to provide appropriate access to assets for ready use.

Which assets are unique? Uniqueness refers to assets which are available only to the firm, and which offer the possibility of securing advantage over direct competitors through their ability to help generate superior products or services.

Are assets balanced? This question refers to the degree to which assets applied bring about complementary results, that is avoiding wasteful counterproductive use of assets in associated activities. A measure of flexibility is also implied in the ability of assets to be employed to meet prevailing uncertainty.

Are assets linked? Michael Porter's concept of the 'value chain' provides a check that company activities are synchronised and consistent in creating value for the firm's customers. This question also addresses the degree to which linkages are distinctive and contribute to sustainable advantage.

What is the comparative utilisation of assets? Historical comparison with previous asset application and comparison with industry trends provides a basis for insight into relative utilisation across time and in relation to industry norms.

Value-creating assets that most readily emerge in a corporate audit, such as the one conducted through the questions raised above, are those having a physical character: money, materials and personnel including their skills. Information follows. Less readily appreciated are intangible assets of a psychological nature: imagination and determination, for instance, are vital strategic assets residing in the mind of the strategist. This point is beyond dispute when considering the strategy of News Corp and its primary strategist, Rupert Murdoch.[11]

In strategic thinking, interdependence among assets and objectives draws attention to further matters requiring consideration:

- *Supply*: To support it in maintaining productive relationships with customers and clients, a firm needs access to requisite financial, material, human and informational assets to undertake the transformations that meet objectives in supply of a product or service. Reliable supply and distribution logistics are essential.
- *Advantage*: Assets are relative. Companies have different assets and ways in which they use them. Efficiency[12] and effectiveness[13] provide one firm with advantage compared with another in terms of application of assets.[14] This enables one firm, for example, to produce a particular product at a lower cost of production than another. This flows on to potential performance advantage.
- *Competitive Intelligence*: Assets are an essential element of competitive relationships. A firm will benefit from information about the assets available to a competitive rival, and how they are put to use. Conversely, a company will benefit from preventing a commercial opponent from forming an accurate picture of its assets and their method of application. Through the process of such competitive intelligence and counterintelligence, relative efficiencies and effectiveness are continuously reduced and recreated for corporate advantage.
- *Vulnerability*: Assets are vulnerable and need to be protected. Supply and distribution are subject to interference by a commercial rival, stocks of assets can be depleted by an aggressive opponent and the means of transformation into products and services can be slowed or rendered ineffective. A firm needs to be alert to these possible intrusions and to develop secure assets, protected from unwanted interference while pursuing objectives.

Let us further note that having an abundance of assets does not necessarily simplify strategic thinking. Nestlé dwarfs its competitors[15] yet it has an aim to become even larger. After concentrating its business in four main activities (confectionery, ice cream, mineral water and pet food) in 1981, the businesses which were themselves the assets comprising Nestlé, had to be realigned so that they could be employed more effectively for strategic objectives.

Maintenance of wherewithal

It is obvious that nothing can be achieved without the availability and application of the necessary wherewithal. However, in strategic thinking, assets also limit and bound strategic aspirations. Assets are a part of the equation that specifies how an objective may be accomplished; they are also a factor that helps define a feasible goal. Most importantly, capability is associated with a potential movement in materials, money and minds for competitive benefit. What motivates this movement; is it leadership?

Leadership[16] in contemporary scholarly literature is commonly regarded as a behavioural phenomenon which brings about distinctive organisational performance through non-rational processes leading to enthusiasm and energy among personnel.[17] Furthermore, it is frequently observed that in top performing companies leadership builds and motivates adaptiveness through fostering distinctiveness in orientation to customer satisfaction, continuous innovation and an attitude of desire for improved performance among all members of a firm's staff.

Here I take a more particular perspective on leadership, viewing it as an asset that gives direction to potential corporate movement through the creation of expectations.

Expectations about the future have an important impact on corporate direction because they influence both what is preferred and what is possible. They evolve, under the influence of leadership, as executives join a firm, at least partly through self-selection, based on a common identification with desirable corporate behaviour. Eventually a sense of identity evolves further through a shared past, present and future. Within a company itself, its own history of accomplishments will influence future expectations. Sony, for example has long been considered an innovator, a company which creates markets rather than responding to them.[18]

There are also external sources of corporate expectation; reference groups such as professional societies and codes of conduct specify acceptable identity and aspirations. And at the broadest level, values of society, often implicit, become incorporated into corporate aspirations and contribute to a sense of direction. These are the values which are held about aspirations for society and what that therefore means about personal and corporate behaviour.

But there is more. Expectations comprise a corporate sense of direction derived from the political processes which, through leadership, marshal the aspirations of senior staff in a firm. Expectations are a guiding component of corporate capability; they are in part, an answer to the question: what can this firm accomplish?

Effective leadership, in Sun Tzu's view, is an issue of the moulding of expectations with competition at its centre. The value of leadership, from his perspective, rests on clear perception and an accurate assessment of the situation in which one is competing. Sun Tzu further emphasises an effective leader's harmony with staff, sound strategy, understanding of circumstances and contingencies and sensitivity to human considerations. In contrast, a general unable to estimate his capabilities when faced with an opportunity will be hesitant and stumbling, foolishly believing unreliable information. His forces, as Sun Tzu suggests, will be '. . . scattered about' and unable to press an advantage:

> . . . the skilful commander takes up a position in which he cannot be defeated and misses no opportunity to master his enemy.[19]

Such expectations are formed through leadership. Machiavelli's[20] outlook on strategic capability is conditioned by his determination to advise the *Prince* on how to gain and maintain control. This in part involves winning honour; honour is an asset. This, Machiavelli proposes, should be accomplished in a number of ways. Great campaigns demonstrate striking personal ability and visible and impressive demonstrations of ability to govern at home draw honour. Expectations derive from honour.

Honour is also won through the appointment of staff which shows esteem for talent. Machiavelli advocates actively encouraging and honouring those who excel in their profession.

Opinion of the *Prince's* intellectual capability is based on the quality of those around him. If they are competent, it is obvious that he selected them and is therefore able to recognise competence. If a *Prince* is to maintain staff performance, then consideration, pay, honour and enrichment will place them in his debt. Machiavelli argues that staff should never be disarmed. One's capability is enhanced by arming staff because those who were suspect become loyal. Disarming causes offence and conveys mistrust.

Von Clausewitz[21] is at one with Master Sun in recognising leadership as one of the main sources of strategic capability; not in the shaping of human behaviour, but rather through the competitive character and ability of the leader. For von Clausewitz, it is *Genius for War* which establishes the basis for a distinctive competitive advantage. Although war lies at the far limit of human competition, the observations made by von Clausewitz are of interest when leadership involves guiding the action of others in ambiguous, stressful and disturbing situations. War is dangerous and frightening and these circumstances demand much of those who lead others into threatening and fearful situations.

Von Clausewitz points out that leadership is not just technical performance. Rather, it brings, together with technical qualifications, the more subtle aspects of deep understanding of the competition and insight which derive more from the soul than from technical training. War, of course, demands physical courage. This involves firmness and boldness in the face of danger. The struggle of competition also calls for moral courage through a leader's willingness to accept responsibility and to exercise judgement based on values and inner conscience.

Formulation of strategy and competitive conflict are both the domain of uncertainty and rapidly changing circumstances. As von Clausewitz observes, chance plays an important part in defining these situations and it calls for special abilities from a leader. In war, as in business, one constantly finds things different from expectations. High levels of uncertainty naturally induce hesitation and an inclination to revise plans, usually with unreliable data. At these times, von Clausewitz identifies three characteristics as indispensable: first, an intellectual ability to see truth in obscurity and inner courage to pursue it. The second is resolution, an act of courage in perplexing circumstances which is a feeling that removes the torment of doubt and the dangers of delay when there are no other sources of guidance. Third is presence of mind, that is, readiness and rapidity of expedient response to sudden danger.

Von Clausewitz calls for strength of mind or soul in the assessment of a great leader. At times of great excitement and when those around are immersed in intense emotion, maintenance of control through understanding is required to avoid loss of balance. Overwhelming forces for distraction, uncertainty and powerful impressions will tend to induce self-doubt and doubt among staff. These require an ability to maintain understanding, stability and consistency. The intellectual lessons of past reflection, conviction and judgement must continue to guide behaviour through tenacity of conviction, even as circumstances bring confusion, bewilderment and approach tumult.

Sight must not be lost of the wholeness of events and circumstances. This calls quite simply for a highly developed imagination which, as von Clausewitz observes, relies on intuitive perception, an extraordinary ability to quickly visualise the whole field of competition and one's place within it.

In von Clausewitz's terms a key strategic asset is the leader. He acknowledges the rare human abilities and traits which are required to maintain direction with decisiveness, imagination, determination, strength of will, courage and presence of mind in the most confusing circumstances. Establishment and maintenance of strategic direction in competitive struggle always involve elements of confusion and distraction. Von Clausewitz establishes expectations for those who are most capable to lead.

To sum up so far, it is misguided to consider material, financial, knowledge and human assets as a minor consideration in strategic thinking. However, inflating the significance of these assets to a point where they are the single centre of attention is also foolish. Moreover, even if a strategically balanced outlook is attained, assets amount to more than mere stock of material, finance, people and information. For strategic significance, assets must be acquired, maintained, protected and deployed for comparative benefit in corporate competition. Leadership is central in this effort. Not only must assets be proportional to strategic objectives; they ought also to be applied with maximum advantage. This is a matter of ability.

Ability

Contemporary thinking about strategy emphasises two important considerations relating to competencies and capabilities.[22] One is commitment to refining a central set of corporate competencies. The other is the capability to encourage an ambitious corporate reach towards the future. While these are valuable contributions to thinking about priorities, the first is exclusively internally focused and the second is abstract and elusive, as we shall see.

In contrast, classic views on strategic ability are direct and straightforward. If the objective is to outwit a competitive rival, then the key abilities are those that, when employed with initiative, leave the rival confused. Such abilities rest on intimate knowledge of what can be achieved with one's own assets; it also depends essentially on knowledge of a competitor's assets and abilities.

Core competencies

The idea that to succeed in business one needs to concentrate on doing what one does best and to build this activity into a source of competitive advantage has been an appealing contemporary theme in strategic thinking. Hamel and Prahalad[23] termed this approach a strategy of concentration on 'core competencies'. So ambitious was this claim for a basis for success, that Hamel and Prahalad framed it in terms of competing for the future.

Its appeal was twofold. First, it resonated with the intuitive sense of concentrating on what one does best, relegating other activities to lower priority, and perhaps reducing costs in the process.

Second, if executives could come to terms with what it actually was that their company did best, then competitive success would simply involve further concentration on these competencies which were already within the firm's domain.

The theme was further reinforced by Michael Porter's provocative 'What is strategy?' article.[24] His answer, like Hamel and Prahalad, was that companies succeed if they concentrate on developing systems of activity that are obscure to competitors and difficult to imitate.

The problem is this: what is implied is that a firm's concentration on refining its own internal processes will lead to competitive advantage.

Not necessarily. Concentrating on refining internal processes is an activity about which a company can organise, but it will not necessarily lead to competitive success.

Bringing again to mind the aircraft manufacturers, both Airbus and Boeing no doubt refine their internal design and production processes, but it is unlikely that these results would be sufficient, by themselves, to enable either firm to be confident of success in competition. If core competencies and systemic differentiation do not positively create strategic benefit, then the claims which support them are overstated.

The French firm Pinault-Printemps-Redoute (PPR) appears to have difficulty identifying its core competencies,[25] not an uncommon problem, even though the idea of core competencies is so appealing. However, if these special competencies were discovered or distilled, and the remaining redundant elements of the firm were disposed of, there is no clear reason to believe that strategic benefits would ensue.

There is no doubt that if a firm does actually have a capability which is unique and which does in fact contribute to an ability to prevail in competition, then it should be incorporated into the calculus of strategy. The problem with the concept of core competencies, and striving to create inimitable and obscure internal process, is that if they are claimed to be the primary sources of advantage, they are simply not competitively oriented.

To illustrate further, De Beers once held a position in the diamond industry which relied on an aggressively defended core competence in diamond purchase and distribution. As a source of long term strategic advantage it was doomed to challenge.[26]

What is required is a concept of corporate ability which, with reference to assets, forms a basis for strategic capability.

Capacity to transform

The Principles of Integrity and Security have already demonstrated, in previous chapters, that success in strategy depends on corporate ability to perform in particular ways designed to unsettle a rival. It should come as no surprise, therefore, that these abilities are once again threaded through the following explanation of strategic ability.

Sun Tzu's chapter on 'Dispositions' refers to strategic ability as the creation of the conditions of one's own invincibility, while at the same time awaiting competitive success through a rival's vulnerability; invincibility in defence, victory in attack. Strategic advantage is created in advance by creating conditions which cannot be defeated.

Perhaps the most important ability which can be employed at a strategic level, therefore, is initiative. In essence this is maintenance of controlled

forward movement in a competitive sense. This ability is designed to establish the terms of rivalry, instead of having them dictated by a competitor.

The essence of Sun Tzu's advice on strategic capability incorporates an
ability to assess circumstances: to understand one's own abilities, those of
one's rival and the ground on which competition takes place.

Sun Tzu's view clearly places great value on foreknowledge as we have
noted previously. An enlightened leader is able to overcome a rival through
the availability of information about the opposition's movements and
accomplishments. He is also clear about the sources of such knowledge:

> ... foreknowledge cannot be elicited from spirits, nor from gods, nor by
> analogy with past events, nor from calculations. It must be obtained from men
> who know the enemy situation.[27]

Sun Tzu identifies flexibility as an ability which is also a central source
of strategic capability. He calls for an ability to apply forces in limitless
variety. Once having accomplished a victory, Sun Tzu recommends never
repeating winning tactics. Reassuringly, he observes that even with very few
elements one can create almost infinite variety in pattern. One aims to
remain unpredictable.

Through interchange of normal forces, which ordinarily confront and
engage, with extraordinary forces, which are more likely to be used in flank-
ing movements, one creates confusion in a rival who has an expectation of
a particular pattern of engagement. Such flexibility calls for extraordinary
abilities of staff who attempt to confuse by convincing a rival that circumstances are different from reality. An ability to create apparent disorder,
cowardice and weakness requires discipline, courage and strength.

Sun Tzu cautions that a leader should not demand accomplishment from
those who have no talent. Victory should be sought from the situation, not
as a demand of staff; the burden of accomplishment is not placed on one's
people alone. For instance, favourable circumstances are created by making
the rival move by creating a situation to which he(she) must conform, to
entice him(her) to something he(she) is certain to take. With a lure of
ostensible profit the competitor is drawn into a trap where he(she) is awaited
in strength. Creation of favourable circumstances, a key strategic ability,
enables staff to exploit situations according to their own dispositions: the
valiant fighting, the cautious defending and the wise counselling.

Much can be achieved even with few resources through careful assessment of three factors: the morale or spirit among one's own staff, the terrain on which a struggle would take place and the rival's state of moral and physical vulnerability or invulnerability. Strategic ability depends on an intelligent assessment of all three. With this knowledge action can be taken to unsettle a rival. Sun Tzu recommends agitating one's rival.

> When the enemy is at ease, be able to weary him; when well fed, starve him; when at rest, make him move.[28]

In Sun Tzu's view a vital strategic ability lies in deception. Sun Tzu recommends having the ability to appear in the least expected places, arriving at a location before a rival while setting out after. And when preparing one's forces this should be performed in such a way as to create ambiguity:

> The ultimate in disposing one's troops is to be without ascertainable shape. Then the most penetrating spies cannot pry in nor can the wise lay plans against you.[29]

A strategist strives to be able to make a rival see one's strengths as weaknesses and one's weaknesses as strengths. If this is successful, and one is aware of a rival's disposition of force, then an opportunity is created to concentrate in areas where a rival is vulnerable. Furthermore, if one can give the impression of posing a threat in many locations a rival will be forced to disperse his(her) force:

> If I am able to determine the enemy's dispositions while at the same time conceal my own then I can concentrate and he must divide. And if I concentrate while he divides, I can use my entire strength to attack a fraction of his.[30]

Speedy movement is an ability which creates strategic advantage. His discussion of *Varieties of Ground* refers to speed, the ability to move quickly:

> Speed is the essence of war. Take advantage of the enemy's unpreparedness; travel by unexpected routes and strike him where he has taken no precautions.[31]

The emphasis throughout is on assessing the circumstances, identifying advantage and being capable of rapid movement to capitalise on this potential:

... at first be shy as a maiden. When the enemy gives you an opening be swift as a hare and he will be unable to withstand you.[32]

And when an engagement takes place:

The enemy must not know where I intend to give battle. For if he does not know where I intend to give battle he must prepare in a great many places. And when he prepares in a great many places, those I have to fight in any one place will be few.[33]

Ability should be maintained. A *Prince's* forces must be continually upgraded in skill, discipline and organisation. This is motivated by Machiavelli's belief that future competitive rivalry is inevitable and preparation, even in times of peace, is essential to future advantage: 'A wise prince . . . must never take things easy in times of peace . . . in order to reap the profit in times of adversity.'[34] Efforts to prepare must be conducted vigorously so that forces become prepared for hardship and struggle. Training must emphasise challenging practice in organisation and assessment of circumstances to enhance flexibility. As part of preparation for inevitable struggle, Machiavelli also recommends the study of history to gain insight into the ways in which others conducted themselves in times of competition.

From these propositions, and with a competitive orientation, organisational design can follow. MacMillan and Jones[35] take such a direction in their discussion of the design of organisations for the main purpose of competition rather than efficiency.

Alliances

Sotheby's alliance with eBay achieved little success, while the alliance between Nissan and Renault has produced outstanding results.[36] Many well-known disappointments and some outstanding successes following formation of alliances raise questions about rationale and method: why alliances and if so, how?

Relative advantage in competition is often attributed to access to superior assets, and greater ability in deploying them. It is not uncommon, therefore, when perceiving a situation of relative disadvantage, to be attracted to forming co-operative relationships with well stocked and able associates.

This argument for forming alliances is as a compensation for strategic deficiency. However, being a dependent partner is risky.[37]

Another argument for formation of alliances is a desire for flexibility, aimed at avoiding the need to acquire assets needed only for temporary purposes. This line of thinking involves securing a bargain whereby a competitor gains access to productive assets and abilities only for a short duration and at an acceptable price. The strength of the alliance is the quality of the contract.

A variety of circumstances arise which entice a firm into collaboration with others. Benefits can be perceived to ensue, for instance, by collaborating with a supplier to create a cost advantage relative to in-house production. Competitors might seek mutual benefit by choosing to collaborate with each other to present a united face to customers. Collaboration might be less costly than acquisition.[38] A firm wanting to establish itself in a foreign location might believe it is in its interests to collaborate with a local ally.

Ohmae[39] goes so far as to proclaim that for any company to achieve global ambitions it must form strategic alliances with others offering access, economy and reach. His argument rests on a comparison with acquisition as the alternative method for global growth. Alliances, he claims, offer the great benefit of maintaining the spirit of both partners, whereas an acquisition carries the consequences of conquest. Ohmae argues for a long term perspective based on a common commitment to collaboration with the aim of mutual benefit.

An alternative view is advanced by Hamel, Doz and Prahalad[40] and by Gomes-Casseres.[41] Their perspective has a more defensive outlook. While they appreciate the potential benefits of an alliance, they also prepare for the risks. The test they set for a successful alliance is whether a focal firm has learned more than it has lost through the relationship.

From a strategic perspective, Hamel *et al.* recognise that what could simply and conveniently begin as an outsourcing relationship with a supplier has the potential for naively providing the manufacturer with the capability to become a formidable competitor. The asymmetrical character of the relationship spawning a new competitor arises when the Focal Firm makes the mistake of assuming that its partner is a passive supplier, whereas the manufacturer seeks to learn from its ally with the ambition of competitive growth.

Hamel, Doz and Prahalad describe two mindsets, one which leads to a predictable loss through alliance, the other to defence against such loss. Loss is almost inevitable, they argue, when an alliance is entered into by a firm with the aim of minimising costly investment or reducing the level of effort needed to take a growth step. Most likely, this Focal Firm will become increasingly dependent on its ally and commercial decline will follow gradually from incremental leakage of information to its partner.

The alternative is based on prior consideration of the aim of the alliance in strategic terms; Gomes-Casseres[42] calls this an alliance strategy, as distinct from strategic alliance. The primary objective should be to learn from the partner, and at the same time to deliberately and effectively protect proprietary skills. Noting how frequently information can be lost inadvertently at an informal level between low level members of allied organisations, outward flow of information should therefore be restricted at all levels.

Japanese firms clearly calculate the risks outlined above in their relationship with their manufacturing suppliers.[43] A concerted effort is made to control technology transfer abroad and to ensure that distinctive competitive capabilities are retained at home. Perhaps there is a deeper significance in alliances for strategic purposes.

Strategic satellites

Alliances comprise assets and sources of ability. Like other assets, competitive advantage derives from the ability to design them for purposeful benefit and to apply them for competitive gain. Such alliances with others, therefore, need to be formed judiciously and with caution. Important questions are: Does this alliance contribute positively to the ability to act for benefit? Can the performance of this alliance be positively controlled?

The strategic benefit of an alliance is a matter of power; from a strategic perspective, it centres on the question of whether an alliance improves a Focal Firm's expectation of competitive benefit.

Kautilya[44] offers recommendations to the king which yield thoughtful insight into motivation for forming alliances. Concerned mainly with maintaining the king's power, Kautilya considers such power to derive from three sources: strength, knowledge and morale. Strength, in turn, is provided by the capabilities of the army, the treasury and by alliances. The purpose of acquiring allies, therefore, is to enable the king to enhance his power. It is also clear that Kautilya favours acquisition of an ally as secondary to gaining control of money or assets.

These priorities are also reflected in Sun Tzu's attitude towards allies. It is interesting to note that his treatise on strategy makes no reference to joint activities with allies. The implication is that the task of strategy is to influence circumstances that enable an army to prevail autonomously.

The only passage in which Master Sun refers to the formation of alliances is in the particular case of approaching a rival on 'focal terrain':

In focal ground, ally with neighbouring states.[45]

Focal ground is a strategically important point of intersection of several neighbouring states. In this situation, Sun Tzu calls for alliances of support to be formed with neighbouring states so that others will not interfere by favouring a rival. This is apparently a course of action designed to reduce risk rather than to enhance efforts to prevail over a competitor.

While Master Sun does not recommend joint action with allies he does offer advice for devising plans against those who have formed alliances. This is clear in his statement of priorities. He favours, first, attacking a rival's plans, next interfering with his alliances, followed by attacking the rival's army, and least favourable, to attack the rival's fortified cities.[46]

As observed earlier, Kautilya is prepared to entertain the promotion of advantage through alliances, so long as they enhance power and can be controlled. This is reflected in Kautilya's considerations for choice of ally:

When there is a choice between two possible allies, both in difficulties, of whom one is constant (based on friendship, not mercenary prospects) but not amenable to control and the other is temporary but controllable, which one should be preferred? Some teachers say that the constant friend, though not controllable is to be preferred because, even if he cannot help, he can do no harm. Kautilya disagrees. The one amenable to control, though a temporary ally, is preferable because he remains an ally (only) so long as he helps.

When there is a choice between two possible allies, both amenable to control, of whom one can give substantial but temporary help and the other a constant help but only a little, which one should be preferred? Some teachers say that a temporary friend giving substantial help shall be chosen because such a friend by giving a lot of help in a short time helps to meet a large outlay. Kautilya disagrees. The constant ally giving smaller help shall be preferred. The temporary friend giving substantial help is likely to withdraw for fear of having to give more or, even if he actually provides the help, will expect it to be repaid. The constant ally, giving a small help continuously, does, in fact, give greater help over a period of time.

Who is better – a mighty ally mobilising slowly or a less mighty one mobilising quickly? Some teachers say that a mighty ally is to be preferred because he adds prestige to the venture and, once he has mobilised, helps to accomplish the task quickly. Kautilya disagrees. An ally mobilising quickly, even if he is less mighty, is preferable because he does not allow the opportune time for action to pass and, being weaker, can be used according to the wishes of the conqueror; a mighty friend with extensive territory is less easy to control.[47]

Kautilya continues with his theme of power and control, reflecting on the most favourable structure of alliances. The partner's strength determines which king to seek as an ally:

- Alliance with two equal kings is better than an alliance with one strong king.
- Alliance with two weaker kings is better than an alliance with a king of equal strength.

Kautilya is above all, a realist. His king will not always be in a position to prevail over a rival. For a weak king facing a strong rival, he recommends as follows:

He who surrenders all lives only a life of despair, like a sheep that has strayed from its herd. (On the other hand) one fighting with a tiny army perishes like one trying to cross the ocean without a boat. It is better to seek the protection of a powerful king or an impregnable fort.

The weaker king will offer, by one means or another, that which the other will, in any case, take by force. It is life that is worth preserving not wealth which, being impermanent, can be given up without regrets.[48]

Both Kautilya and Sun Tzu advise against promoting the power of others. This advice is particularly pertinent in quickly developing industries:[49]

. . . he does not contend against powerful combinations nor does he foster the power of other states.[50]

Machiavelli agrees; he is especially averse to the idea of alliances with auxiliaries and mercenaries:

Mercenaries and auxiliaries are useless and dangerous. If a prince bases the defence of his state on mercenaries he will never achieve stability or security. For mercenaries are disunited, thirsty for power, undisciplined, and disloyal; they are brave among their friends and cowards before the enemy; they avoid defeat just so long as they avoid battle; in peacetime you are despoiled by them, and in wartime by the enemy.[51]

Furthermore:

Auxiliaries, the other useless kind of troops, are involved when you call upon a powerful state to come to your defence and assistance. . . . In themselves, auxiliary forces can prove useful and reliable, but for the one who calls them in they are almost always a disaster. You are left in the lurch if they are defeated, and in their power if they are victorious.[52]

In contrast with Alvarez and Barney,[53] Machiavelli is particularly cautious about the formation of alliances with those more powerful:

. . . a Prince should never join in an aggressive alliance with someone more powerful than himself, unless it is a matter of necessity. . . . This is because if you are victors, you emerge as his prisoner; and princes should do their utmost to escape being at the mercy of others.[54]

Moreover, neutrality in matters of relations with other states is not advisable. Commitment and decisiveness in terms of alliances is important: being a true friend or a true enemy will bring greater reward than neutrality. As Machiavelli observes, the conqueror does not want doubtful friends and a loser will repudiate you for being unwilling to help them:

A Prince . . . wins prestige for being a true friend or a true enemy, that is, for revealing himself without any reservation in favour of one side against another. This policy is always more advantageous than neutrality. For instance, if the powers neighbouring on you come to blows, either they are such that if one conquers, you will be in danger, or they are not. In either case it will always be to your advantage to declare yourself and to wage a vigorous war; because, in the first case, if you do not declare yourself you will always be at the mercy of the conqueror, much to the pleasure and satisfaction of the one who has been beaten, and you will have no justification nor any way to obtain protection or refuge. The conqueror does not want doubtful friends who do not help him when he is in difficulties; the loser repudiates you because you were unwilling to go, arms in hand, and throw in your lot with him.[55]

Alliances are powerful strategic assets if they are directed towards a Focal Firm's goals and if they can be properly controlled. Conversely, a rival's alliances are a point of vulnerability, commonly available for exploitation for strategic advantage by a Focal Firm.

To conclude, feasibility in strategic thinking involves the question of whether what would be achieved, can be achieved. Some things are possible and others are not. And with a creative outlook, what might have been considered impossible might not be so. The view taken here is that the conventional wisdom about the relevance of the availability of assets, abilities and alliances to feasibility requires review. Three particular points are important. One is the significance of thinking for strategic thinking; cognitive skills are surely an underestimated strategic ability. Second is the character of the strategist. Third is the motivation for alliances: are they for friendship, fashion or competitive function?

Table 6.2 *Elements of strategic capability.*

Strategic Capability	**Feasibility**: *Strategy ensures that the enterprise acquires and maintains sufficient* **capability** *to accomplish aims*		
	Assets	Ability	Alliances
1. Identified beginning and end states		Ability to assess current situation and specify objective for strategic initiative	Objective of Focal Firm
2. Requisite energy	Sufficient assets to transform current situation into end state		Provision of transformative assets to enhance Focal Firm assets
3. Control of energy		Ability to control the direction of energy	Control by Focal Firm
4. Internal intelligence		Ability to sense progress towards end state	Internal intelligence of the Focal Firm
5. Reserve capability	The outcome would be a false gain if the effort to achieve this particular outcome disabled the company in the process. Capability needs to anticipate subsequent strategic objectives.		

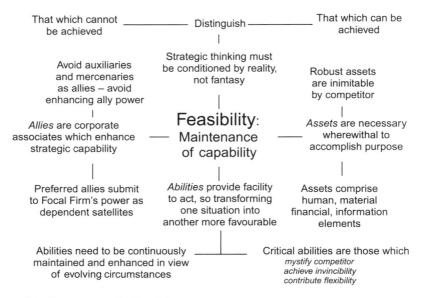

That which cannot ———————— Distinguish ———————— That which can be
be achieved   achieved

Avoid auxiliaries   Strategic thinking must
and mercenaries   be conditioned by reality,   Robust assets
as allies – avoid   not fantasy   are inimitable
enhancing ally power   by competitor

Allies are corporate   **Feasibility**:   *Assets* are necessary
associates which enhance   —   Maintenance   —   wherewithal to
strategic capability   of capability   accomplish purpose

Preferred allies submit   *Abilities* provide facility   Assets comprise
to Focal Firm's power as   to act, so transforming   human, material
dependent satellites   one situation into   financial, information
                             another more favourable   elements

Abilities need to be continuously ———————— Critical abilities are those which
maintained and enhanced in view   *mystify competitor*
of evolving circumstances   *achieve invincibility*
                                                contribute flexibility

Figure 6.1 Concept map for Feasibility.

Finally, after the preceding discussion of assets, ability and alliances, Table 6.2 demonstrates and explains links back to the capability proposition, offered at the beginning of the chapter. Assets refer specifically to the requirement for energy or effort to secure capability. Ability is broader. It refers to matters of control; specification of aims, control of application of assets and feedback of information about progress from internal intelligence. The main point about alliances, as the Table shows, is their contribution to strategic capability through the application of power.

Once again, a concept map is offered above to help summarise the main points arising in this chapter:

Reflection

In commerce, as in all competition, the simpler the strategy, the better. Does simple strategy rely on simple assets?

What is a corporate disability?

Risks associated with an alliance put any competitive enterprise in jeopardy.

7

Morality

Principle of Morality: Strategy ensures that the enterprise acts consistently with ethically principled judgement in achievement of aims.

Strategy will be judged on whether its aims and associated actions are good and right. Strategic thinking therefore needs to be ethically defensible.

It is common knowledge among those close to the fashion and cosmetics industries that behind the elegance and taste displayed in their products, exists, barely hidden, bitter commercial rivalry.[1] Virtuous products do not necessarily reflect virtuous corporate behaviour. Is this bad? And what is good?

The struggle for supremacy among firms in the developing cosmetics industry during the twentieth century is largely the story of competition between Helena Rubinstein and Elizabeth Arden. Both companies began from modest origins to become very successful and highly profitable businesses, driven by two determined and ruthless women. For both Rubinstein and Arden, the very existence of the other seemed to be a source of immense irritation. In a world of fashion and flair, both companies sought industry domination.

Alongside continuous efforts in both companies to set style and invent trend-setting products, all the time aiming for ever higher levels of profitability, there was also, apparently, a corporate mindset in each firm, determined to seek advantage by disrupting the balance of their rival. In an industry where image is all important, a loss of balance, even for a short while, might be enough to gain a commercial edge.

In 1937, there began a sequence of events which illustrates this point. Helena Rubinstein acquired a stylish building in New York and invested heavily in refurbishing it to rebuild and consolidate the company's brand. At the time it made good commercial sense. But it was also a bold step, an intrusion; it was designed simultaneously, to offend Arden who, Rubinstein knew, considered New York her home territory. At Elizabeth Arden, Rubinstein's initiative succeeded in causing dismay; temporarily. Very soon afterwards, Arden recruited 12 of Rubinstein's senior executives, including the man who instigated the New York offensive. Helena Rubinstein responded by securing a flood of eye-catching articles through friends at Vogue, friends secured through a deliberate and dramatic increase in advertising budget with the publisher. The spotlight was further concentrated on Rubinstein as a result of public and industry interest in her arrival in New York with a new husband, a Prince, no less. Soon after, Elizabeth Arden released plans for her company's grand presence at the 1938 World Fair in New York. Rubinstein responded by releasing the world's first waterproof mascara at a magnificent synchronised water ballet performance. Deuce.[2]

While Arden and Rubinstein occupied themselves with the strategic offensives and counter-offensives, activities of a third important competitor building a potentially threatening position in the industry went almost unnoticed by both women. Charles Revson began to build his Revlon Empire on a product which was then of little interest to either Arden or Rubinstein: nail varnish. Revson was as ruthless as his rivals. Intensely interested in his competitors, it is believed that his competitive intelligence activities extended to phone tapping. Espionage became linked with the industry.

Irritating a rival by distracting and unsettling the thinking of its senior executives, its strategists, in the ways we have seen, clearly serves the purpose of commercial advantage in this industry where image is so vitally important. Loss of focus can easily lead to a rival's temporary loss of direction, so strategic initiative calls for consideration of courses of action such as the ones we have seen in the cosmetics industry. Those potentially distracted strategists need a defensive posture incorporating the ability to choose from responsive alternatives which mitigate such attempts at causing loss of balance. Both assertive and defensive postures are clearly seen in the competition between Rubinstein and Arden.

Stepping back momentarily for a broad perspective, the theme presented in previous chapters about strategic thinking is that understanding competition between businesses is comprehension of the scope for manoeuvring. Both defence and assertion are designed to permit the focal firm to prevail in competition.

But what does *prevail* actually mean? Does it mean pre-empting a rival's new product launch so that an initiative in market leadership can be secured? Does it mean seizing control of vital supplies to a competitor by acquiring the firm that supplies them? Does it mean inducing a competitor to make an investment in a business direction which will eventually lead to the downfall of the firm? Does it mean poaching key staff from a competitor, thus depriving the rival of expertise which is critical to the firm's future? Does it mean taking legal action which would cripple a rival through the cost of defence and drive the firm to financial ruin? Does it mean propagating rumours about a rival's commercial reputation which will lead to loss of a sustainable business?

Prevail can mean many things. In sport the outcome of competition is clear: one team, the one that prevails in the competition according to the rules of the game, is pronounced the winner. In commerce there are also *rules of the game*. Legal constraints limit the range of competitive behaviour and the scope of strategic thinking; such rules differ from one country to another.

Returning to the cosmetics industry, there is a line which can clearly be drawn separating legal from illegal competitive behaviour; phone tapping is illegal. It goes without saying that strategy should surely be constrained by relevant law. If illegal activity is unacceptable for strategy in commerce, is this the only limit on competitive behaviour? No.

Poaching staff was, and probably still is, a popular strategic ploy in the cosmetics industry. It is not illegal, but is it unethical? Where is the line between the morally acceptable and unacceptable?

Strategy should be restricted by moral principles.[3] Why? Philosophically speaking, competition between businesses is a form of human interaction; purposeful, instrumental and restricted. Other forms include sport, international relations and interpersonal behaviour. In general, methods for untangling incompatible human goals range from negotiation[4] to force.[5] At both ends of the continuum, from negotiation and persuasion to force, participants conduct themselves according to commonly accepted, even if implicit, rules of behaviour. Competition is limited by rules of engagement and by moral agreement.

Moral agreement is by far the most controversial element because it stems from negotiation about what distinguishes *right* behaviour from *wrong*. In sport such as hockey, fair and therefore *right* play excludes action deliberately designed to harm an opposing player. In boxing, where punching is designed specifically to disable an opponent, there is a limit. Rules of fair play exclude deliberately harmful action executed after an opponent is unable to defend. It is interesting to observe that even in struggles between nations, wars are rarely fought to the outright destruction and devastation of one state by another. A moral limit intervenes.

Prevailing in competition with moral constraint usually implies that both rivals permit each other to survive beyond the conflict, albeit in a different relationship. One does not destroy the other. In time, through history, warring states resume diplomacy and trade; they even become allies.

Liddell Hart distinguishes between the objectives of states, on one hand, and military aims, on the other; from the viewpoint of a state's Policy objective,

> The object in war is a better state of peace – even if only from your own point of view. Hence it is essential to conduct war with constant regard to the peace you desire. That applies both to the aggressor nations who seek expansion and to peaceful nations who only fight for self-preservation – although their views of what is meant by a better state of peace are very different.[6]

The essential idea here is that military aims do not have objectives other than those defined by Policy. Military action is *right*, therefore, to the degree that it is consistent with Policy objectives.

Carse also refers to levels of objectives. The reader will recall that he defines two kinds of games: 'A finite game is played for the purpose of winning, an infinite game for the purpose of continuing the play'.[7] Importantly, the Infinite game involves continuous attention to defining rules of play, negotiation to maintain play. The moral imperative in Carse's view is that what is *right* is that which maintains the game:

> The rules of an infinite game must change in the course of play. The rules are changed when players of an infinite game agree that the play is imperilled by

a finite outcome – that is, by the victory of some players and the defeat of others.

The rules of an infinite game are changed to prevent anyone from winning the game and to bring as many persons as possible into the play.

If the rules of a finite game are the contractual terms by which the players can agree who has won, the rules of an infinite game are the contractual terms by which the players agree to continue playing.[8]

No company functions entirely independently of others. Inevitably relationships will exist in supply and distribution networks, manufacturing and service standards. Some will be relationships of convenience, others of necessity. The view offered by Iansiti and Levien[9] refers to such sets of relationships as a *business ecosystem*. To the degree that such interdependencies are inevitable, they argue that the health of the ecosystem is as important as is the health of a firm within it. Benefits accrue to all from investment in promoting the health of 'the commons'.

Why would a firm want to commit itself to restraint through moral agreement? Perhaps one of the most compelling reasons relates again to the distinction between the finite and infinite games; between the short and long term. Unwillingness to participate in an infinite game where rules are negotiated risks relegation to the status of outsider who can only play finite games; where there is only winning and losing, and there is no long term, no longevity.

Put more simply, reputation is the very least, and most, that is lost through violation of commonly agreed standards of behaviour. And bad reputation is bad for business.

All would be straightforward if the argument could stop at this point. But the source of this idea of *commonly agreed standards of behaviour* is problematic. Where and when does this negotiation about moral standards occur? Specifically, who participates? Is it a purely abstract notion, unrelated to reality?

Which community? Agreement might be implied thorough membership of a particular cultural entity.[10] But what happens when commercial competitors are members of different cultures?[11] As Chin-Ning Chu[12] points out, much can go wrong when strategy, and indeed, commerce generally, is interpreted differently from different cultural perspectives. Intention and capability, key strategic elements, will take different attributes in different cultures. So also will appreciation of acceptable standards of behaviour.[13]

To go further, a deeper philosophical discussion is needed but this is not the place to conduct it. Permit me to draw this idea to a close with the assistance of Simon Blackburn who addresses this problem in his small book called *Being Good*:

> We need standards of behaviour, in our own eyes, and we need recognition in the eyes of others . . . From within our self-understanding, we can admit that those standards are ours – just ours. We legislate them for ourselves, and also for others, when we demand respect or civility or forbearance from them.[14]

To conclude, strategy in commercial competition is not a game played in abstract with imaginary rivals. It is a game played among humans having consequences felt by the competitors themselves, other third parties and the environment in which the competition is conducted. Direction resulting from strategic thinking therefore has impact on competition, immediate and in the future; on current players, and on those who will follow. Ethical responsibility in strategy, that is, consideration of the moral merit of alternative courses of action, is therefore inescapable.

Figure 7.1 Concept map for Morality.

We dwell here on the idea that strategic thinking needs to be enveloped within rules of behaviour defined at the Policy level. Business competition must therefore be constrained by Policy and the moral terms by which firms agree to continue to participate in a commercial community, based on commonly accepted standards.

The concept map in Figure 7.1 offers a preliminary sketch of these considerations.

Reflection

Are good and right the same?

8

Conclusion

The theme of this book is now fully developed. Competitive aspects of business, which require strategic thinking, are of vital concern. Clear and competent strategic thinking enhances business progress and reduces the prospect of interference by competitors.

This is not to say that strategy is the only matter on which executives dwell. Unless a firm addresses its market with appropriate products and services, it will not succeed. Likewise, a firm will not survive if effective and efficient management of its people, money, materials and knowledge is overlooked.

However, the consequences of overlooking or trivialising strategy are too important to neglect. If, in times of confrontation, strategy were to be displaced by focus only on markets or internal corporate development, then opportunistic rivals could seize whatever lay open to them. Exploitation of points of commercial vulnerability by others could at least result in inconvenient loss; at worst, it might bring about the demise of the firm as an autonomous enterprise. Willingness to take at least a defensive posture is essential. And growth of a business enterprise requires the complementary mindset: an assertive strategic outlook. Both mindsets are threaded through the Principles I have offered in previous chapters.

I have so far explored the Principles one by one for convenience, however it is intended that they exist as a combined interdependent set; no one

Principle has priority over the others. To present this point and demonstrate their integration, I have chosen to show how the Principles relate to each other while employed together, by discussing my interpretation of events which occurred in one of the most famous campaigns of corporate acquisition.[1] This is the campaign of Alexander III of Macedon which began in 334 BC.

Alexander's strategy

Even today, nearly two and a half thousand years afterwards, the accomplishments of Alexander III of Macedon (Alexander the Great) are universally judged outstanding in scale and scope.[2] His reputation among scholars in modern times ranges between that of an admirable empire builder[3] to distastefully ruthless conqueror.[4] Nevertheless, there is no doubt that Alexander remains most highly regarded as a strategist.[5]

Over an eleven-year period, Alexander formed and consolidated a vast empire that extended from the Balkans, across the Middle East from modern day Libya to the Indus River bordering India, and from the Black and Caspian Seas to the Persian Gulf. In metaphorical terms, this is equivalent to successfully managing the rapid growth of a very large and diversified corporation. Adopting Alexander's eleven-year campaign in Asia Minor, ending prematurely as it did in 323 BC, as a metaphor for business growth, there is good reason to dwell on explanations of strategic thinking using inferences from Alexander's strategy.[6]

Although no direct evidence remains to provide a modern scholar with a concrete record of Alexander's thoughts, ancient sources do offer points of consistent agreement about his action as a leader and strategist and the rationale for the actions which followed. My interpretation draws from these well-documented activities where there is also general agreement in interpretation by modern scholars.

Policy objectives

Alexander's Policy objectives were inherited from his father, Philip II, who was preparing a campaign in Asia Minor before he died in controversial circumstances in 336 BC. These objectives were economic, political and moral:

Enhancement of economic wealth
Internal struggles over more than a century had depleted the resources of
the Greek city states. While Macedonia grew in political, economic and
military influence under the leadership of Philip II, Greece needed further
economic growth to consolidate its political stability.

Stabilisation of the alliance of Greek states
Unless the Greek city states could be engaged together in some wealth-
creating enterprise, forcing them to set aside their mutual antagonism, they
would continue to consume Macedonian resources in maintaining control.

Liberation of Greek cities in Asia Minor
In recent history, Persia had twice invaded Greece causing serious blows to
pride and considerable moral offence when the Persian army violated religious sites. Persia remained a potential threat. Philip had persuaded the
Hellenic League of Greek states to embark together on a campaign to 'liberate' the Greek cities on the coast of Asia Minor which had been forcefully
acquired by Persia. A campaign to recover control of these Greek cities was
a powerful moral imperative. It was a matter of pride and honour.

Strategic thresholds

Two features of Alexander's strategic thresholds during his campaign are
particularly noteworthy. First, in my judgement, there were *only four* of them
in the eleven years of his campaign.[7] Second, they are *not* the most cele-
brated incidents in Alexander's campaign.

Yet, these were choice points that were absolutely essential to accomplishment of his Policy objectives. These were the critical times when
Alexander's thinking could easily go unnoticed, especially when compared
with the colourfully documented force and fury of the great battles and sieges
that were tactical measures implementing his strategy.[8]

Threshold of internal security

Internal security was needed in Greece before Alexander could safely embark
on the campaign to Asia Minor. Action taken before he embarked on his
Asian campaign showed that he had a keen sense of the motives, interests

and power of those who remained behind. He was wary of leaving the potential for trouble behind him as he set off in his quest for wealth.

How to embark on the campaign with confidence in a secure base?

Alexander's resolution: Immediately after his father had been assassinated and Alexander had been accepted by the Macedonians as King, he called for an assembly of the League of Greek states. Alexander took this step to ensure that there was no opportunity for the alliance, which had been forged by his father, to break apart following Philip's death. For the Macedonians to maintain control of the Greek states, the previous agreement to moral, political, economic and military support for the campaign to liberate the Greek cities in Asia Minor had to be ratified.

All this, Alexander swiftly accomplished, and by such a move he maintained command of the armies of Greece under Macedonian leadership. The significance of this task should not be underestimated in view of the autonomy, which had long been traditional in the democratic Greek city states. Alexander required that his leadership be acknowledged and accepted.

Once this had been accomplished, his thinking turned to requirements for the expedition across the Aegean Sea. Threat of invasion by tribes bordering Greece had persisted for some time. Alexander was aware that his absence would provide an opportunity for leaders of these tribes to gain advantage. It was essential that he leave a secure base behind him to permit freedom of movement while he was abroad. He achieved this by reinforcing his Northern and Western borders. With his Macedonian army, he conducted short campaigns to the Danube to secure the Balkans and a campaign on the Western frontier to enforce Illyrian loyalty.

While he was away securing borders, Alexander received word that Thebes had ejected the Macedonian garrison posted there. Its leaders believed a rumour that Alexander had been killed while in the North. If this rebellion was permitted any level of success, it could well encourage other Greek states to take similar action. With great speed, and before the city was aware of his approach, he returned to Thebes to reclaim control. The city was razed to the ground in an unambiguous demonstration of Alexander's authority. Alexander wanted to implant the idea that mutiny would not be tolerated in the minds of any who were disenchanted by his leadership.

Alexander's departure for Asia Minor was arranged so as to leave behind a finely balanced equilibrium. Antipater, a trusted general, was delegated responsibility for the army he left in Greece to maintain control. Olympus, Alexander's very politically powerful mother, balanced Antipater's influence. The army which was left behind was itself finely balanced against the requirements of strength of the expeditionary force. The army which embarked on the campaign was comprised of contingents from the Greek states; sufficient to be a useful fighting force, sufficient also to constitute a suitable group of hostages should the states consider revolt after Alexander had gone abroad.

Threshold of naval threat

A Persian alliance with Phoenicia controlled the Mediterranean Sea and the Aegean. At any time, therefore, Persia had the capability to land an army in Greece and to stir trouble in Alexander's home base. At the same time, Alexander's communications with Greece could be cut from the sea leaving him isolated and without support. Alexander was apparently aware of both these possibilities and he was therefore obliged to make a strategic choice to limit Persian interference with his plans.

How to accomplish reduction of the naval threat?

Alexander's resolution: The reduction of the Phoenician naval threat was essential to accomplishment of Alexander's Policy objectives. But it was a costly and difficult strategic imperative.

Counterintuitively, rather than reinforce his naval strength, Alexander chose to disband his fleet. He had the option of enlarging his own navy through support from resources secured from Athens. But this would mean placing the fate of his campaign in the hands of the possibly mutinous Athenian navy. This was a risk he was apparently not prepared to take. His own military strength lay in his land army and Athens could not be trusted as a thoroughly reliable ally.

Rather than compete with his rival at sea, Alexander's plan was to do his fighting on land while depriving the Phoenicians of access to supply from coastal ports.[9] He accomplished this by systematically moving south down the coast of modern day Turkey, securing control of each city and port in turn.

By one method or another, whether by force, siege or persuasion, Alexander proceeded relentlessly around the Eastern Mediterranean. Major battles were fought along the way and cities that resisted him were besieged;

eventually he took control of the city of Tyre which was the seat of Phoenician naval strength.

Valuable elements of his army had to remain distributed along the coast
to secure the ports, which he progressively controlled. Fighting and sieges
further diminished his fighting strength. Most of all it cost Alexander time.
Yet there were benefits. He was no longer committed to the cost of maintenance of an uncompetitive naval fleet. Each city he 'liberated' became a
source of contributions to his army, even if the riches of the Persian Empire
were still beyond his reach.

Threshold of assimilation

The strategic question which Alexander faced was: how to maximise the
growth of economic wealth by means of forced acquisition?

Alexander's resolution: Alexander was fully aware that he could not control a
large and diverse empire by pure domination. The success of the campaign of
acquisition against Persian rule depended on being able to take control
through the vast array of existing Persian institutions by keeping them intact.

He demanded loyalty and recognition of his authority in each city he
encountered. Once he received this, Alexander installed two structures
reporting directly to him: a military presence to maintain order, and a
treasury to control contributions.[10] Alongside these structures, he typically
permitted a local satrap to maintain traditional administrative, cultural,
religious and political arrangements.

The process of assimilation took two further progressive forms. As he
acquired control, region by region, Alexander invested in growth through
public works, building many cities, each named *Alexandria* to symbolise his
authority.[11] Assimilation also took another form; his army became increasingly multi-ethnic as he integrated soldiers into his force as he moved from
one region to another. This reinforced the common cause through the soldiers fighting together for Alexander. Looting by his soldiers was forbidden:
to do so would be to steal the King's property.

He demanded loyalty and rewarded it generously once it was offered. This
initiative helped ensure that seeds of discontent were not sown, reducing
the likelihood of revolution blooming behind him as his campaign took him
further and further from home.[12] Although his rule was not oppressive,

Alexander was ruthless in suppressing resistance to his authority. Defiant resistance anywhere was eliminated.

Threshold of peace

The Battle of Issus was a tactical victory for Alexander in 333 BC. Darius, the Persian King, was defeated and fled. His army, which was much larger than Alexander's, was scattered. This was a moral and military defeat for Darius, and with it he lost pride and prestige.

For Alexander, the resulting strategic threshold unfolded in two questions:

Whether to be tempted to pursue Darius and the defeated remnants of the Persian army?

How to respond to an offer made by Darius to negotiate a peace?

Alexander's resolution: The question of pursuit was resolved without difficulty in view of Alexander's Policy objectives. A chase after the weakened Persians would be a distraction from his commitment to secure the Eastern Mediterranean coast against the continuing threat from the Phoenician navy. However, if he did not give chase, there would remain a possibility of harassment by regrouped elements of the Persian army.

Alexander chose, therefore, to continue to neutralise the Phoenician threat, seeking long term benefits rather than a risky short term gain. He knew that if he did not pursue Darius immediately, the Persian King would assemble another army to fight him again. Confident that he would win when that day came, Alexander moved on to secure the Phoenician coastal strongholds, eventually reaching Egypt.

The second question involved an attempt by Darius to negotiate a peaceful settlement and discourage Alexander from advancing further into Persia.

Soon after Issus, Darius offered Alexander generous terms for peace and cessation of hostilities. This included an offer of all the territory Alexander had so far acquired. It comprised an area of Asia Minor which exceeded the geographic extent of Philip's original ambition.

Alexander declined. He called Darius' bluff, knowing that with his refusal, the Persian King now had no option but to once again assemble an army for a another battle. This would be difficult for him in the light of his recent loss of prestige.

A final decisive battle was what Alexander wanted and he knew that circumstances compelled Darius to offer it. For Alexander it would represent a conclusive engagement, a final demonstration to Persians and Greeks alike, of his army's superiority. He was determined to win the whole Empire and was not content with negotiating to accept a portion of it. But first he had to wait; wait until Darius was ready.

Principles of strategy

Having outlined the four strategic thresholds and the ways in which Alexander responded, the next step is to reconsider these situations, in detail, from the viewpoint of the Principles of Strategy. I point out here that nobody actually knows what Alexander thought, although his decisions are well-documented and have been thoroughly studied. My following interpretation of his strategic thinking is necessarily speculative.

Principle of Competition

Purpose: Alexander was apparently single-minded in his concentration on objectives. At a strategic level they were essentially simple. Before leaving Greece, his aim was to ensure that the Greek states were not going to rebel in his absence. Elimination of the possibility of a threat by the Phoenician navy to his lines of communication with Greece was necessary. As he succeeded in progressively acquiring control of portions of the Persian Empire, Alexander aimed to secure their loyalty to him, not have them defect once again to Darius. Finally, his objective in negotiating with Darius after defeating him at Issus was to confuse him.

Context: In order to leave Greece without the concern that there would be an uprising to displace Macedonian influence while he was away on his Persian campaign, Alexander appreciated the sensitivity of both Greek borders and independent aspirations of the Greek states. The way he was to advance against Persia was also of importance in defining the competitive context of the campaign; Alexander knew that his strength lay in his army and his navy was relatively weak.[13] As he moved from city to city once crossing into Asia Minor, he was aware that resistance to his advance would be strong in some quarters but not others, so his approach to competitors would be conditioned by circumstances. After the battle of Issus,

Alexander's appreciation of his competitive context was that Darius would have lost considerable prestige and this would be an important factor to consider in deciding his next steps.

Competitive intelligence: Alexander's appreciation of competitive intelligence was both instinctive and learned. Trained by his father to fight and by Aristotle to understand the practical and metaphysical nature of people and things, Alexander knew the importance of knowledge. He therefore understood full well the possibility of the Greek city states rebelling on his departure; more than this, he knew which were likely to lead and how strongly. In Asia, his progress was led by advance parties instructed to gather all relevant information about the route and those he would encounter on his way. At each step he was well informed in preparation for confrontation.

In Alexander's youth he was known to hold court from time to time in his father's absence. On these occasions he took great interest in conversation with envoys from the East, enquiring into the nature of the countryside and in the people who lived there. He was particularly interested in learning about the character of Darius; he knew that such intelligence would serve him well in the future. And it did, helping him to choose direction after the Battle of Issus.

Principle of Assessment

No documentary evidence exists explicitly showing Alexander's analytical method for assessing strategic thresholds. But ancient literature shows clearly that he relied at such times on conferences he called with his senior executives. At these meetings, Alexander presented the information available and invited discussion of alternative courses of action. He trusted his senior staff to express their honest points of view, which, together they weighed. There was often disagreement and debate, which Alexander encouraged. These were clearly points of choice, not decisions imposed by a dictatorial leader, although of course, he was general (and King), and therefore Alexander's discretion was the final decision.

Issues would have been presented in terms of the clear objectives defined by Policy. Circumstances would have been taken into account from the best competitive intelligence available, revealing insight into both the terrain and rivals. Alexander depended for successful progress on the tactical activities of his subordinates, so it was important for them to receive a compelling argument for any particular course of action.[14]

Principle of Integrity

One of the most impressive aspects of Alexander's strategic thinking was his ability to bring together a combination of initiative, flexibility and balance in his conduct of competition with his rivals.

Initiative: Before leaving Greece, he immediately seized control of political circumstances left after his father died, confirming with the Greek states an agreement which they had previously reached as the Hellenic League, under Philip's direction. Alexander secured agreement, a second time, that all the city states accepted responsibility for enforcing the principles of the League. His initiative was also well illustrated by the timing of his crossing into Asia Minor, at a time when Darius was otherwise occupied in Egypt. Equally decisively, he disbanded the Greek navy shortly afterwards and with great determination, Alexander proceeded to Tyre and Gaza. Here he conducted sieges designed to secure control of cities which were the main bases of his opposition, the Phoenician navy. Assimilation of cities he acquired also demonstrates his initiative; in clear and decisive terms, Alexander invested in reconstruction of damaged buildings, especially religious sites to indicate his commitment to alliance. Equally decisively, he ruthlessly eliminated any defiant resistance. Although Alexander's choice of course of action after the Battle of Issus was *not* to follow up immediately to bring an already defeated king to his knees, his action was all the same decisive. It demonstrated his securing the initiative for any further struggle by boldly provoking Darius who would have felt sure Alexander would have accepted his generous offer.

Flexibility: Alongside decisive initiative through which Alexander maintained control of competitive momentum, his thinking also exhibited outstanding flexibility. To secure Greece while he was absent, Alexander had to ensure that both his boundaries were safe and the Greek city states were stable and compliant. Achieving this joint objective required him to simultaneously secure the Northern borders with the Balkans, the Western border with Illyria, and rapidly respond to the show of rebelliousness at Thebes. All this he accomplished with great swiftness, but without placing his Policy tasks at risk. After crossing into modern day Turkey and moving down the coast of the Eastern Mediterranean, Alexander further demonstrated his flexibility by adapting his approach to circumstances, using force, siege or persuasion as appropriate. Perhaps even more impressively demonstrating both his determination and flexibility, he showed no hesitation in rapidly returning to secure cities which revolted after Alexander had moved on. This element of flexibility enabled him to ensure that he moved to eliminate the threat in the Mediterranean as quickly as possible. Once cities had been secured, his flexibility was once again called for in ensuring their loyalty. He recognised local systems of administration, political arrangements, and cultural and religious practices. Alexander returned administrative control to willing supporters of his influence. Furthermore, he demonstrated flexibility by progressively integrating tribal soldiers into his army. His final threshold was met after engaging Darius in a battle which interrupted his progress in securing the city ports on the Mediterranean coast. After his victory at Issus, Alexander flexibly redirected his attention to neutralising the threat from the Mediterranean before confronting the Persians again.

Balance: At each threshold, Alexander's chosen course of action demonstrated balance. Before setting out on his campaign, he balanced leadership influence in Greece by leaving *both* Antipater, a senior general, *and* Olympus, his mother in charge. He *balanced* the size and strength of the army he left behind in Greece *against* the size of his expeditionary force. Alexander also left behind him a political arrangement which featured *both* control *and* democratic freedom. Neutralising his opposition in the Mediterranean also reveals his attention to balance. He weighed the need for rapid forward progress *against* systematically seizing control of ports, one by one. He balanced the size of his army's land capability *against* the need for naval power. The assessment of the size of garrison to leave behind in acquired cities had to be balanced *against* the strength of army needed to progress to meet further rivals. Furthermore, Alexander balanced the very high cost of acquiring Tyre, the seat of his naval opposition, in terms of the expense and time needed for siege, *against* the value of controlling the Phoenician navy. Assimilation of successive cities into his expanding empire involved further attention to balance. *On one hand* further liberation of cities in Asia Minor progressive fulfilled his Policy objective, but *on the other*, each additional acquisition increased the vulnerability of the enterprise by extending lines of communication with Greece. In each acquired city, Alexander balanced traditional administration *against* his military's control of the treasury. Alexander was also obliged to balance investment of funds for military growth *against* investment to consolidate his acquisitions. After Issus, balance was also a prominent feature of his thinking about responding to the peace proposal offered by Darius. The value of waiting for a later decisive confrontation was balanced *against* immediately pursuing a weakened Persian army. Control of the Persian Empire, long term, was balanced *against* the value of short term benefit. Alexander chose to risk losing the next battle as *against* immediate peace. Most of all, he balanced the likelihood of acquisition of the wealth of the entire Persian empire *against* the generous Persian offer after the battle.

Principle of Security

Prominent in Alexander's mind, no doubt, was the idea of psychological domination of his rivals. To accomplish this he exploited time at each of his strategic thresholds, managing his adversaries' impressions of confrontations, and crafting their perceptions of their dependence on him, thus securing power.

Time: Most impressive in his manoeuvring prior to leaving Greece was Alexander's pace of movement in securing his borders, and even more so, the astonishing speed with which he arrived at the walls of Thebes when he heard that this city had challenged his authority. Speed of movement is one thing, but strategically what Alexander achieved was a sense of shock and dismay, even terror, among the leaders of Thebes who, at first, simply could not believe that he had even arrived when he did, such was their perception of time. As Alexander moved from city to city it was important for him to impress on the inhabitants of each that what he demanded was their loyalty; indefinitely. Although he could not neutralise the Phoenician navy as quickly as he had journeyed from the Greek frontier to Thebes, it was necessary that his defeat of the navy be framed in terms of time. On this occasion, the impression he succeeded in creating in his opposition was that time was limitless; Alexander would maintain his siege of Tyre for however long was needed to bring the city under his control. Resistance by Tyre was determined, but eventually Alexander prevailed. Darius would have been unsettled, no doubt, about Alexander's refusal to accept his terms for peace after Issus. As Alexander continued his progress south towards

Egypt, the Persian King concluded that he now had the task of assembling an even more powerful army to meet Alexander again; but when, and how much time did he have to prepare? The answers were not in his hands.

Deception: Alexander's strategic thinking employed some of the craft of a magician. He left leaders of the Greek states with the impression that he trusted them not to revolt in his absence, but he did not in fact trust them. He kept precautions in reserve. Alexander commenced his campaign with his own naval support. As such it was a challenge to his Mediterranean adversary. Soon after crossing to Asia Minor, he disbanded his fleet. From the Phoenician perspective, his intentions would have been difficult to fathom: is Alexander protecting his advance with a navy or not? As he left each city which he had acquired for his expanding empire, Alexander left the impression that he was near; he named many new cities Alexandria as a reminder. But he travelled far away; yet he returned very rapidly if there was a sign of disloyalty. Where was Alexander? His influence was pervasive yet obscure. Perhaps the most dramatic piece of theatre orchestrated by Alexander was his response to the Persian peace plan. From the perspective of Darius, Alexander's response was probably a foregone conclusion; it was an offer too good to refuse. But he didn't accept it. Instead he moved away from the Persian centre of power, rather than towards it. What was he really trying to do?

Power: It was necessary for Alexander to leave no doubt in the minds of his Hellenic League that they were dependent on his influence. This he achieved by his decision to leave an army of substantial strength behind him when he departed for Asia Minor. But his impression of dependence was no doubt reinforced by the ruthless treatment of the Thebans who dared to defy his authority. One of Alexander's most impressive demonstrations of strategic power was his complete commitment to elimination of threat by the Phoenician navy to cut his communication lines back to Greece. This exhibition of power was shown in the final dependence the navy perceived on Alexander's activities as he held it captive in Tyre under siege. His exertion of power over those who administered the cities he acquired was achieved in a similar manner; he left garrisons of soldiers charged with keeping order. Order meant ensuring that city populations kept clearly in mind their dependence on Alexander for their welfare. Disloyalty was not going to be tolerated. As Alexander moved south towards Egypt after defeating Darius at Issus, it would have been clear to Darius that he was dependent on Alexander for the next initiative, whatever that might be, in their confrontation. He was securely in Alexander's power, dominated by him at a psychological level, already defeated and demoralised after the last battle.

Principle of Feasibility

Alexander's main strategic assets and abilities, demonstrated throughout his campaign, were his own charismatic influence over his increasingly successful army. He was an intelligent and empathetic leader, tuned to the needs and expectations of his subordinates. This disposition was extended to those who pledged loyalty to him and his ambitions, and soon his allies included many who had previously been his rivals.

Assets: Alexander was a source of cohesion and confidence for his soldiers, even though his tactical confrontations were typically undertaken when his rival had a numerical advantage. Alexander was always able to place his enterprise in a position where it was most likely to succeed. To do this he ensured that he was informed both about the strategic significance of his surroundings, and about the attributes of his rivals. He repeatedly penetrated the intentions of his rivals, and well understood their capabilities. Needless to say he also fully understood the capabilities of his own organisation.

Ability: An important part of Alexander's genius was his strategic ability to see beyond present circumstances. For example, he set off with his small army into Asia Minor with supplies which would support him for no more than 30 days. This would be enough to daunt most leaders, but Alexander had sent his most senior general, Parmenio, ahead and with intelligence received, he knew that he could win sufficient assets to support his campaign well beyond its initial time horizon. His counterintuitive decisive step to demobilise his own navy at a time of threat from his Phoenician rivals was taken with the confidence that beyond present circumstances, he would prevail on land. Acquiring cities also took a long term perspective; Alexander saw the prospect of a thriving empire comprising these new acquisitions. So each city was assimilated for this future vision. Alexander saw beyond the immediate benefits offered by Darius; he perceived a time when the Greeks would rule Asia.

Alliances: Alexander's attitude towards allies suggests, at a superficial level, that he formed collaborative relationships with many so that he could progress in assembling his empire. But at a deeper level, Alexander was single-minded in his own Policy agenda. In reality, his allies were recruited (or sooner or later forced) to become loyal subjects, faithfully serving his purpose; otherwise he destroyed them. The citizens of Thebes took what they thought was an opportunity to step outside Alexander's alliance in the Hellenic League. This was unacceptable so the city was razed to the ground. His relationship with those who led the cities and territories he acquired became extensions of his own influence; subordinates not allies.

Principle of Morality

Was Alexander's campaign objective right, and were his methods right? These are the questions of ethics to be addressed to Alexander's strategic thinking.

Alexander's Policy objectives embodied two values. The first was economic growth. Its aim was to enhance the wealth and well-being of the Greeks. This would be justifiable using Western moral reasoning only if three conditions were met: that no others suffered violation of their rights as a consequence; that fairness and equity were not threatened; and that actions and outcomes were just, and benefits outweighed costs.

Unification of the Greek city states was Alexander's second Policy objective, also addressing the value of wealth. This was motivated by the value of stabilising relationships between the city states, to secure the wellbeing of all Greeks. Again, this aim was one of enhancing the lives of the Greeks, notwithstanding effects on others.

The second value motivating Alexander's campaign was the moral imperative based on revenge. The Persians had attacked the Greeks in the past and caused great offence by interfering with religious sites. This wrong, in its own contemporary terms, simply had to be put right.

Today, the claim is made that there was no justification for Alexander's campaign.[15] The fact that it can be characterised as an eleven-year era of brutal oppression and wanton destruction of the Persians and their culture should come as no surprise, especially when Alexander's empire building is judged according to today's Western moral values. Certainly, people died in the process and therefore both the Policy objectives and the methods by which Alexander accomplished them can be judged wrong.

However, a moral argument based on the Principle of Utility could be mounted in reply, making the claim that there was moral justification for his campaign. This could be based on the fact that the overall value of Alexander's campaign was substantial and long lasting, outweighing the costs. Considerable economic benefits flowed to the region extending from Greece to modern day India through Alexander's introduction of a common currency, a common language of trade and secure routes for trading of goods between East and West. This was the beginning of an era of Hellenic influence[16] which supported and enhanced cultural and economic exchange, enhancing widespread well-being and welfare.

The fact that his influence was long lasting is illustrated by the fact that today the name of the city of Kandahar (which Alexander established as Alexandria Arachoton) in Afghanistan is derived from the name Sikandar which Alexander was called in this region. In fact there are many villages called Sikandarpur ('Alexanderville') throughout the Punjab.[17]

But long lasting influence does not by itself constitute moral justification. Neither is conquest universally wrong. Add to this impasse the viewpoints of other contemporary moral philosophies, and most importantly, the prevailing moral argument in Alexander's own time, and there is little prospect for a final resolution about whether Alexander's empire building campaign was right. However, it is clear that Alexander's argument for the campaign was judged right and good in his time, by his constituency. Perhaps this is the best that can ever be achieved in moral justification.

Alexander's campaign for corporate growth over two thousand years ago was conducted as a sequence of successfully assimilated acquisitions. For this reason Alexander's campaign is a valuable metaphor for contemporary business strategy. It provides the opportunity to show how the six Principles of Strategy combine, and it illustrates the value of these Principles for both design and evaluation of strategic thinking.

But it would be an overstatement to assert that Alexander's accomplishment was simply a result of his exemplary strategic thinking. Alexander's successful strategy is one contributor to explanation of his success, however it is also necessary to ask: why did Alexander's rivals fail?

This is an important question, because it cannot be assumed that Alexander's rivals were simply incompetent. Each thought they could win in their major confrontations with Alexander, and they had good reason for believing so. Three examples support the point.

First, the capture of Tyre was an important tactical event for Alexander because it supported his strategy of securing Phoenician ports in the Mediterranean. However, for the Tyreans, securing their port was the primary strategic objective supporting their policy of survival. The Tyreans thought they were safe; their city was an island approximately 1 km offshore, with strong defensive walls and two secure harbours. All that was needed in the minds of Tyrean strategists was to outwait Alexander since they could be continuously re-supplied by sea. The Tyreans misjudged Alexander's resolve. Although it took him 10 months, Alexander successfully secured control of the city. His successful tactics centred on construction of an enormous rock fill causeway to the island, and fabrication of siege weapons for attacking the walls from both the sea and from the causeway. The Tyreans failed because they underestimated the engineering capability of Alexander's army, and they overlooked Alexander's sheer determination.

Second, the final great battle between the Persian and Macedonian armies at Gaugamela in 331 BC was a tactical victory for Alexander and a Policy defeat for Darius. For Alexander it was a further step towards control of Asia; for Darius his kingdom was at stake. Because of the importance of the battle, Darius assembled an enormous army which outnumbered Alexander's force many times over. Based on reasonable calculations of relative strength, Darius would have had reason to expect that he would be successful in defeating Alexander. He was not. Darius lost because he did not anticipate the combination of Alexander's deceptive battlefield tactics and his deployment of his highly disciplined and well trained army.

Last, in the years 330 to 328 BC Alexander encountered a form of competitive resistance which nearly prematurely ended his campaign. Having defeated Darius and later found him betrayed by his own generals, Alexander assumed the Persian throne. Afterwards he took his army to the northeast to secure control of the mountainous area in modern day northern Afghanistan. He was resisted in turn by Bessus, one of Darius' former generals, and Spitamenes, a local warlord. Both were determined to retain their independence and resist Alexander's efforts to subdue them. Here, for the first time, Alexander encountered what would today be called guerrilla warfare. In rugged country, difficult to traverse, with food in short supply, Alexander was faced by fighters who attacked by surprise then simply vanished. On this occasion Alexander had no tactical advantage. However, even though it took more than two years he claimed success. This time his opponents underestimated only one factor: Alexander's apparently unlimited determination.

Taking the perspectives of Alexander's adversaries, we see more and different explanations for Macedonian success. Each of his competitors was able, talented and purposeful; yet they lost. Their failures arose from a combination of miscalculation of their rival's capability in engineering operations, in tactical prowess and in clever leadership. However, most of all, Alexander's rivals underestimated one telling factor: Alexander's inexhaustible determination. They misjudged Alexander's character.

Finally . . .

Strategy is a psychological engagement between those in charge of competing firms. At its best, strategic thinking anticipates the intentions and capabilities of a rival, and incorporates the purposes and capabilities of the strategist's own enterprise, in full appreciation of the circumstances of the confrontation. The outcome of strategic thinking is its definition of tactical objectives which are designed to shape a rival's behaviour. Strategic thinking is being able to think through a competitor's thinking. As such it is truly a mind game.

It is a way of thinking which centres on four concepts which were identified in Chapter 1: purpose, reason, advantage and future. In this book I offer a set of Principles defining strategy which is constructed upon these four essential concepts.

Principles help to guide the main tasks of strategic thinking. They are intended as guides to creative thought, guides which flow together towards improving the likelihood of prevailing in competition. These are most definitely *not* checklists of necessary elements, factors or considerations which drive out imagination and intuition. Rather, they offer a framework for analysing the benefits and limitations of alternative creative possibilities.

Together, the Principles define an idea of strategy which is holistic: strategy is one coherent idea comprising interrelated themes and threads. Each part should be considered in view of all the others. Table 8.1 represents this holistic view of strategy, demonstrating combined relationships among the Principles. Two competitive orientations are depicted in the table: an assertive perspective below the northwest-southeast diagonal, and a defensive posture above the shaded diagonal.

In concluding, let us return briefly to Nokia whose situation we considered at the beginning of this discussion of strategy. The reader will recall that I speculated about what might be occupying the thoughts of Jorma Ollila and his senior executives as they considered Nokia's competitive relationship with Sony Ericsson, Motorola and LG, among others. This speculation can now be sharpened.

Strategy is a mindset . . . more correctly *two* mindsets: at the threshold of threat to vital interests, both the mindset of an assertive competitor, and of a defensive competitor.

Adopting an assertive mindset, the questions which might come to mind in Nokia are: How might Nokia create competitive momentum in this business? How might Nokia mislead its competitors about its real business direction? How to ensure Nokia's capability to prevail in this business competition?

What might be Nokia's resolution of these questions?

An assertive competitive posture might bring to mind many possibilities designed to create competitive momentum exploiting vulnerabilities and unbalancing a rival's strategic thinking: identify points of competitor vulnerability, including recognition of any weakness in internal cohesion; induce competitors into a sense of false security; disconcert them with ambiguous signs of direction; advance to capitalise on competitor weaknesses with stealth and speed, while avoiding their strengths; move forward with a simple and uncomplicated plan, supporting Policy and consolidating accomplishment at each step.

An assertive posture is one mindset; a defensive outlook is the other. Defensively, Nokia's executives might also be asking: How to evade their competitors' attempts to disrupt Nokia's balance? How to penetrate Nokia's competitors' attempts to mislead? How to deny Nokia's competitors their capability to prevail?

Nokia's defensive resolution would be designed to prevent its competitors from successfully shaping its commercial activities: developing a deep understanding of competitors' sensitivities; recognising indications of competitors' intentions, and anticipating their courses of action and competitive thrusts; securing points of known vulnerability;

Table 8.1 *Relationships among Strategy Principles for assertive and defensive competitors.*

Principles of Strategy	Competition	Assessment	Integrity	Security	Feasibility	Morality
Competition: Orientation to those with rival claims	**Purpose, context and intelligence designed to: Protect wealth Enhance wealth**	*Initiate direction on valid logical argument derived from appreciation of rival strength*	*Design initiative to avoid being unbalanced by rival through flexible response to circumstances*	*Employ competitive intelligence to secure corporate sense of reality and avoid fantasy*	*Ensure sufficient capability to secure and maintain security*	*Initiate action designed to discourage rival's aggressiveness*
Assessment: Compelling logical case for direction	Initiate direction on valid logical argument derived from appreciation of rival vulnerability	**Appraise situation and choice of action to: Protect vulnerability Exploit opportunity**	*Appraise situation for rival's relative weakness and strength, securing points of vulnerability*	*Appraise situation for rival assumptions and preconceptions, seeking evidence of creation of false impressions of reality*	*Appraise situation for relative capabilities, circumventing points of rival strength*	*Appraise situation for rival's comparative ethical standards, securing against unexpected initiative*
Integrity: Concentration on advantage	Design initiative to unbalance rival through flexible response to circumstances	Appraise situation for rival's relative weakness and strength, exploiting vulnerability and avoiding strength	**Blend initiative, flexibility and balance: Secure balance Unbalance rival**	*Prepare for rival initiative to disconcert through disturbing sense of time, reality and dependence*	*Prepare for rival initiative to ensure that purpose is achieved with no loss to capability*	*Prepare defensive position consistent with ethical standards of acceptable behaviour*

Principles of Strategy	Competition	Assessment	Integrity	Security	Feasibility	Morality
Security: Psychological control of impressions	Employ stealth and speed to induce rival into sense of false security	Appraise situation for rival assumptions and preconceptions, creating false impression of reality	Design initiative to disconcert rival through disturbing sense of time, reality and dependence	Appreciate value of impressions of time, reality and power: **Achieve dominance**	*Employ sufficient capability to ensure that requirements of avoiding a misleading indirect rival approach are met and sustained*	*Be alert to false impressions by rival sufficient to cause dislocation yielding advantage*
Feasibility: Maintenance of capability	Ensure sufficient capability to secure and maintain advantage	Appraise situation for relative capabilities, undermining rival sources of robustness	Design initiative to ensure that purpose is achieved with no loss to capability	Employ sufficient capability to ensure that requirements of a misleading indirect approach are met and sustained	Secure and maintain assets, ability and alliances: Secure defense **Develop offence**	*Develop and employ capability with defensive but not aggressive potential*
Morality: Action consistent with principled standards of behaviour	Initiate action designed to maintain rival's continued competitiveness	Appraise situation for rival's comparative ethical standards, securing against unexpected response	Design initiative consistent with ethical standards of acceptable behaviour	Influence false impressions in rival sufficient to cause dislocation yielding advantage without aggression	Develop and employ capability with assertive but not aggressive potential	Be vigilant to differences in standards of behaviour: Appreciate values **Secure values**

Assertive strategic posture
Defensive strategic posture

and inducing competitors to disperse and thus reduce their points of strength.

Ultimately strategy is a state of mind towards competition which incorporates an ambition to prevail. It builds on determination, perseverance, energy, judgement and detachment. It is deeply personal and intellectually demanding . . .

. . . may the best strategist prevail.

Endnotes

Chapter 1

1 'The giant in the palm of your hand', *The Economist*, 10 February 2005.
2 Porter, M.E. (1980) *Competitive Strategy*, New York: The Free Press.
   Porter, M.E. (1985) *Competitive Advantage*, New York: The Free Press.
3 Hamel, G. and Prahalad, C.K. (1994) *Competing for the Future*, Boston Mass.: Harvard University Press.
4 Johnson, G., Scholes, K. and Whittington, R. (2005) *Exploring Corporate Strategy*, 7th edn, Harlow: Pearson.
5 Mintzberg, H., Ahlstrand, B. and Lampel, J. (1998) *Strategy Safari*, London: Prentice Hall.
6 Calori, R. (1998) *Essai*: 'Philosophizing on strategic management models', *Organisation Studies*, 19(2): 281–306.
7 Freeman, R.E. (1984) *Strategic Management: A Stakeholder Approach*, London: Pitman.
8 Mintzberg, H., Ahlstrand, B. and Lampel, J. (1998) *Strategy Safari*, London: Prentice Hall.
9 Gilbert, D.R., Hartman, E., Mauriel, J.J. and Freedman, R.E. (1988) *A Logic for Strategy*, Cambridge, Mass.: Ballinger.
10 Evans, D. (2000) *War: a matter of principles*, Canberra: Aerospace Centre offers a comparison of such principles across a variety of military organisations.
11 Mitroff, I. (1982) 'Marrying Two Schools of Policy Research'. In Grant, J.H. *Strategic Management Frontiers. Monographs in Organisational Behaviour and Industrial Relations*, 10: 33–42.
12 Crouch, A.G.D. (1998) 'Reframing the strategic problem: An accommodation of harmony and belligerence in strategic management', *Journal of Business Research*, 41(1): 3–13.
13 Sun Tzu, *The Art of War*, Tr. Griffith S.B. (1963), London: Oxford.
14 Kautilya, *The Arthashastra*, Tr. Rangarajan L.N. (1987), New Delhi: Penguin.
15 Arrian, *The Campaigns of Alexander*, Tr. de Selincourt A. (1958), Harmondsworth: Penguin, pp. 108–29.
16 Machiavelli, N. *The Prince*, Tr. Bull G. (1981), Harmondsworth: Penguin.
17 Von Clausewitz, C. *On War*, Tr. Howard, M. and Paret, P. (1976), Princeton, NJ: Princeton University Press.

[18] If this list were to be extended it should include Xenophon, *The Persian Expedition*, Tr. Warner, R. (1949) London: Penguin; and Thucydides, *History of the Peloponnesian War*, Tr. Warner, R. (1954) London: Penguin.

[19] The reader will note that it is this writer's intention to bring to light the strategic thinking of early sources using texts which are sympathetic to the original contexts in which insights were derived. This leaves the sources uncontaminated by spurious modern interpretation. Be aware that there are bodies of interpretive work which attempt to bring historical sources to the attention of contemporary executives; *this writer advises against them, recommending instead that the reader forms a personal evaluation of historical sources viewed from their place as they were written, in their own historical times.* Among such contemporary interpretations of classic sources are the following: Bose, P. (2003) *Alexander the Great's Art of Strategy*, Sydney: Allen and Unwin; Krause, D.G. (1995) *The Art of War for Executives*, London: Nicholas Brealey; Von Ghyczy, T., von Oetinger, B. and Bassford, C. (2001) *Clausewitz on Strategy*, New York: John Wiley & Sons, Inc.

[20] Machiavelli lived from 1469 to 1527.

[21] Perhaps not surprisingly since the Papal States were an active competitor, along with Florence, Venice and Sienna, among others, in rivalry for power in his time.

[22] For example, Skinner, Q. (1981) *Machiavelli*, Oxford: Oxford University Press.

[23] Bull, G. (1981) Introduction to *The Prince*.

[24] Published posthumously by his wife in 1832.

[25] Brown, M.E., Coté, O.R., Lynn-Jones, S.M. and Miller, S.E. (eds) (1998) *Theories of War and Peace*, Cambridge, Mass.: MIT Press; Kagan, D. (1995) *On the Origins of War*, London: Pimlico; Blainey, G. (1988) *The Causes of War*, 3rd edn, Melbourne: Macmillan.

[26] Von Clausewitz ('Friction in War').

[27] . . . at least one would imagine Ollilla hopes they do not know what he thinks.

[28] Bracker, J. (1980) 'The historical development of the strategic management concept', *Academy of Management Review*, 5(2): 219–24.

[29] Terms such as 'marketing strategy' or 'human resource strategy' are misnomers; they do not refer to competitive rivals. Nokia, no doubt, has plans for marketing and plans for human resource management. Related to strategy though they might be, here they will not be referred to as 'strategies'.

[30] Adapted from Andrews, K.R. (1980) *The Concept of Corporate Strategy*, New York: Irwin.

[31] Fahey, L. (1999) *Competitors*, New York: John Wiley & Sons, Inc.

[32] Strictly speaking a third aspect should follow: planning, the translation of aims into action. I choose not to explore planning in this book because it would draw discussion on from strategy into tactics and operations.

[33] This concept map and others which follow should be read in the spirit of Tony Buzan's method: Buzan, T. (1993) *The Mindmap Book*, London: BBC Books.

Chapter 2

[1] Brenner, J.G. (2000) *The Emperors of Chocolate*, New York: Broadway Books.

[2] The 'cola wars' between Coca Cola and Pepsi are well known (see for example, Ramsey, D.K. (1987) *The Corporate Warriors*, Boston: Houghton Mifflin). Less publicly appreciated, but equally, if not more vicious, are the bitter struggles between competitors in confectionery. Rivalry between Mars and Hershey is of particular interest in the United

States where these two control the major share. On a global basis the players are different, including Nestlé and Cadbury, but the character of competition is no less intense.

3 'Light tears', *The Economist*, 5 March 2005.
4 Porter, M.E. (1980) *Corporate Strategy*, New York: Free Press.
5 Ansoff, I. (1987) *Corporate Strategy*, Harmondsworth: Penguin.
6 Andrews, K.R. (1987) *The Concept of Corporate Strategy*, Homewood Ill.: Irwin.
7 Andrews (1987) p. vii.
8 Miles, R.E. and Snow, C.C. (1978) *Organisational Strategy, Structure and Process*, New York: McGraw Hill.
9 Miles and Snow (1978).
10 Ansoff (1987).
11 Andrews (1987).
12 Porter (1980) and Porter, M.E. (1985) *Competitive Advantage*, New York: Free Press.
13 Henderson, B. (1979) *Henderson on Corporate Strategy*, Cambridge Mass.: Abt Books.
14 Henderson (1979).
15 Porter (1980).
16 Kay, J. (1993) *Foundations of Corporate Success*, Oxford: Oxford University Press.
17 Miles and Snow (1978).
18 Porter (1980).
19 Porter (1985).
20 Henderson (1979).
21 Kay (1993).
22 This discussion is drawn from Crouch, A.G.D. (1998) 'Reframing the strategic problem: An accommodation of harmony and belligerence in strategic management', *Journal of Business Research*, 41(1): 3–13.
23 Porac, J.F., Thomas, H., Wilson, F., Paton, D. and Kanfer, A. (1995) 'Rivalry and the Industry Model of Scottish Knitwear Producer', *Administrative Science Quarterly*, 40: 203–27.
24 Hannan, M.T. and Freeman, J.H. (1977) 'The Population Ecology of Organisations', *American Journal of Sociology*, 82(5): 929–84.
25 Chen, M.-J. and MacMillan, I.C., (1992) 'Nonresponse and delayed response to competitive moves: The roles of competitor dependence and action irreversibility', *Academy of Management Journal*, 35: 539–70. Chen, M.-J. and Miller, D., (1994)'Competitive attack, retaliation and performance: An expectancy-valence framework', *Strategic Management Journal*, 15: 85–102. Chen, M.-J. and Hambrick, D., 'Speed, stealth, and selective attack: How small firms differ from large firms in competitive behaviour', (1995) *Academy of Management Journal*, 38: 453–82.
26 Davis, J. and Devinney, T. (1997) *The Essence of Corporate Strategy*, Sydney: Allen and Unwin; Mintzberg, H., Ahlstrand, B. and Lampel, J. (1998) *Strategy Safari*, London: Prentice Hall.
27 Kay (1993).
28 Henderson, B. (1984) *The Logic of Business Strategy*, New York: Ballinger.
29 Kay (1993).
30 Krohn, F.B. (1987) 'Military metaphors: semantic pollution of the market place', *Et Cetera*, 44(2): 141–5.
31 'Softwar or hard?' *The Economist*, 26 March 2005.
32 'See you in court', *The Economist*, 26 March 2005.
33 'Shaking up corporate Japan', *The Economist*, 26 March 2005.
34 Peacock, W.E. (1984) *Corporate Combat*, New York: Facts on File.

[35] Ramsey, D.K. (1987) *The Corporate Warriors*, Boston: Houghton Mifflin; James, B. (1985) *Business Wargames*, Cambridge Mass.: Abacus.

[36] Clemons, E.K. and Santamaria, J.A. (2002) 'Maneuver Warfare', *Harvard Business Review*, 80(4): 57–65.

[37] Cohen, W.A. (1986), 'War in the Marketplace', *Business Horizons*, 29: 10–20.

[38] Kotler, P. and Singh, R. (1981), 'Marketing warfare in the 1980s', *Journal of Business Strategy*, 1: 30–4.

[39] Ansoff (1987).

[40] Miles and Snow (1978).

[41] Clark, I. (1988) *Waging War*, Oxford: Clarendon.

[42] 'Attack of the BlackBerry killers?', *The Economist*, 19 March 2005.

[43] Henderson (1979).

[44] Porter (1980).

[45] Gordon, I. (1989) *Beat the Competition*, Oxford: Blackwell.

[46] Sun Tzu, *The Art of War*. Tr. Griffith, S.B. (1963) Oxford: Oxford University Press.

[47] O'Dowd, E.O. and Waldron, A., 'Sun Tzu for strategists', *Comparative Strategy*, 10(1991): 25–36.

[48] Von Clausewitz, C. *On War*. Ed. and tr. Howard, M. and Paret, P. (1976) Princeton, NJ: Princeton University Press.

[49] Porter (1980).

[50] Henderson (1979).

[51] O'Dowd and Waldron (1991).

[52] Von Clausewitz.

[53] Porter (1980).

[54] Henderson (1979).

[55] Henderson (1979).

[56] Ramsey, D.K. (1987) *The Corporate Warriors*, Boston, Mass.: Houghton Mifflin.

[57] Sun Tzu p. 66.

[58] Sun Tzu p. 93.

[59] Von Clausewitz. p. 198.

[60] Liddell Hart, B.H. (1967) *Strategy*, 2nd edn, London: Faber and Faber.

[61] Henderson (1979).

[62] Liddell Hart (1967) p. 338.

[63] Sun Tzu p. 77.

[64] Porter (1985).

[65] Henderson (1979).

[66] Lao Tzu, *Tao Te Ching*, Tr. Lau, D.C. (1963) Harmondsworth: Penguin, p. 131.

[67] Machiavelli, N., *The Prince*, Tr. Bull, G. (1981) Harmondsworth: Penguin, p. 40.

[68] Machiavelli p. 87.

[69] Machiavelli p. 129.

[70] Valuable insights for competition in business come from high level competitive sports; Walker, S.H. (1986) *Winning: The psychology of competition*, New York: Norton, provides an example, as does Charlesworth, R. (2001) *The Coach*, Sydney: Pan Macmillan.

[71] 'Growing pains', *The Economist*, 16 April 2005.

[72] Andrews, K.R. (1980) 'The concept of corporate strategy'. In Mintzberg, H. and Quinn, J.B. (1996) *The Strategy Process*, 3rd edn, London: Prentice Hall, pp. 47–55.

[73] Henderson, B.D. (1991) 'The Origin of Strategy'. In Montgomery, C.A. and Porter, M.E. (eds) *Strategy*, Boston, Mass.: Harvard University Press, pp. 3–9.

[74] Porter, M.E. (1980) *Competitive Strategy*, New York: The Free Press.

[75] Porter, M.E. (1996) 'What is strategy?' *Harvard Business Review*, 74(6): 61–78.

76 Wernerfelt, B. (1984) 'The resource based theory of the firm', *Strategic Management Journal*, 5(2): 171–80; Grant, R.M. (1991) 'The resource-based theory of competitive advantage: implications for strategy formulation', *California Management Review*, Spring: 114–35; Barney, J.B. (1991) 'Firm resources and sustained competitive advantage', *Journal of Management*, 17(1): 99–120.

77 Hamel, G. and Prahalad, C.K. (1994) *Competing for the Future*, Boston, Mass.: Harvard University Press.

78 McGee, J. and Thomas, H. (1986) 'Strategic Groups: A useful link between industry structure and strategic management', *Strategic Management Journal*, 7: 141–60.

79 Stalk, G. and Lachenauer, R. (2004) 'Five killer strategies for trouncing the competition', *Harvard Business Review*, 82(4): 63–71.

80 Carse, J.P. (1986) *Finite and Infinite Games*, New York: Ballantine.

81 Fahey, L. (1999) *Competitors*, New York: John Wiley & Sons, Inc.

82 Powell offers an interesting complementary perspective on the logical structure of competition in commerce (Powell, T.C. (2001) 'Competitive advantage: Logical and philosophical considerations', *Strategic Management Journal*, 22: 875–88; Powell, T.C. (2002) 'The philosophy of strategy', *Strategic Management Journal*, 23: 873–80; and Powell, T.C. (2003) 'Strategy without ontology', *Strategic Management Journal*, 24: 285–91) in debate with Durand (Durand, R. (2002) 'Competitive advantages exist: a critique of Powell', *Strategic Management Journal*, 23: 867–72.) and Arend (Arend, R.J. (2003) 'Revisiting the logical and research considerations of competitive advantage', *Strategic Management Journal*, 24: 279–84).

83 Dixit, A.K. and Nalebuff, B.J. (1991) *Thinking Strategically*, New York: Norton.

84 For further interest in the game perspective, see as examples, Ghemawat, P. (1997) *Games Businesses Play*, Cambridge, Mass.: The MIT Press; Romp, G. (1997) *Game Theory*, Oxford: Oxford University Press.

85 Fahey (1999) p. 18.

86 Blainey, G. (1988) *The Causes of War*, 3rd edn, Melbourne: Sun Books.

87 Bolton, R. (1979) *People Skills*, London: Prentice Hall; Nelson-Jones, R. (1986) *Human Relationship Skills*, Sydney: Hold-Saunders; Fisher, R. and Ury. W. (1981) *Getting to Yes*, Harmondsworth: Penguin; Smith, M.J. (1975) *When I say no, I feel guilty*, New York: Bantam.

88 Note that I have stopped short of saying submission is wrong, in my view. Some will take exception even to this weaker position because submission could include a *Harvest* business direction which might be deliberately chosen to maximise value through outright sale of an enterprise. In my view, a fairly negotiated price for sale of a business is not submission, because it is not foregoing stakeholder interests by giving the enterprise away for nothing.

89 'The alchemist of paper', *The Economist*, 16 April 2005.

90 Andrews (1980).

91 'The alchemist of paper', p. 62.

92 Sun Tzu.

93 Kautilya, *The Arthashastra*, Tr. Rangarajan, L.N. (1987), New Delhi: Penguin.

94 Von Clausewitz.

95 Machiavelli.

96 Sun Tzu ('Attack by Fire', pp. 18, 19).

97 'Consumer republic', *The Economist*, 19 March 2005.

98 'Consumer republic', p. 63.

99 Johnson, G., Scholes, K. and Whittington, R. (2005) *Exploring Corporate Strategy*, 7th edn, Harlow: Pearson.

[100] The Appendix to this chapter is a brief outline of the practice of competitive intelligence.

[101] Ferrier, W.J. (2001) 'Navigating the competitive landscape: The drivers and consequences of competitive aggressiveness', *Academy of Management Journal*, 44(4): 858–77.

[102] Gilad, B. (1995) 'Where are your blindspots?', *World Executive's Digest*, November, 44–5; Neugarten, M.L. (2003) 'Seeing and Noticing: an Optical Perspective on Competitive Intelligence', *Journal of Competitive Intelligence and Management*, 1(1): 93–104; Zahra, S.A. and Chaples, S.S. (1993) 'Blind spots in competitive analysis', *Academy of Management Executive*, 7(2): 7–28; Zajac, E.J. and Bazerman, H.M. (1991) 'Blind spots in industry and competitor analysis: Implications of interfirm (mis)perception to strategic decisions', *Academy of Management Review*, 16: 37–46.

[103] 'Combination therapy', *The Economist*, 26 February 2005.

[104] Sun Tzu ('Employment of Secret Agents', p. 3).

[105] Sun Tzu ('Employment of Secret Agents', p. 4).

[106] Sun Tzu ('Employment of Secret Agents', p. 23).

[107] Sun Tzu ('Terrain', pp. 22–4).

[108] Fahey presents an exceptionally thorough treatment of the rationale and analytical apparatus needed to forecast a competitor's future activity and its implications for the Focal Firm. West concentrates on informing the strategist of the methods and techniques available for gathering information about competitors. Fahey, L. (1999) *Competitors*, New York: John Wiley & Sons, Inc and Gilad, B. (2004) *Early Warning*, New York: AMACOM; Nolan, J. (1999) *Confidential*, New York: HarperBusiness; and West, C. (2001) *Competitive Intelligence*, Houndmills, Hampshire: Palgrave.

[109] Sun Tzu ('Offensive Strategy' pp. 31–3).

[110] *Competitive intelligence* is a broad field which refers to competitors and their context, whereas *competitor intelligence* refers to enquiry about the intentions and capabilities of a specific rival.

[111] West, C. (2001) *Competitive Intelligence*, Houndmills, Hampshire: Palgrave.

[112] At this point, to help simplify the following discussion, it is convenient to distinguish between the *Focal Firm*, that is, the firm with which we identify as if it were ours, and a *Competitor*, a commercial rival.

[113] Fahey, L. (1999) *Competitors*, New York: John Wiley & Sons, Inc; West, C. (2001) *Competitive Intelligence*, Houndmills, Hampshire: Palgrave.

[114] Mitnick, K.D. (2002) *The Art of Deception*, Indianapolis: John Wiley & Sons, Inc.

[115] Winkler, I. (1997) *Corporate Espionage*, Rocklin CA: Prima Publishing.

[116] Pattakos (1997) 'Keeping Company Secrets Secret', *Competitive Intelligence Review*, 8(3): 71–8; Waters, R. (1998) 'In the Mind of Judas: Why Employees Give Away Company Secrets', *Competitive Intelligence Review*, 9(3): 9–14.

Chapter 3

[1] Roddick, A. (2000) *Business as Unusual*, London: Thorsons.

[2] 'Has Kodak missed the moment?', *The Economist*, 30 December 2003; 'Kodak changes the picture', *The Economist*, 23 January 2004.

[3] Van Der Heijden, K. (1996) *Scenarios – The art of strategic conversation*, Chichester: John Wiley & Sons, Ltd, pp. 53–111.

[4] Porter, M.E. (1980) *Competitive Strategy*, New York: Free Press.

[5] Fahey, L. and Randall, R.M. (1998) *Learning from the Future*, New York: John Wiley & Sons, Inc. 'What is scenario learning', pp. 3–21, 'Integrating strategy and scenarios', pp. 22–38.

[6] Schwartz, P. (1996) *The Art of the Long View*, Chichester: John Wiley & Sons, Ltd, pp. 241–8.

[7] Hamel and Välikangas explore the idea of resilience in some detail in Hamel, G. and Välikangas, L. (2003) 'The quest for resilience', *Harvard Business Review*, 81(9): 52–63. The reader will see parallels in their article with the logical relationships presented here among Purpose, Business Model, Competitors, Trends and Scenarios.

[8] Chrisman, J.J., Hofer, C.W. and Boulton, W.R. (1988) 'Towards a system for classifying business strategies', *Academy of Management Review*, 13(3): 413–28; Miller, D. (1992) 'The generic strategy trap', *The Journal of Business Strategy*, 13(1): 37–41.

[9] Johnson, G., Scholes, K. and Whittington, R. (2005) *Exploring Corporate Strategy*, 7th edn, Harlow: Pearson.

[10] Johnson, Scholes and Whittington (2005) p. 243.

[11] Derived from Johnson, G., Scholes, K. and Whittington, R. (2005) *Exploring Corporate Strategy*, 7th edn, Harlow: Pearson.

[12] Rumelt, R.R. (1980) 'The Evaluation of Business Strategy'. In Glueck, W.F. (1980) *Strategic Management and Business Policy*, New York: McGraw Hill.

[13] 'Incredible shrinking plants', *The Economist*, 21 February 2002; 'The day of the Panda', *The Economist*, 4 September 2003; 'The party's over', *The Economist*, 30 January 2003; 'The three F's', *The Economist*, 4 March 2004; 'Going east', *The Economist*, 4 March 2004.

[14] No calculations can be made here to compare the three courses of action because no financial data is available in the sources.

[15] Mitchell, T. (2003) *The Integrated Business Planning Process*, unpublished manuscript.

[16] Rumelt, R.R. (1980) 'The Evaluation of Business Strategy'. In Glueck, W.F. (1980) *Strategic Management and Business Policy*, New York: McGraw Hill.

[17] Tiles, S. (1963) 'How to evaluate corporate strategy', *Harvard Business Review*, July–August, pp. 111–21.

[18] Hofer, C.W. and Schendel, D. (1978) *Strategy Evaluation: Analytical Concepts*, St Paul, MN: West.

[19] Johnson and Scholes (2002).

[20] Mitchell (2003).

[21] This is not intended as a remark about the likely gender of strategists, rather an observation that in Sun Tzu's world strategists were male.

[22] Langley, A. (1995) 'Between "Paralysis by Analysis" and "Extinction by Instinct"', *Sloan Management Review*, Spring, 63–76.

Chapter 4

[1] Warner, P. (2001) *The Battle of France*, London: Cassell.

[2] *The Fundamentals of Land Warfare*, Commonwealth of Australia, Australian Army, 1993. Principles of War, pp. 24–9.

[3] Nelson's history, including examples of initiative in Napoleonic naval warfare, is described in detail in many sources, including: 'Nelson, Vice Admiral Horatio'. In Holmes, R. (ed.) (2001) *The Oxford Companion to Military History*, Oxford: Oxford University Press; Pocock,

T. (1994) *Horatio Nelson*, London: Pimlico; Hibbert, C. (1995) *Nelson*, London: Penguin; and Coleman, T. (2001) *Nelson*, London: Bloomsbury.

[4] On two of these three occasions (Cape St Vincent and Copenhagen) Nelson acted on his own outside the orders of his senior officer. For this he was liable for court marshal because such action was illegal. Had it not been for the publicity he generated himself through the newspapers of the day, about these glorious events, he would have been in serious trouble. It should be pointed out, therefore, that initiative does not require or condone illegal activity.

[5] 'Nestlé: A dedicated enemy of fashion', *The Economist*, 29 August 2002.

[6] 'Barclays' big ambitions', *The Economist*, 16 November 2000.

[7] Liddell Hart B.H. (1967) *Strategy*, 2nd edn, New York, Meridian. pp. 326–9.

[8] Sun Tzu, *The Art of War*, Tr. Griffith, S.B. (1963), London: Oxford. ('Nine Varieties of Ground' pp. 59–61).

[9] Sun Tzu ('Energy' pp. 13–15).

[10] Adapted from von Clausewitz, C. *On War*, Tr. Howard, M. and Paret, P. (1976), Princeton, NJ: Princeton University Press. (Book 7 – 'Attack').

[11] Von Clausewitz 'Boldness'.

[12] In commerce, a distinction can be made between two types of initiative:

Uncontested Initiative: In a new venture involving uncontested corporate action, initiative is commonly termed *first mover advantage*. It offers a firm the benefit of establishing the framework for future competition by being first to define the terms of rivalry. Benefits include the psychological influence of establishing identity, commanding assets and defining relevant terms for future development. A first mover can aim to cause a potential rival to be discouraged to the point where they decide not to compete.

Contested Initiative: Initiative is also relevant, as a slightly different concept, beyond the conditions of the first mover's monopoly. This is termed here, contested initiative, and in the following discussion, it will be simply referred to as *Initiative*. In an ongoing competition, such initiative is aimed at bringing about the psychological state whereby a competitor rationally concludes hope of advantage is lost and that future rivalry is pointless.

[13] MacMillan, I.C. (1982) 'Seizing the initiative', *Journal of Business Strategy*, 2(4): 43–57.

[14] Smith, K.G., Ferrier, W.J. and Grimm, C.M. (2001) 'King of the hill: Dethroning the industry leader', *Academy of Management Executive*, 15(2): 59–70.

[15] Lynn, M. (1998) *Birds of Prey*, New York: Four Walls Eight Windows. Chapter 5: 'Le Défi Américain'.

[16] 'Mobile telecoms: Emergency Calls', *The Economist*, 26 April 2001.

[17] Santé, *The Economist*, 23 April 2005.

[18] Sun Tzu, *The Art of War*. Tr. Griffith, S.B. (1963), London: Oxford. ('Weaknesses and Strengths' pp. 13–24).

[19] Raynor, M.E. (2004) 'Strategic flexibility', *Competitive Intelligence Magazine*, 7(1): 6–13.

[20] Ansoff, H.I. (1975) 'Managing strategic surprise by response to weak signals', *California Management Review*, 18(2): 21–33.

[21] Courtney, H., Kirkland, J. and Viguerie, P. (1997) 'Strategy under uncertainty', *Harvard Business Review*, 75(6): 67–79.

[22] Courtney *et al.* (1997).

[23] Porter, M.E. (1996) 'What is strategy?' *Harvard Business Review*, 74(6): 61–78.

[24] Sun Tzu ('Manoeuvre' pp. 26–31).

[25] Machiavelli, N. *The Prince*, Tr. Bull, G. (1981), Harmondsworth: Penguin. XVIII.

[26] Machiavelli XXI.

[27] Sun Tzu 'Offensive Strategy' pp. 10–17.

[28] Mintzberg, H. and Waters, J.A. (1985) 'Of strategies, deliberate and emergent', *Strategic Management Journal*, 6: 257–72.

[29] Sun Tzu 'Weaknesses and Strengths' pp. 27–30.

[30] Raimond, P. (1998) 'Where do strategic ideas come from?' In Hamel, G., Prahalad, C.K., Thomas, H. and O'Neal, D. (eds) (1998) *Strategic Flexibility*, New York: John Wiley & Sons, Inc.

[31] Mintzberg, H. (1994) 'The fall and rise of strategic planning', *Harvard Business Review*, 72(1): 107–14.

[32] Holsti, O.R. (1978) 'Limitations of cognitive abilities in the face of crisis', *Journal of Business Administration*, 9(2): 39–55.

[33] Janis, I.L. (1989) *Crucial Decisions*, New York: Free Press.

[34] Sun Tzu 'Offensive Strategy' pp. 24, 25.

[35] Sun Tzu 'Energy' pp. 5–12.

[36] Sun Tzu 'Weaknesses and Strengths' p. 26.

[37] Chen, M.-J. (1996) 'Competitor analysis and interfirm rivalry: Toward a theoretical integration', *Academy of Management Review*, 21(1): 100–34.

[38] Hambrick, D.C. and MacMillan, I.C. (1982) 'The product portfolio and man's best friend', *California Management Review*, 25(1): 84–95.

[39] Markides, C. (2001) 'Strategy as balance: From "either-or" to "and"', *Business Strategy Review*, 12(3): 1–10.

[40] Mintzberg, H., Ahlstrand, B. and Lampel, J. (1998) *Strategy Safari*, London: Prentice Hall.

[41] Mintzberg, H. (1994) 'The fall and rise of strategic planning', *Harvard Business Review*, 72(1): 107–14.

[42] Langley, A. (1995) 'Between "Paralysis by Analysis" and "Extinction by Instinct"', *Sloan Management Review*, Spring, 63–76.

[43] Freeman, R.E. (1984) *Strategic Management: A Stakeholder Approach*, Boston: Ballinger.

[44] 'Losing the HP way', *The Economist*, 19 August 2004.

[45] Von Clausewitz 'Intelligence in War'.

[46] Liddell Hart (1967) 'The Theory of Strategy'.

[47] Gray, C.S. (1998) *Explorations in Strategy*, Westport: Praeger.

Chapter 5

[1] Napoleon Bonaparte. In Holmes, R. (ed.) (2001) *The Oxford Companion to Military History*, Oxford: Oxford University Press; Chandler, D. (1965) *The Campaigns of Napoleon*, London: Weidenfeld and Nicholson.

[2] Borges, Jorges Luis (1964) 'A new refutation of time'. In Yates, D.A. and Irby, J.E. (eds) (1964) *Labyrinths*, Harmondsworth: Penguin; Butler, R. (1995) 'Time in organisations: Its experience, explanations and effects', *Organisation Studies*, 16(6): 925–50; Flood, R. and Lockwood, M. (1986) (eds) *The Nature of Time*, Oxford: Blackwell; Jaques, E. (1982) *The Form of Time*, London: Heinemann; Waugh, A. (1999) *Time*, London: Headline.

[3] Johnson, G., Scholes, K. and Whittington, R. (2005) *Exploring Corporate Strategy*, 7th edn, Harlow: Pearson.

[4] Eisenhardt, K.M. and Brown, S.L. (1998) 'Time pacing: Competing in markets that won't stand still', *Harvard Business Review*, March–April.

[5] Hamel, G. and Prahalad, C.K. (1994) *Competing for the Future*, Boston Mass.: Harvard University Press.

[6] Hamel and Prahalad (1994) p. 50.

[7] Chen, M.-J. and Hambrick, D.C. (1995) 'Speed, stealth and selective attack: How small firms differ from large firms in competitive behaviour', *Academy of Management Journal*, 38(2): 453–82.

[8] Carse, J.P. (1986) *Finite and Infinite Games*, New York: Ballantine.

[9] 'The big picture', *The Economist*, 22 July 2004.

[10] 'Hovering higher', *The Economist*, 27 May 2004.

[11] Sun Tzu, *The Art of War*, Tr. Griffith, S.B. (1963), London: Oxford. 'Weaknesses and Strengths' pp. 19–23.

[12] Sun Tzu ('Nine Varieties of Ground' pp. 59–61).

[13] Sun Tzu ('Energy' pp. 13–15).

[14] This diagram is a variant of the well known OODA (Observe-Orient-Decide-Act) loop.

[15] Von Clausewitz, C., *On War*, Tr. Howard, M. and Paret, P. (1976) Princeton, NJ: Princeton University Press, 'Strategy'.

[16] Von Clausewitz 'Genius for War'.

[17] Paquette, L. (1991) 'Strategy and time in Clausewitz's *On War* and Sun Tzu's *The Art of War*', *Comparative Strategy Review*, 10: 37–51.

[18] Wulfstan (1014). Homily Number XX(EI). In Bethurum, D. (1957) (ed.) *The Homilies of Wulfstan*, Oxford: Clarendon Press, pp. 267–75.

[19] Brewer, G. (1993) 'Be Like Nike?' *Sales and Marketing Management*, September, pp. 67–74.

[20] 'Qantas denies Olympic ambush', *The Australian*, 30 May 1997, p. 23.; Lloyd, S. (2000) 'The unfriendly skies', *Business Review Weekly*, 20 October, pp. 82–4.; 'Steal a deal', *The Australian*, 20 September 2000, p. 21.

[21] 'Sneaky shots the goal in World Cup ambush', *The Australian*, 22 May 2002, p. 28.

[22] Sun Tzu. 'Manoeuvre' 12.

[23] Sun Tzu 'Estimates' 17–20.

[24] For instance, Godson, R. and Wirtz, J.J. (2000) 'Strategic denial and deception', *International Journal of Intelligence and CounterIntelligence*, 13: 424–37 and Bell, J.B. (2003) 'Toward a theory of deception', *International Journal of Intelligence and CounterIntelligence*, 16: 244–79.

[25] Whaley, B. (1982) 'Toward a general theory of deception', *Journal of Strategic Studies*, 5(3): 178–92.

[26] *Empires of Industry: Cola Wars*, video documentary 2002.

[27] Sun Tzu 'Energy' pp. 3–12.

[28] Sun Tzu 'Energy' pp. 6–9.

[29] Sun Tzu 'Energy' pp. 18–19.

[30] Tanzer, A. (1993) 'The students who rose up and ate their teacher', *Business Review Weekly*, 12 February, pp. 60–2.

[31] Leavitt, H.J. (1978) *Managerial Psychology*, 4th edn, Chicago: University of Chicago Press; Mitchell, T.R. (1982) *People in Organisations*, 2nd edn, New York: McGraw Hill.

[32] 'Turbulent skies', *The Economist*, 8 July 2004.

[33] 'Stiff competition', *The Economist*, 19 August 2004.

[34] MacMillan, I.C. (1983) 'Preemptive strategies', *Journal of Business Strategy*, 4(2): 16–26.

[35] 'Turbulent skies'.

36 MacMillan, I.C., van Putten, A.B. and McGrath, R.G. (2003) 'Global gamesmanship', *Harvard Business Review*, 81(5): 62–71.
37 MacMillan, I.C. (1980) 'How business strategists can use guerrilla warfare tactics', *Journal of Business Strategy*, 1: 63–5.
38 'A big week for Apple', *The Economist*, 29 July 2004.
39 'Of monkeys and penguins', *The Economist*, 30 August 2003; 'Microsoft at the powerpoint', *The Economist*, 13 September 2003.
40 Macmillan, I.C. and Jones, P.E. (1986) *Strategy Formulation: Power and Politics*, St Paul, MN: West.
41 Kautilya, *The Arthashastra,* Tr. Rangarajan, L.N. (1987), New Delhi: Penguin.
42 Sun Tzu.
43 MacMillan, I.C. (1988) 'Controlling competitive dynamics by taking strategic initiative', *Academy of Management Executive*, 11(3): 111–18.
44 'The cartel isn't for ever', *The Economist*, 15 July 2004.
45 'A big week for Apple'.
46 . . . such as is fostered by Mintzbert and his colleagues in Mintzbert, H., Ahlstrand, B. and Lampel, J. (2005) *Strategy Bites Back*, London: FT Prentice Hall.
47 Mintzberg, H. (1994) 'The Fall and Rise of Strategic Planning', *Harvard Business Review*, 72(1): 107–14.

Chapter 6

1 Caesar, Caius Julius. In Holmes, R. (ed.) (2001) *The Oxford Companion to Military History*, Oxford: Oxford University Press; Grant, M. (1969) *Julius Caesar*, London: McGraw Hill; Needham, C.P. (1968) *Caesar – Politician and Statesman*, London: Blackwell.
2 *Commentaries* of Caesar cited in Fuller, J.F.C. (1965) *Julius Caesar: Man, Soldier and Tyrant*, London: Eyre and Spottiswoode.
3 'Opening the throttles', *The Economist*, 8 July 2004.
4 Johnson, G., Scholes, K. and Whittington, R. (2005) *Exploring Corporate Strategy*, 7th edn, Harlow: Pearson.
5 Wernerfelt, B. (1984) 'The resource based theory of the firm', *Strategic Management Journal*, 5(2): 171–80; Barney, J.B. (1991) 'Firm resources and sustained competitive advantage', *Journal of Management*, 17(1): 99–120; Grant, R.M. (1991) 'The resource-based theory of competitive advantage: Implications for strategy formulation', *California Management Review*, 33(3): 114–35.
6 In Grant's terminology, 'resources' refer to a broad range of a firm's attributes including the skills of staff, specialized machinery, ownership of sources of raw materials, and a sales network.
7 Grant (1991).
8 Porter, M.E. (1996) 'What is strategy?' *Harvard Business Review*, 74(6): 61–78.
9 'Global TV', *The Economist*, 8 July 2004.
10 The questions which follow comprise what many authors of texts on *business development* refer to as a survey of 'strategic capability': for example, Johnson, G., Scholes, K. and Whittington, R. (2005) *Exploring Corporate Strategy*, 7th edn, Harlow: Pearson; Hill, C.W. and Hill, G.R. (2004) *Strategic Management*, 6th edn, Boston, Mass.: Houghton Mifflin; White, C. (2004) *Strategic Management*, Hampshire: Palgrave Macmillan.
11 'Yesterday's papers', *The Economist*, April 23 2005; Chenoweth, N. (2001) *Virtual Murdoch*, London: Vintage.

[12] Economy of application of assets to reach an objective.

[13] Degree to which objectives are reached through application of assets.

[14] Note that efficiency and effectiveness are useful measures of the application of assets ONLY after the appropriate objective has been established; a company can be exceptionally efficient and effective in pursuing the wrong objectives.

[15] 'Daring, defying, to grow', *The Economist*, 5 August 2004.

[16] . . . as distinct from management.

[17] See for instance, Bass, B.M. (1985) *Leadership and Performance beyond Expectations*, New York: Free Press.

[18] Luh, S.S. (2003) *Business the Sony Way*, Oxford: John Wiley & Sons (Asia) for Capstone Publishing Ltd.

[19] Sun Tzu, *The Art of War*, Tr. Griffith, S.B. (1963), London: Oxford. 'Dispositions', p. 13.

[20] Machiavelli, N., *The Prince*, Tr. Bull, G. (1981) Harmondsworth: Penguin.

[21] Von Clausewitz, C. *On War*, Ed. and tr. Howard, M. and Paret, P. (1976) Princeton, NJ: Princeton University Press.

[22] The terms competencies and capabilities are frequently used both interchangeably and with implied separate significance in the contemporary strategy literature. Both in essence, refer to *ability*, the facility to act to bring about performance outcomes.

[23] Prahalad, C.K. & Hamel, G. (1990) 'The core competence of the corporation', *Harvard Business Review*, May–June, 68(3): 79–91.

[24] Porter (1996).

[25] 'PPR tries to reinvent itself', *The Economist*, 22 July 2004.

[26] 'The cartel isn't for ever', *The Economist*, 15 July 2004.

[27] Sun Tzu 'Employment of Secret Agents', p. 4.

[28] Sun Tzu 'Weaknesses and Strengths', p. 4.

[29] Sun Tzu 'Weaknesses and Strengths', p. 24.

[30] Sun Tzu 'Weaknesses and Strengths', p. 13.

[31] Sun Tzu 'Nine Varieties of Ground', p. 29.

[32] Sun Tzu 'Nine Varieties of Ground', p. 61.

[33] Sun Tzu 'Weaknesses and Strengths', p. 14.

[34] Machiavelli 'How a prince should organise his militia', XIV.

[35] MacMillan, I.C. and Jones, P.E. (1984) 'Designing organisations to compete', *Journal of Business Strategy*, 4(4): 11–26.

[36] 'With allies like these', *The Economist*, 22 April 2002.

[37] Das, T.K. and Bing-Sheng Teng (1999) 'Managing risks in strategic alliances', *Academy of Management Executive*, 13(4): 50–62.

[38] Dyer, J.H., Kale, P. and Singh, H. (2004) 'When to Ally and When to Acquire', *Harvard Business Review*, July–August, pp. 109–15

[39] Ohmae, K. (1989) 'The global logic of strategic alliances', *Harvard Business Review*, March–April, pp. 143–54.

[40] Hamel, G., Doz, Y.L. and Prahalad, C.K. (1989) 'Collaborate with your competitors – and win', *Harvard Business Review*, January–February, pp. 133–9.

[41] Gomes-Casseres, B. (2000a) 'Alliances and risk', *Financial Times*, 9 May 2000.

[42] Gomes-Casseres, B. (2000b) 'Strategy must lie at the heart of alliances', *Financial Times*, 16 October 2000.

[43] '(Still) made in Japan', *The Economist*, 7 April 2004.

[44] Kautilya, *The Arthashastra*. Tr. Rangarajan, L.N. (1987), New Delhi: Penguin.

[45] Sun Tzu 'Nine Varieties of Ground', p. 13.

[46] Sun Tzu 'Offensive Strategy', pp. 1–7.

[47] Kautilya X.iv 'Allies and Vassal Kings' (Choice of Allies).

48 Kautilya X.x 'The Weak King' (Attitude towards a stronger king).
49 'Battling for the palm of your hand', *The Economist*, 29 April 2004.
50 Sun Tzu: 'The Nine Varieties of Ground' (pp. 52, 53).
51 Machiavelli: XII 'Military Organisation and Mercenary Troops'.
52 Machiavelli: XIII 'Auxiliary, Composite and Native Troops'.
53 Alvarez, S.A. and Barney, J. (2001) 'How entrepreneurial firms can benefit from alliances with large partners', *Academy of Management Executive*, 15(1); 139–48.
54 Machiavelli XXI 'How a prince must act to win honour'.
55 Machiavelli XXI 'How a prince must act to win honour'.

Chapter 7

1 See, for example, the history of commercial competition between Helena Rubinstein and Elizabeth Arden in Woodhead, L. (2003) *War Paint*, London: Virago.
2 A moment in a game of tennis when both players have won three points each.
3 Peter Singer, a prominent moral philosopher, argues strongly in the affirmative. To illustrate he presents a succinct argument about strategic thinking as it applies to globalisation, building on ethical criteria rooted in Western moral philosophy; Singer, P. (2002) *One World*, Melbourne: The Text Publishing.
4 Ury, W. and Fisher, R. (1981) *Getting to Yes*, Harmondsworth: Penguin.
5 Clark, I. (1988) *Waging War: A Philosophical Introduction*, Oxford: Oxford University Press.
6 Liddell Hart, B.H. (1967) *Strategy*, 2nd edn, New York: Meridian, p. 338.
7 Carse, J.P. (1986) *Finite and Infinite Games*, New York: Ballantine, p. 3.
8 Carse (1986) p. 11.
9 Iansiti, M. and Levien, R. (2004) 'Strategy as Ecology', *Harvard Business Review*, March.
10 A substantial literature is available on business ethics, viewed from the particular perspective of Western moral philosophy. Examples include: Grace, D. and Cohen, S. (1995) *Business Ethics*, Melbourne: Oxford University Press; Kitson, A. and Campbell, R. (1996) *The Ethical Organisation*, London: Macmillan; Solomon, R.C. (1993) *Ethics and Excellence*, New York: Oxford University Press; Velasquez, M.G. (1992) *Business Ethics*, 3rd edn, Englewood Cliffs, NJ: Prentice-Hall. The majority of issues discussed in this literature refer to internal activities, not to strategy.
11 Where, for example, *The Upanishads*, *The Bhagavad Gita*, *Mahabharata*, *The Analects of Confucius* or the *Koran*, might provide guidance for right behaviour.
12 Chu, C.-N. (1991) *The Asian Mind Game*, New York: Rawson Associates; Chu, C.-N. (1992) *Thick Face Black Heart*, Beaverton, OR: AMC Publishing.
13 Tung, R.L. (2001) 'Strategic Management Thought in East Asia', *Organisational Dynamics*, Spring, 22(4): 55–65.
14 Blackburn, S. (2001) *Being Good*, Oxford: Oxford University Press. p. 133.

Chapter 8

1 The following discussion of Alexander's campaign is based, in part, on a paper presented by the writer at the 19th Annual International Conference of the Strategic Management Society, October 3–6, 1999, in Berlin.
2 'Alexander the Great'. In Holmes, R. (ed.) (2001) *The Oxford Companion to Military History*, Oxford: Oxford University Press.

[3] Hammond, N.G.L. (1980) *Alexander the Great*, 3rd edn, London: The Bristol Press.

[4] Bosworth, A.B. (1988) *Conquest and Empire*, Cambridge: Cambridge University Press.

[5] From the viewpoint of military strategy, Fuller (Fuller, J.F.C. (1960) *The Generalship of Alexander the Great*, New York: Da Capo) is the most prominent source.

[6] Current scholarly insight benefits directly from the research findings of ancient historians including Arrian, Curtius, Diodorus and Plutarch. Each studied this Macedonian King's life in considerable depth and offers a contribution to contemporary knowledge. However, Alexander's history presented by Arrian (De Sélincourt, A. (1958) (Tr.) Arrian: *The Campaigns of Alexander*, London: Penguin) is commonly regarded as most reliable. This comes about, in part, because it is based on the writing of Ptolemy who was one of Alexander's most trusted generals. Contemporary analysis of Alexander's methods and accomplishments are drawn from Bosworth (1988), Hamilton, J.R. (1973) *Alexander the Great*, Pittsburgh: University of Pittsburgh Press, Hammond (1980), Hammond, N.G.L. (1997) *The Genius of Alexander the Great*, Chapel Hill: The University of North Carolina Press, Fox, R.L. (1973) *Alexander the Great*, Harmondsworth: Penguin; and Green, P. (1991) *Alexander of Macedon, 356–323BC*, Berkeley: University of California Press.

[7] A fifth critical incident occurred at the River Beas, located at the most Easterly margin of his campaign on the frontier with modern day India. Here he faced the frustrating possibility that his tired Macedonian soldiers might refuse to follow him any further east; it was not quite a mutiny, but almost. The issue was dissolved by Alexander consulting the gods who conveniently called for a halt to expansion in this direction, thus allowing Alexander to avoid a direct confrontation with his army. This is not classed here as a Strategic Threshold because it was an internal organisational matter, not an issue of competition with a rival.

[8] More commonly prominent also than strategy in the popular histories of the campaign, Alexander's cavalry and infantry, which comprised the most advanced military technology of the time, showed his outstanding operational capability. Unfortunately, his impressive logistical and engineering feats are often overlooked.

[9] Fighting ships were dependent on landing daily for supplies.

[10] Alexander demanded tax of each city he acquired, but a sum never greater than the taxes previously imposed by the Persian King Darius.

[11] . . . and to establish a 'brand'.

[12] It is worthy of note that Alexander's willingness to progressively gather in supporters to join him in his administration and army eventually fuelled discontent among his own Macedonian colleagues. As the campaign progressed they lost their superiority in numbers and found their access to Alexander increasingly restricted by the presence of newcomers. As the King's countrymen, they resented being displaced. This posed a further tactical dilemma for Alexander in deciding how to maintain an equitable balance in influence among his ethnically diverse advisors.

[13] . . . and possibly unreliable since his navy was mainly in the hands of the Athenians, a potential rival at home.

[14] Modern scholars would approve of this decision-making method where issues were vitally important and the commitment of his staff was required for effective implementation: Vroom, V.H. and Yetton, P.W. (1973) *Leadership and Decision-Making*, Pittsburgh: University of Pittsburgh Press.

[15] See Bosworth, A.B. (1988) *Conquest and Empire*, Cambridge: Cambridge University Press.

[16] Olmstead, A.T. (1948) *History of the Persian Empire*, Chicago: University of Chicago Press.

[17] Green, P. (1991) *Alexander of Macedon, 356–323BC*, Berkeley: University of California Press.

Index